A WARSAW
DIARY
1978-1981

A WARSAW DIARY

1978 – 1981

KAZIMIERZ BRANDYS

TRANSLATED FROM THE POLISH BY

RICHARD LOURIE

RANDOM HOUSE
NEW YORK

Grateful acknowledgment is made to the following for permission to reprint previously published material:

Penguin Books Ltd. for permission to reprint an excerpt from Stendhal: *The Charterhouse of Parma*, trans. M.R.B. Shaw (Penguin Classics, 1958), p. 19. Copyright © Margaret R. B. Shaw, 1958. By permission of Penguin Books Ltd.

The University of Colorado for permission to reprint an excerpt from Mikhail Lermontov, *The Demon and Other Poems*, translated by Eugene M. Kayden, Antioch Press, 1965.

A portion of this work previously appeared in the *New York Times Magazine*.

Library of Congress Cataloging in Publication Data

Brandys, Kazimierz.
    A Warsaw diary: 1978-1981.

Translation of: Miesiące.
    1. Brandys, Kazimierz—Biography. 2. Authors, Polish—20th century—Biography. I. Title.
PG7158.B632A3513   1984   891.8′58703   [B]
83-42782
ISBN 0-394-52856-5

Manufactured in the United States of America

9 8 7 6 5 4 3 2

First American Edition

A Warsaw Diary: 1978-1981 is a selection of passages from two volumes of my journals, the complete text of which appeared in a Polish edition under the titles *Miesiące 1978-1979* and *Miesiące 1980-1981*.

—K.B.

A WARSAW DIARY

1978–1981

■ OCTOBER
1978

It has been a barren stretch. Not an empty one, for there's been a lot going on. But barren as far as work goes. I haven't written anything for fifteen months now. Not a line, with the exception of the story I had to stop working on. I finished *Rondo* in April 1977; I was abroad from October to May. Paris: illness, the hospital. Berlin: illness, the hospital. Warsaw: the hospital, an operation.

It wasn't I who was sick. Physically I felt fine; yet the calamity I experienced was real: the life I shared with another person was destroyed. The arrangement of our days and nights, our everyday ways, our calendar life, our meals and sleep—all went up in a single explosion. Like the outbreak of war, illness shatters the structure of time, the order of thought and reality. With the sole difference that war is a universal calamity, whereas illness selects an individual, seeming to stalk him out, and then does to him what war would, but stealthily, obliquely. Then add to that being out of one's element, a foreign language, a looser connection to the world around you. Every day, as I covered the distance between home and hospital, I felt that I had become the target of some menace. A bomb could fall on me at any second, and I was not free of the feeling even at night, for then the telephone could bombard me. Without any prior discussion of this, M.* and I both hit on that same comparison of illness and war. "They're turning the big guns on us now," she said to me one day.

All that would seem explanation enough for the long gap in my writing. I knew, however, that there were other factors mak-

---

* Maria, the author's wife. (All footnotes in this book have been added by the translator.)

ing it impossible for me to work and that those factors would not disappear so soon. Our journey, her illness and the obligations it created, were a pretext for self-justification, a long-standing alibi that I could use to legitimize not working. But I was fully aware that when my alibi expired, I would still be unable to write. I also realized that it was only when the obstacles fell away that I would find myself in real danger, threatened not by external circumstances but by the void within me.

I had been prepared for this for a long time. These periods of enforced unproductivity always follow the completion of a large piece of work, and sometimes even occur while I'm still writing. As I grow older, it becomes increasingly difficult for me to bear these barren stretches, and though they took me by surprise at first, in time I learned to anticipate them, knowing they had to come. The wisest thing would have been to get used to it, but that's impossible. It's a psychological and physical state that might be defined as a subclass of depression—if giving it a name solves anything—or as a state of nonbeing. I prefer the latter description—it says more. The intermissions in one's life as a writer resemble nervous breakdowns. The days are lifeless, no circulation, no pulse; your head feels empty, sucked dry. Those days are about as different from the writer's normal life as crawling is from walking. You do what has to be done with the pitiful remnants of your strength, with a galley slave's sense of impotence and humiliation. The head, the arms, the legs, are weighed down by a question—for what? Things only improve when the day is half over. Night approaches. Night brings relief because sleep is, of course, a release from the necessities of the waking world. Obligations and goals vanish; there is no responsibility. In those bad months my dreams are pleasant and peaceful, and sometimes I fall asleep with a glimmer of curiosity about what I will dream. I remember one dream I had not long ago. I was making a phone call from a post office in some small town in the Far East. It was a poor, primitive building, with a dingy interior and a window that looked out onto snow-covered peaks. I was calling Warsaw, calling her. I shouted to her not to worry about me, my troubles were over, I had a job: I was a mountain horse working for some smugglers, whom I carried across the border to the other side of the mountains. I explained all this to her in a state of joyous emotion.

But in those periods it is especially difficult to leave the world of sleep. Just before dawn, when you're only half asleep, the nightmares come. They are realistic. Every association and image is menacing. A pattern, a chair, an incident from years back, a word, a geometric shape, become suffocatingly absurd, somehow sinister. You want to go back to sleep, to retreat into the depths, into that interrupted, better reality. Sleep becomes a life more real and pleasant than the one to which you return, which starts gnawing at you with anxiety from daybreak on. Most likely, those specters are born of the body's own fear, and it is possible that those predawn nightmares are all symbols of a single menace that writing protects me against but that can get to me in the months when I am idle. I am apparently on closer terms with death than might have seemed the case.

Johanna Schopenhauer, the philosopher's mother, was born in Gdańsk in 1766. I read her memoirs recently. She was a friend of Goethe, a literary woman; her home in Weimar was known as an intellectual salon. Describing her childhood years in Gdańsk, she often speaks of Poland with feeling and a sense of attachment and recalls the first partition of Poland as a catastrophe. Gdańsk, annexed by Prussia, was then cut off from its lifeblood, Polish grain, whose shipments fell to one fifth of what they had been. As a republican and a citizen of the Free City,* she hates Prussia and finds militaristic absolutism repugnant. She frequently stresses her sympathy for the Poles, admiring both the flamboyance of the nobility and the people's naïveté and simplicity. These pages make for moving reading. Gdańsk was a piece of the West linked to Poland by real interests, and at the same time, it

---

* In the sixteenth and seventeenth centuries, Gdańsk had risen to great wealth and fame as a trading post between East and West, and Polish kings granted it extensive rights of autonomy.

was the eye of the West for several hundred years, viewing Poland from close up. There had to be something fascinating for the merchants of Gdańsk in the disintegrating colossus of the Polish republic, as if, with the clashes and revolts now past, they suddenly realized that some insufficiently prized value was dying in Europe along with Poland. Arthur Schopenhauer's mother was a progressive, a child of the enlightened bourgeoisie, who greeted the storming of the Bastille with enthusiasm. What did she find attractive in that republic of noblemen? Most likely it was the image of an exotic democracy with an elected king, a democracy in colorful Eastern garb (which she describes fondly), one with free and easy customs. Warmly, benignly, she depicts the Vistula raftsmen bringing the grain into Gdańsk. For her, those were innocent, simple, happy creatures. Those people of the Vistula, ingenues walking up and down Długi Targ selling clay pots, were confident, cheerful, drunk. Happy because they were unaware of their misfortune. The memoirist has pity for them and, at the same time, is certain that she need not fear any harm from them. The royal republic of Sarmatians clad in Turkish costumes had reared a childlike people on its plain. That image of the republic was to last for quite some time in the West. A few years later, the French historian Jules Michelet called Poland a great, peaceful country, where travelers felt safe even in the forests.

Shortly after reading Johanna Schopenhauer's memoirs, I spent half a day in Gdańsk. We had come in from Sopot.* The weather was foul, windy, rainy; people were wearing sweaters and coats. The day before, I had given up working on a story and felt like a man deceived and abandoned, with nothing left in his life but movies and walks. We bought a full-length coat for me (too long, it didn't fit well), and later we went for a look at the old center of the city.

All the rebuilt historical parts have the charm of a miracle

---

* A resort town on the Baltic, near Gdańsk.

about them, a charm that only restoration can provide. The rows of narrow apartment buildings, bright shades of plaster reflecting the light (Gdańsk had not been such a very bright place), buildings with the elegant design of old engravings, seemingly untouched for centuries; copper drain pipes ending in the faces of beasts, baring their teeth from the front steps; intricate gratings, sculptures, balustrades, the insignia and crests of merchants, masterly baroque blacksmith work, the rhythm of windows and roofs—everything re-created immaculately, with wonderful care to both detail and the whole. I retraced Joanna Schopenhauer's childhood as if across an empty stage where the sets remain after the play has been performed and the actors have left. A drizzle fell through the gray air; a west wind kept gusting. A series of resurrected buildings let our steps pass in silence. A group of schoolchildren on a field trip were being led down the middle of the street between the facades. There weren't too many pedestrians. Two rolled-up umbrellas stood in solitude in front of something that was probably a wine shop. A man who looked like an out-of-work circus performer, with an enormous Tatra sheepdog in a harness, stood in the middle of this tourist attraction. I could have my picture taken with the white mountain dog on the front steps of Johanna Schopenhauer's apartment building. I could drink a bottle of beer under a drooping umbrella or go down a few steps and buy a little ship made of amber. Everywhere, on both sides of the street, the windows were closed, no eyes peering out from them. If large wax dolls lived here, I would not have thought them out of place. There were no human neighborhoods on that street, no crowds chattering in a dozen different languages, no peddlers, matrons, wood-carvers, patriarchs, sorcerers. Only little groups of bored, slovenly boys in short jackets and jeans roamed that street, boys with country faces. It occurred to me that the vanished world of Johanna Schopenhauer's youth, that venerable, harmonious way of life filled with form and light, had left an ironic posthumous trace. In the features of those roaming boys and the children toddling around on their field trip, Johanna Schopenhauer would have recognized the faces of the old Vistula raftsmen, those confident, carefree, simple souls whom she had liked to gaze down upon from the windows of her house. How astonished she would be to see that those cheerful, honest people, who had never planted the tree of liberty anywhere, those good, drunken neanderthals procreating over the years and multiplying, had become, in the end, the masters of the old port city of her birth.

> First of all, nearly every page of his work emanates the conviction that philosophy is supposed to reveal a truth of uncommon importance. Man's needs are not only physical; his innate characteristics also include a sense of metaphysical need, that is, a dissatisfaction with knowledge about relations, a striving to know the essence of things. So as not to lose his way in the world around him, man needs a compass in the form of some absolute truth; the sciences, however, only furnish him with relative knowledge. Religion used to satisfy this metaphysical need. But since Kant not only pointed out the nullity of the proofs of God's existence thus far proffered but, in addition, the fundamental impossibility of carrying out any such proofs, religion as a basis for relating to the world became unacceptable for a worldly person. Its legacy went to philosophy. For man, who has been ultimately deprived of his belief in a Providence that watches over the world, in supernatural reason using death and suffering for higher purposes known only to itself, philosophy was to answer the question of the meaning of life. If it is not equal to that task, all moral order will collapse like a house of cards and man will prove to be completely defenseless against the world, condemned to an incessant fear of suffering that he cannot avoid, with the specter of inevitable death before his eyes. Because of the bankruptcy of religion, only philosophy can save man from despair.

So wrote Jan Garewicz in his book on Schopenhauer. The mother's memoirs aroused my curiosity about her son, as happens now and again with reading. My bookshelves are not burdened with works of philosophy, and so I went to the library and selected a volume entitled *Schopenhauer* from the card catalog— Garewicz's book. Frankly, I was not so much moved by a desire to acquaint myself with the German philosopher's thought as by my interest in his family home. What influence did that bright and vital woman have on him as he was growing up and maturing beneath her intelligent eye? Had she played an important role in his life? I already felt a certain attachment for Johanna Schopenhauer, an affection, a closeness. I desired something more than what she said of herself. What had she been to her son? How had he viewed her? How had she remained in his memory? How much did he owe to her? I was disappointed. He had broken with her; he ran away, wrote her a letter, and they never saw each other again. He could not forgive her for her liaison with a certain man. Frau Schopenhauer, a court councillor, was living at the time in Weimar and had been a widow for years.

Even the reading of a book has a fate of its own. I read the mother's memoirs to calm myself, to tear free of myself and the evil spirits molesting me. To prolong the healing effect of her narrative's pleasant flow, which had already enticed me and drawn me in, I hit upon the son. And then, all of a sudden, the son pierced me straight through by pointing a finger at the source of my shameful defeats, escape from which I had sought in his mother's memoirs. What he said to me was: "Your distress does not flow from the biological anxiety that you call the fear of time but from a lack of belief in Providence: you have no God. God can be replaced by philosophical ideas: you have no philosophy. There is nothing in you to protect you against despair and the thought of death. I foresaw this a hundred years ago."

And I in turn could reply to this: "What you foresaw a hundred years ago is the stuff of journalism today. The sense of meaninglessness and despair, the loss of inward identity, doubt, and the ignorance of the Essence of Things have become part of our normal consciousness. There is so much talk about all this that it sounds a bit comical now. The only thing you did not foresee was that philosophy would not fulfill your expectations. It has turned its gaze from the mystery of existence and taken up other matters. And thus things have reached their worst, as you warned they would. Everyone is defenseless against the world, condemned to anxiety and pain. But since we all know this, if each person feels poisoned by his own and by interpersonal consciousness, does that not signify the beginning of a purification? Perhaps it is just to detoxify myself from the fumes of those images and words that have seeped into my mind that I attempt to replace them with others—to replace hopelessness with hope, and existential despair with a biological fear of transience. This contains less resignation. And to live in resignation is the last thing I want. And your precept that a belief in Providence as the basis for a relation to the world is impossible for a thinking person to accept does not seem self-evident to me."

A belief in Providence? I would express myself otherwise in my secular way—an inner certainty that beyond earthly life there exists a higher law and a singular value that contains the purpose of human life and justifies suffering and death. Millions of people have lived their lives in that state of inner certainty. They joined together, creating religions and churches, praying in them, giving their lives for them, converting others. I am using the past tense here. Many such people are alive now. However, now, when saying "faith, religion, the church," we have in mind the religions and churches that we associate with our received notions of religion and church. Faith and the church are for us what tradition defines as a faith and a church. We call a religion "with a past" a religion.

But good God, why should that be so? Our epoch resounds with new religions swirling among the old churches, a throng of them in passionate turmoil amid debate and gunfire! There are already martyrs to the new faiths, immolations, excommunications, apostates . . . There are fanatic preachers and cruel monks. Let us see things for what they are—religion is closer now. Let us think a little, ask what religion is in our times and whether the smoke from its fire has to be the smoke of hallowed candles. Haven't you heard? Don't you read? People are descending into the catacombs, the prisons; they are tearing one another to pieces over dogmas; they are perishing for their faith or killing one another for it. They do battle using the written and spoken word, the names of their saints on their lips. Who are they? Young people, girls, sometimes practically children. Beaten and tortured. Or murdering and torturing. And sometimes both.

The contemporary world does not belong to the Age of Reason; it is convulsed by a desire for faith. As a layman living outside the church, my epoch ages me. I feel an anachronism in it, sometimes alien, superfluous. Especially since I usually felt distaste for the type of person and the kind of life that express themselves through religion. I was a student when I halted in front of the steps of a rather old temple, asking myself, Should I turn back or enter? I entered. For me socialism was not a confession of dogmatic faith; I went in because it was battling against a barbaric church that was hostile to me—fascism. Socialism's nineteenth-century past had earned my respect, attracted me with its legends, the lives of its heroes, its ethical tension. And also by its modest liturgy, its simple ways. A table, a chair, a speaker, a discussion. And so, though I professed no dogmas, I already had a gospel. It is without irony that I think of this today. And I have no intention of reducing the significance of socialism in my life. And not only in my life. In history, culture. If I had to name the most important phenomena in our era, I would say the Roman Catholic Church, the Reformation, and socialism. I would further add that these constitute the historical trinity that delineates my idea of Christianity.

Thus, when saying "church," I am using the word in a broader sense. For me it includes ideological orders and organized state religions. Today, the universal Catholic Church is carrying out its mission in a world terrorized by new inquisitions and crusades. The churches of anarchism and nationalism are killing people. The churches of the totalitarian states are killing life itself. Both the former and the latter use torture. And both have their believers and their unbelievers. Society seems to be conscious of the religious character of contemporary life. It is no accident that the protesting democrats in the countries of Eastern Europe are called dissidents.

Two young German pastors expressed their protest against the tyrannies and intolerance of the East German authorities. They set themselves on fire—burned to death of their own free will. I ask myself, To which religion, which church, should this highest act of self-sacrifice be ascribed? The Evangelical or Reformed Church? The Calvinist Church? Or were they perhaps Baptists?

It's beside the point. In all likelihood they were professing the same faith for which ten years earlier the Czech Jan Palach had set himself on fire on Wenceslas Square in Prague. Today the old Christian religions are concerned with finding an intelligent cure for the evils attacking the human community. They make a point of participating intelligently in all areas of life; they proclaim social, civic, and humanitarian virtues; they defend their own believers against the clutches of political tyranny; they tame the beast. The old churches have ceased to burn with the fire of holy madness. I don't know what sort of baptism Palach received— Catholic, Marxist, or Protestant—and I have made no effort to find out. His act was sufficiently clear: he committed it as a believer in the restored church of freedom. But both the Czech Palach and the two German pastors must have had a strong sense of innate certainty in the existence of some absolute value that gave meaning to their deaths. And so . . . a lack of belief in Providence? A lack of absolute truth? Councillor Schopenhauer's brilliant son did not foretell everything to a tee one hundred years ago. He failed to take the changing nature of life into account.

There is no golden autumn this year; a constant cold grayness, rain, and lines at the stores. I had to go to Wola* at seven o'clock

---
* One of the boroughs of the city of Warsaw.

in the morning. The taxi driver, his face likably morose, asked me if I had seen the "prosperity hour." "What?" I said, not having understood. He had been referring to the evening news. I smiled. He didn't . . .

In May 1977 fifteen people declared a hunger strike against the imprisonment of KOR* activists. The strike took place in a Warsaw church, St. Marcin's on Piwna Street. The strikers included scientists, writers, humanists from the university, and young women, one of whom was a worker's wife; the seventy-year-old father of one of the KOR people also took part. People of different generations and with different world views—Catholics, intellectuals who practiced no religion, former Marxists, young men who not long before had been in the boy scouts, and young women students. Their family trees or personal pasts reached back to the Home Army,† the January Uprising,‡ the Polish left, and the Catholic Church, as well as the ZMP.§ Their number included a Catholic clergyman and the translator of Marx's *Das Kapital.* They were on strike for a week, in a nave at the side of the church, their only nourishment water and salt. The press treated the strike with derision, sparing neither slander nor lies. Television predicted in no uncertain terms that the imprisoned KOR people would be brought to trial. Walking down Piwna Street, I could observe plainclothesmen dressed as tourists keeping watch in the vicinity of the church, ice-cream sandwiches in hand to look the part better. The street was also filled with real tourists, of course, who knew nothing of what was going on or who didn't want to know or who were simply interested in other

---

* Komitet Obrony Robotników (Workers' Defense Committee). Founded in September 1976 by a group of Polish intellectuals to help workers being persecuted by the authorities in the wake of the June 1976 workers' riots, KOR gradually developed into an open opposition movement.
† The Polish underground resistance force fighting the Germans during World War II, under the leadership of the Polish government-in-exile in London.
‡ The 1863 armed insurrection against Russia.
§ Związek Młodzieży Polskiej (The Association of Polish Youth), a Communist youth organization.

things. The Old City, with its little bars and cafés, spaghetti joints, Parisian-style boutiques, and Canadian-style frankfurters, its hurdy-gurdies, parrots, and roaming street bands, was entering its summer season.

The hunger strike was an act of protest and solidarity in a moment of danger. At the time, no one was able to foresee what would happen next. At any moment hundreds of people could have been arrested, and their trials would necessarily have resulted in long sentences. Everyone I spoke with at once defined their relation to the hunger strike. It had been clear for some time that the social defense movement to which the hunger strikers belonged brought out certain traits in people that had been effaced and covered over by years of silence. Now many "mutes" had begun to speak; proselytizers also surfaced, people who had been skeptical or indifferent before. There was also the chorus of the anxiety-ridden, who warned of provocations: the miracle seemed too dangerous for them to believe in. People were experiencing spiritual dilemmas, despair, euphoria.

This was already the realm of religious experience, free of historical suggestion. The image of God is not necessary in such experience, whose essence is the subordination of the changing time of events to the eternal time of values. The hunger strikers in the church on Piwna Street evoked the same thought in different people: Was there any value that endures beyond events and is independent of their historical time? One could spend a long time reflecting on whether any more important question has ever been addressed to man.

■ NOVEMBER
1978

The window can still be kept open—the first days of November
are warm and it is quieter this time of year in the Old City, and
even quieter at night. During the day, however, the area around
the Market and the Cathedral is crawling with secret police. The
Primate gave a public address in the Cathedral after his return
from Rome. The election of Pope John Paul II and the approach
of November 11 (the sixtieth anniversary of Polish independence) have gotten the police moving again. Last year their as-
signments were boring—following individual KOR people,
writing anonymous letters, seizing mimeograph machines, and so
on. Now, things have started to bubble, and they're everywhere.
Julek S. came to see us one evening, having walked with an enormous crowd headed for the Cathedral. A mass will be held there
on the eleventh, followed by the laying of wreaths at the Tomb of
the Unknown Soldier. The announcements of the ceremonies are
posted on the churches and torn off by the secret police at night.
By day the secret police are less enterprising and usually cannot
be told from their colleagues, who buy hard currency and pester
tourists for dollars or marks. Both have that certain insolence in
their eyes and a tainted look to their faces. The local drunks have
a different sort of face—tearful, with pink eyelids. This symbiosis
of elements—tourists, alcoholics, police, and currency buyers—
extends the entire route from where the Constitution of May 3*
was ratified, past points where executions occurred during the

---

* In 1791 the Polish parliament and King Stanisław II August Poniatowski
ratified the first democratic constitution in Europe.

German occupation, along the streets where the Targowicians*
were hanged, and up to Traugutt Park, where a cross marks the
place where the members of the National Government of 1863
were executed.† Yesterday I walked that way with the writer
Adolf Rudnicki whose hair is now completely gray. He complained that the censors were mutilating his work. In his recollections of the writer Witold Gombrowicz, Rudnicki described a
walk they had taken on Wiejska Street before the war when,
passing the Sejm,‡ Gombrowicz confessed that he was tormented
by a desire to go inside during a session, take the rostrum, and
ask, "Gentlemen, when is the next partition?" The censor had
crossed out those words.

I read Nabokov after the evening news; television is also cele-
brating the sixtieth anniversary. With expressions of joy, their
gazes intent, the announcers bend over backwards to prove that
we owe the recovery of our independence in 1918 to the Bolsheviks.

The P.E.N. Club celebrated the sixtieth anniversary of independence. The ceremonies took place on the day before the anniversary of the miracle, on Friday, November 10, at six o'clock in the
evening. The hall was filled to overflowing: many were standing;
the younger people were sitting on the steps to the little gallery
that rose above the seats opposite the entrance, well inside the
hall. An audience composed of intellectuals. There were many
older people with well-known names (Stanisław Lorentz,
Krzysztof Radziwiłł), women of various generations, quite a few
connected to literature by family tradition (Monika Żeromska,
Maria Korniłowicz, Henryk Sienkiewicz's granddaughter, Miss

---

* A pro-Russian faction of the Polish aristocracy whose members were sen-
tenced to death for treason during the 1794 nationalist insurrection led by
Tadeusz Kościuszko.
† After the collapse of what is called the January Uprising of 1863 against
Russia, members of the provisional rebel government were tried and exe-
cuted. Romuald Traugutt was the government's leader.
‡ The Polish parliament.

Grabska, Bronisława Ostrowska's daughter), a few KOR people, some former members of the POW* and Home Army men, ex-Communists, Catholic activists, scientists, writers ... And, it seems, not a single party member. I was among the older segment of the audience. Not the oldest, for I was not there on November 11, 1918, and there were still a few people in the audience who could recall that day; but certainly I belonged to the older generation whose youth coincided with the years between the wars. Sitting there, I realized that forty-six years ago I had seen Piłsudski† during a parade on Saxon Square. It had been a cold and cloudy day. My father and I were standing in the crowd not far from the reviewing stand, and I recall the moment the parade began—the band of the First Regiment of Light Cavalry galloped to the stand on gray horses with a flourish of trumpets. Piłsudski waved his white-gloved hand to them, and I remember that gesture, cordial and aristocratic. He was sixty-five then. Nothing in his appearance foreboded any illness: his movements were brisk; he greeted the French ambassador, Laroche, with a smile. In silhouette, despite his broad sloping shoulders, he had a certain defiant ease, and the hand in the white glove was slender. I realized yet another thing: that at that time barely fourteen years had passed since November 11, 1918, exactly as many years as had passed between 1964 and the present. Independence was fourteen years old on that day. But then for me, the period before independence was the stuff of legend, remote, a

---

* Polska Organizacja Wojskowa (Polish Military Organization), an underground organization founded in the years preceding World War I in Austrian-occupied Poland by Józef Piłsudski. Its purpose was to prepare Poles for battle.

† Józef Piłsudski (1867–1935), originally a Socialist, gained fame as a military leader and organizer of armed opposition to Russia. Elected chief of state at the end of World War I, he went on to wage war with the Soviet Union (1919–1921), defeating the Soviet army outside Warsaw on August 15, 1920. He retired from public life in 1923, but in 1926, appalled by what he considered to be rampant factionalism and corruption of the parliamentary system, he staged a coup and installed himself in power. Until his death, he was the virtual dictator of Poland. His name is associated with the brief period of Polish independence (1919–1939).

part of history, like the age of the Jagiełłons.* Probably the period of Piłsudski's rule is like that for sixteen-year-olds today. An
odd calculation.

Several generations and a variety of lives had gathered in the
P.E.N. Club's auditorium. There were quite a few young people
born after Stalin's death, as well as those who (like my wife) had
in childhood heard direct accounts of the battles fought during
the Uprising of 1863 from their grandfathers, who in turn could
remember people who had seen Napoleon. The audience could
also have been categorized according to time and place of imprisonment. I counted a dozen or so people who had been imprisoned by the Germans during the occupation and a similar
number of others who had passed through Soviet camps. There
were also people who had been imprisoned in Poland after the
war: in 1949–1955 and later, in 1968, and still later, in 1977. Even
among the officers of P.E.N. itself there were writers whose lives
had been quite different: a member of the Home Army (six years
in prison in People's Poland), an officer cadet who served at
Monte Cassino, two reserve officers from before 1939 (who had
been in a German prisoner-of-war camp for officers), a poet who
had been a woodcutter in Siberia during the war. I have not, of
course, mentioned them all. There were others—those who came
under the racial clause and who had spent the war in hiding
or in the forests as partisans. And there were also those who
after the war, in the years of the trials and persecutions, "were
carried in sedan chairs" (an expression I heard) and who had
jumped down to go on foot in the opposite direction. For the
sake of order I should add that many a time the same person
belonged to two or three of the categories. I also noticed an elegant old woman in the third row, who a few years back when
buying postage stamps—at the time beautiful stamps were being
issued depicting newts and salamanders, in addition to those
commemorating political events—said with a Wilno accent, "I

---

* The second Polish royal dynasty, ruling from the end of the fourteenth
century to the end of the sixteenth.

would like two amphibians, three reptiles, and one Third Congress."

Whatever the particulars of their lives, all those present at the P.E.N. Club on that November evening had come with one common purpose and, I would say, in a common state of mind. They were guided by similar feelings and wanted to share the same experience and emotions, specifically, to express their desire for an independent Poland and to honor its memory. But then, right at the beginning, the ceremonies took a rather unexpected turn, one that did not occasion much satisfaction and seemed to be at odds with the prevailing mood. I am thinking of the first of the three speeches, that by Professor Stefan Kieniewicz.

To understand the situation, you have to imagine yourself there. Four gray-haired men were seated at a table, four heads that represented the best traditions of the Polish intelligentsia. The ceremony was opened by the newly elected chairman of the P.E.N. Club, the son of a poet who had been in Piłsudski's Legions, the nephew of one of the leaders of the old PPS.* Among those invited to speak were two eminent historians, professors at Warsaw University. One had published excellent studies on the January Uprising;† the other, besides being an expert on the history of the Slavs, also had a splendid past as an active member of the Home Army underground. They were facing a few hundred people sitting and standing, people tired of the official lie, bored by daily absurdity, and united in a common need for a miracle and by a hunger for a legend that would give them strength. Nowadays such ceremonies conclude with the singing of "O God, Who So Long Has Protected Poland . . ." with a distinct stress on the refrain "Lord, deign to return us our homeland free!" (different than when we sang it in school before the war: "Lord, deign preserve . . .").

I listened closely to Professor Kieniewicz's ideas. He spoke

---

* Polska Partia Socyalistyczna (Polish Socialist Party).
† See note on p. 13.

without glancing at his notes. From his opening words I was drawn by the calm, cohesive, and at the same time, free form his speech took. He spoke of the two decades between the wars in something like an autobiographical sketch. He characterized the period's conditions and its social atmosphere, interspersing broader reflections with the story of his life. He was the son of a landowning family in the Eastern Territories, a student of history and, later, an archivist. He spoke of himself as an apolitical intellectual, a liberal democrat. He recalled that he had imbibed his liberalism from Professor Marceli Handelsman while taking his seminars. Among Handelsman's students some were pro-Fascist, some pro-Communist; Handelsman didn't allow the slightest shade of difference to be felt in his relations with the two groups. In describing the successive phases of his life and work in independent Poland, Kieniewicz set them against the background of contemporary reality. He did not pass over in silence the period's shortcomings—social inequality, economic backwardness, arbitrary rule. Even back then, he said, when publishing his first scholarly studies, he had experienced both external and internal censorship. Neither did he fail to mention that after the first years of intoxication had passed, many of the activists who had favored an independent Poland grew disenchanted with the form Polish statehood had taken, less than ideal and not entirely just. On the other hand—and this he emphasized—the intelligentsia liked that Poland and felt at home in it. There was a sense of normalcy at that time, a sense that Poland had an authentic life as a nation. The intelligentsia shifted the responsibility for the country's fate onto the people who ruled it and made the decisions of state. But, after the catastrophe of September 1939,* when Kieniewicz was traveling on a suburban train to Milanówek the whole car was cursing. People weren't only cursing the *Sanacja* government,† they were execrating the people

---

* The German-Soviet conquest of Poland at the start of World War II.
† *Sanacja* ("purification") was the name bestowed upon the military regime installed by Marshal Józef Piłsudski in 1926 (see also note on p. 22).

who had felt at home, at ease in pre-September, independent, Poland.

I have not reproduced Kieniewicz's speech in its chronological order. He spoke of traveling to Milanówek after the September defeat at the beginning of his talk. But he referred to that incident in his conclusion as well, sounding a note of warning: Doesn't the Polish intelligentsia of today, present company included, with their daily bread and butter and tenured positions, also not feel responsible for the actions of the authorities? Will we not one day hear similar curses and will not the complaints against us be, to some degree, valid?

I felt anxious at that moment, shocked by the final note in Kieniewicz's argument. How, in what form, is the intelligentsia to take responsibility for the condition the country is in if every impulse that accords with responsible citizenship results in repressions, in being tossed overboard, in the loss of work, or in the prohibition of practicing one's profession? I know many people who took such responsibility (a dozen or so of them were there in the hall) and, as a result, learned the taste of prison bread; I assume that Kieniewicz did not have them in mind. So who was he thinking of then? No doubt the others, perhaps the majority of those present there at P.E.N. Who knows, he may have been thinking of himself. If so, that would have attested to a scrupulous honesty on his part. Either way, his final formulation struck me as unjust.

But his speech was serious, and that's how I took it. The speaker had wished to transmit his experience, to express the truth of those years falsified so many times in journalism and propaganda, years already remote and that today produce nostalgia, a nostalgia that, of course, embellishes and idealizes. As I have said, I belonged to that part of the audience that could recall those years. The speech had seemed to me a tallying up of difficult thoughts. And what pleased me most about it was its sobriety, its self-criticism, its anxiety. It is worth noting here that Kieniewicz had begun his argument with a prediction made half in jest: "It could be that what I am going to say here will shock some of you ladies and gentlemen." And so he was aware that he was going to antagonize the audience and set it against him. But that in itself was deserving of respect.

There was no applause. "During Professor Kieniewicz's speech," said Jacek Woźniakowski, the third speaker, "I notice how gloomy you grew, ladies and gentlemen, how long your faces became." As for me, I interpreted that absence of applause as ceremonial seriousness: clearly people desired to experience this anniversary evening in concentration and silence. It proved, however, to be the silence of the grave. The audience felt stung and shocked. During the break I heard some highly irritated remarks, and a few days later the board of the P.E.N. Club began receiving indignant letters. About what, for what? Because of the perhaps less-than-fortunate last few remarks? Not at all. For failing to show respect for patriotic sentiments.

Truly astonishing . . . How could it be, the same thing all over again? That age-old Polish "don't desecrate the sacred"? There was something of a caricature about all this, a grotesque repetition of the nation enslaving itself. After so many critical lessons exposing that defect in verse and epigram, after Boy, after Gombrowicz . . . But the public knew those writers by heart, delighted in them, and besides, some of them had become a part of the national tradition, required reading. And it was enough to assemble the elite of the Polish intelligentsia in an auditorium, to give the floor to a person who spoke his mind on matters of importance, like a free man speaking to free men, not adapting himself to the mood, feelings, and wishes of his audience, that was enough for the elite of the Polish intelligentsia immediately to react with a genetic twitch and for 300 people to cry inwardly, "Disgraceful!" Tolerance, liberalism, respect for other people's opinions, the decalogue of civic virtues (which is exactly what we are demanding!)—all that went out the window in one minute. Afterward, I heard that someone—I don't know who—had said, "I felt like hitting him." That made me shudder.

Only the third speech brought the audience any relief. After some informational remarks by Aleksander Gieysztor, who acquainted the audience with the principal trends in historical thinking under the Second Republic,* Jacek Woźniakowski, an art historian and Catholic intellectual, took the floor. His talk was splendid and focused on the culture of the two decades between the wars. He also discussed the country's legal system, making liberal use of examples of violations of law in today's judiciary; barely a few days before, he had been present at a trial in Katowice, where Kazimierz Świtoń, one of the active oppositionists, was the defendant. At last the room swelled with feeling. It was actually happening, at the end to be sure, but happening nonetheless. What people had been anticipating. The desired words were spoken, the moment of satisfaction had arrived . . . There was a whiff of the miraculous in the air. And thunderous applause.

I record my impressions without any sarcasm. Sarcasm toward whom? The greater part of the audience consisted of my friends, acquaintances, people who were utterly decent (Dostoevsky was very fond of that word) and who thought like I did. But among those with whom I spoke during the intermission and the next day, only two or three expressed any respect for the first speaker. Two others expressed theirs discreetly, as if it were only for my information. At bottom, they considered the first speaker unseemly, somehow offensive. Why? After all, he had spoken the truth about those years, and what was truly offensive was to live in a society where the truth can be considered unseemly. One way or the other, I found myself nearly isolated, since to express such opinions in Warsaw and Kraków causes eyes to goggle or doleful half-smiles to appear. And in the end I myself said to someone, "Why are you surprised? That wasn't the bird they wanted. They came to hear the flutter of eagles and what they got was the rapping of a woodpecker. A wise woodpecker though . . ."

---

* The name given to the period of Polish independence between the two world wars. The period before the eighteenth-century partitions of Poland by Austria, Prussia, and Russia is known as the First Republic.

But still . . . what can be done about this? This need for an inviolable myth so deeply rooted in intellectually refined people. Kieniewicz could have said more, much more. He passed over the internment camp at Bereza, the "pacification" of nationalist uprisings in the Ukraine, the rigged elections, the seating ghettos in universities, the numbers of unemployed. Nevertheless, he wounded the majority of the audience. The nation's sensitivity has become more acute after several decades of offenses; the irritations have swelled. And, as a result, all that was good and evil, bright and dark in the past, today glimmers with a varnish of miraculous imagery. All the spirits of the past are venerated; even Dmowski* is showered with praise, and for the Polish intelligentsia he had been a truly sinister figure, one who had done more spiritual damage than a partitioning power, for he had infected the minds of three generations. Today he is set alongside Piłsudski and ranked as the nation's second teacher. Piłsudski was not a teacher either but, rather, a supreme authority. There was greatness in him, and he truly did outgrow his partners, but there was also a good deal that was small about him, and an impartial witness who admired Piłsudski wrote this of him: ". . . for Piłsudski Poland was a sort of great big Zułow or Pikiliszki† through which he went grumbling and acting eccentrically, driving his stewards and farmhands with a gnarled stick, urging them on. With his Renaissance exuberance and his Lithuanian stubbornness, the breadth of his ideas and his petty vengefulness, his person and legend have covered and overwhelmed an entire period of Polish history and intruded into all our lives."

One time Andrzej Kijowski was arguing with me: "That shouldn't be touched, that's the instinct for self-preservation

---

* Roman Dmowski (1864–1939), founder of the National Democratic Party, a right-wing conservative movement that by the 1930s had come to resemble, in its ideology and political strategy, the Fascist and Nazi movements in Italy and Germany. One of the goals of the National Democrats (or *endecja*, as it became known) was that Poland must become an ethnically homogeneous country and that the Jews represented the greatest obstacle to the realization of that goal.
† Lithuanian villages in the district where Piłsudski was born.

thanks to which the nation has continued to exist." The instinct for self-preservation, all right, but what to do if one is a writer—submit, keep silent, write about sex? A constantly recurring dream: to live in a normal country . . .

To live in a normal country . . . in Iceland! But I once made a note of a remark by Jonas Salk, the American biologist, to the effect that it is in the areas where life's normal structure is disturbed that we come to know the essential laws of the species.

That "abnormality" contains a certain opportunity for literature: a renewed possibility for being aristocratic. It is the writer's clash with the regime that creates this opportunity. A new vitality is revealed in the descent into his private underground, his semivoluntary isolation: this is the impulse to exclude himself from mass culture, to separate himself from the creativity that is bought and paid for. The status of regime writer is offered to anyone who satisfies the conditions stipulated by the authorities. Literature replies: a writer is a person who does not accept offers. History provides us with a warning in that regard—in the opinion of Pliny the Younger, the decline of literature in Rome was caused, among other things, by its duplication, public readings, which destroyed the old elite literature of circumvolutions.

I'm reading *The Idiot* again (Nabokov's *The Defense* put me in the mood) and I came across the following sentences: "The world is starting to become too noisy and industrial, there is not enough spiritual peace . . . That may be, but perhaps the rumble of wheels carrying bread for hungry humanity is better than spiritual peace . . . I don't trust those wagons carrying bread for humanity! Because the wagons carrying bread for humanity can, if there is no moral basis for their action, eliminate a significant portion of humanity."

It is more difficult to be a writer today than it was a hundred years ago, when the novel offered itself to everyone, like a mirror on a busy highway, when literature had not yet confronted bare empty spaces full of frightening spectral questions. And in Poland it is even harder to be a writer because here literature is constantly burdened by the legacy of the Romantic poets, who have bequeathed to literature the duty of creating a national miracle. There is honor and beauty in that. But it cramps things, encumbers personality and individuality. Rooted in our collective otherness, our profiles are none too clear; how much we lose in comparison even with the Russians and their extreme, well-defined types: with Dostoevsky, Gogol, Tolstoy, Mayakovsky, with Yesenin and Solzhenitsyn, with their suicides, penal colonies, madness. I once explained to an Englishman who had become interested in Poland that emigration was bound up with the tradition of our literature much as the Russian tradition was bound up with exile and hard labor. But still he didn't seem to understand much of what I was saying. A short while later I tried to explain to someone in Warsaw the role of the miracle in Polish culture. I spoke of Polish fiction's lack of power, which we often mock ourselves (the Polish Aeolian harp . . .), and the fact that we had not passed through the school of historical plot development, which created the literature of the countries that possessed a court, a bourgeoisie, colonies, and police. The court was the school for intrigue, the bourgeoisie the school for careers, the colonies the school for adventure, and the police the school where crimes are reconstructed. Those are the fundamental elements of a story: intrigue, career, adventure, crime. Those countries produced Molière, Balzac, Defoe, and Sir Arthur Conan Doyle. In Poland there was no court like that at Versailles, a central focus for grand intrigues; the bourgeoisie developed late here and was weak; we had no colonies (Robinson Crusoe could not have come into being in a country without colonies); and we had no criminal police of the Scotland Yard variety. But we had the Miracle. Only in Polish does the word "miracle" (*cud*) rhyme with "the people" (*lud*). Miracle was rooted in church liturgy; the Catholic service itself is an irrational, surreal plot structure. In addition, we had the consciousness of being unfree, with its sublimations—the contempt for death, loyalty, honor—its theme of revolt, compromise, and defeat, and we had eruptions of genius feeding and reinforcing the age-old hope for a miracle. And perhaps that is why Polish literature has so few novels with precise structures and so few well-constructed plays.

The Baroque and Romantic predilection for the miraculous has been encoded into Polish thinking about life and literature. It grows darker, then dawns again; it is oppressive, then radiant again. We feel its tickle on our heels, that breathtaking possibility of leaping beyond ourselves, above reality, into dreams and the heroic . . . The resurrection of an independent Poland, wasn't that a miracle? God himself seems to encourage us. As if in response to the party slogan "A Pole Can Do It," He points a finger at Wadowice.* Become Pope? A Pole can do it.

A hundred paces from my gate. For twenty years excursions for foreign tourists have been stopping there and for twenty years I have been hearing the same scratchy baritone voice saying in English, "That is the old Gothic door of fifteenth century!" That sets the tourists twittering, and the group examines my gate. I have been cursing that scratchy voice for twenty years. Only a month ago, on my way home, did I see the guide for the first time. An aging woman with dark, smiling eyes that squinted without warmth at me as if understanding my old vexation. She was wearing muddy boots. Since then, whenever the baritone reaches me from below, I feel no hatred.

For a few months the shortage of medicine has been making itself painfully apparent throughout the country. Many pharmacies have put up little signs with the hated words "Closed for Repairs"; the hospitals are short of cardiological drugs. At some level in the ministry, expenditures for imports have been cancelled: ingredients essential to Poland's own drug industry are not being imported either. This has people very upset. Meanwhile, as usual, the greatest fury is caused by the mass media's hypocrisy. As far back as September, a conversation among sev-

---

* A small town near Kraków and the birthplace of Karol Wojtyła, Pope John Paul II.

eral well-known physicians had been broadcast on television. The topic—the mania for medications plaguing Poland and its harmful effects on society. The conversation had a certain civic, didactic air about it, but there was not a single word about the difficulties in obtaining medicine. The dominant tone was that of benign persuasion: my dear ladies and gentlemen, what do you need so many prescriptions for? Medicine taken too often can be injurious to health ... And that more than anything drives people wild—the dishonesty of the manipulation, the dirty tricks of such sophistry. It's somehow even worse than a lie.

I recently read *My Century,* a volume edited by Czesław Miłosz from tape recordings of his conversations with Aleksander Wat.* Wat was suffering from an inability to write, but he was a genius of a conversationalist. He always reminded me of both the monologists from *The Magic Mountain* (I called him a cross between Naphta and Settembrini), and in those autobiographical tapes he created an unparalleled, fascinating oral essay. *My Century* tells of a humanist's experiences with communism, of self-hypnosis in the closed circle of ideology, of interrogations, prison cells, deportations. This is an oral text, a voice turned into writing, and for that reason it unintentionally acquired the naturalness of a macabre tale told under a linden tree, an intellectual nobleman's stories about his adventures in Turkish captivity.† Besides narration, the book contains constant reflection and analysis. In one of his digressions, Wat speaks of the essence of the Communist system and the "betrayal of language" that is ingrained in it, and in one place—I'm relying on memory here—he defines this Mephistophelian trick as the replacement of the lie with the truth.

It would have been a lie to maintain that the hospitals and pharmacies had sufficient supplies of medicine. And so the tele-

---

* Polish poet (1900–1967).
† The reference is to a seventeenth-century figure from a trilogy of historical novels by Henryk Sienkiewicz (1846–1916), who in his old age used to recount his grisly wartime experiences in a joking, anecdotal manner.

vision and the newspapers do not lie. They only say that people in Poland are using an excessive amount of medicine. And, of course, there is some truth to that. But when there is a shortage of medicine on the market, that sort of truth fulfills the role of the lie.

Wednesday, an afternoon tea with Mademoiselle R., whom I knew from Paris, my wife, myself, and several other friends. The conversation constantly interrupted by Pik's drunken roarings, "Who's the bitch sleeping with?!" He had put away a quarter liter before he arrived. Thin, dark, he sits across from me; he has a small wolfish face, new white teeth, and speaks no French. We try to smooth over the awkwardness of the moment with desperate conversation. Julek S. tells of the anniversary ceremonies at the Tomb of the Unknown Soldier, where thousands of people had come together (the police were out of sight, hidden in side streets). Thousands of people sang "O God, Who So Long Has Protected Poland" and Konopnicka's anti-German "Rota" ("The Unit"). A moment later we are talking about Sartre. A month before in Montparnasse, Mademoiselle R. had passed a gray-haired *clochard* in dark glasses who she thought looked like Jean-Paul Sartre. Last week, on the day before her departure, she was walking through Montparnasse again, and not far from the Coupole café she spotted Simone de Beauvoir leading the same *clochard* by the arm. Sartre was blind, small, unshaven, wearing frayed trousers. I had read his interview in *Le Nouvel Observateur* back in 1976. That was after his first hemorrhage and after he had lost his vision. He said that the hemorrhage resulted from working too intensely on his book on Flaubert: he had been writing it on stimulants. "Hey, you!" cries Pik. "I don't give a shit about Frenchmen!" He bares his pearly teeth at me. "Why are you sucking up to that Parisian bitch?" Someone tries to calm him down. Artur, wishing to save the situation, seizes on the theme of Mediterranean culture. Pik removes his dentures to show them to the women. "Look at these, you bitch; I paid three thousand for them!" Fear, silence. Mademoiselle R. expresses her admiration for the reconstruction of Warsaw's monuments. In the end, Pik begins abusing me and someone else. "Balls!" he howls. "Goddammit, you write with your balls!" And now let's start singing, I thought. Let's sing a chorale so that the Frenchwoman can have a complete picture of our artistic life.

Meanwhile, and this is perhaps oddest of all, Mademoiselle R. seems content and clearly pleased by this Warsaw intellectual salon. I could already see the gleam of discovery in her eye as she lands at Orly: *"On est très slave là-bas, vous savez; c'était comme de Mrożek ... de Gombrovitch ..."* ("It was very Slavic there, you know; it was like something from Mrożek ... from Gombrowicz ...") When we said goodbye at the door, we could hear from the room behind us: "I give a fuck for that whore ..."

■ DECEMBER
1978

There has been frost for a week now. In the morning the temperature goes down to 10 degrees. Two months, more than two months spent in Warsaw, sixty-odd days without traveling and packing suitcases or any change in my way of life. Two full months: a bath at eight, three hours of work, a little rewriting or correspondence, lunch at the Writers' Club, then a walk, someone stops by, or a movie, and in the evening a couple of phone calls, records, television, and then, at last, quiet hours, reading ... Midnight. How blessed is this repetition. Each day practically identical to the day before and the day after—one doesn't feel the passage of time. The minutes and hours are transformed into another more secure structure made of objects, acts, words—homogeneous, stable, sealed absolutely tight. Not a single chink to let the fear in. A well-run life at peace with the world. Not a second's worth of feeling that it will come to an end, no despair over its meaning.

A letter arrived from the Executive Board of the Writers' Union requesting replies to a few questions about the collaboration of writers with publishing houses, film, radio, and television. The letter contained the following sentence: "For purposes of documentation we wish to obtain a reliable picture about the giving of short answers containing specific information." A typist's error? But that letter with its nonsensical sentence had gone out to the members of the Writers' Union. Sometimes one has dreams about senseless sentences like that. Perhaps the office director is an adherent of surrealistic prose. A couple of weeks ago I saw that same director throwing a mentally ill poet from the Writers' Club. He was dragging him by the collar, kneeing him along and being quite professional about it. A small man with pale eyes and a bulging forehead. A difficult face to forget.

I gave the following answers to the questionnaire's five questions:

1. *What form has your work with publishers taken in recent years?*
For six years no publisher in the country has offered to sign a contract with me for a new book.

2. *With film?*
For ten years all my proposals have been rejected (not by the film directors).

3. *With radio?*
I have not received any offers for six years.

4. *With television?*
No offers for seven years.

5. *What problems would you like to bring to the attention of the Executive Board of the Polish Writers' Union?*
The censorship. The censorship's criminal actions with respect to persons and texts. The censorship, but not only as an agency. As an activity destructive of public property—the culture of the nation.

It took me less time to fill out the form from the National Census. The blanks concerned the apartment's usable areas. "Rooms and spaces not used as rooms. Be specific."
Very simple: two rooms and a kitchen with no windows.

Lines, lines ... The closer it is to the holidays, the longer and denser the lines. It has snowed. Snow means mud in the stores. People stand in wet, darkened coats and splash dirtily along. The line at the fish store stretched down Wąski Dunaj Street. Some herring was supposed to have been delivered. The line was excited, and people were close to being sociable. The possibility of herring had evoked the idea of herring, and that idea had created a sense of community. A gray-haired man with a cane and a sack hanging over his arm was wheezing on about prewar herring. He might have been talking about Piłsudski. He was stirred by some wild and pious emotion. "They were beautiful! They gleamed! A slice was like twenty-four-carat gold!" There was a light frost; a few snowflakes were falling. The line listened respectfully as the old-timer, stooped with age, told of the herring, hero of the days of yore. The store opened at eleven o'clock. I learned that the people at the head of the line had been there since two o'clock in the morning. Later I walked down Piwna Street to Castle Square. There was also a line at the meat store on Piwna Street. People were packed tightly on the sidewalk, crowding up against the steps. Everyone was silent, leaning forward together, pushing fiercely—a real squeeze. I came back by there in the afternoon. They were still standing there, still packed together, but now they seemed to be bending backward, their heads held high, looking upward at the steps. The entrance was being stormed. They were breaking into the store. People had started shouting. Fights broke out in the line before the store closed; a few faces were bloodied. That evening on television the Premier's speech in the Sejm on the fulfillment of the economic plan was applauded by the deputies—literary men, scientists, journalists. The same people who two years before had sent me letters in reply to my appeal that a Sejm commission be convoked. After the strikes in

Ursus and Radom,* when the police beat up the workers they had arrested, a dozen or so deputies were requested to speak out in the Sejm and introduce a motion for an investigation of the matter and for the bringing of the guilty parties to justice. The appeal was addressed to the deputies from the world of science and culture and was signed by 175 people, who also represented science and culture. In the letters I sent to the deputies I guaranteed the authenticity of the signatures. At my request, the appeal was also sent to two deputies who were doctors from the provinces. I was anxious that the appeal reach them. I thought that the type of doctor who was sensitive to human injustice, the socially conscious doctor, still existed, especially in the provinces. After all, I knew such doctors, not only from reading Żeromski,† and they were more than childhood memories for me: doctors like that were still alive and practicing after the war. And here was a case of physical injustice, of broken jaws and ruptured spleens.

Of the seventeen deputies contacted, four sent no reply; the rest sent letters to me. They were all refusals. Diplomatic or complex-ridden, self-justifying or argumentative, but all refusals. Their arguments? They made for a rich collection. "The Polish People's Republic's Sejm is not a parliament of the West European sort." "To convoke such a commission would be against the interests of the state." "It was the police who had been beaten and provoked." "How do you know," asked one of the deputies in his letter, "that I have not taken appropriate steps in this matter already?" Nearly all the letters had the same tone of solidarity, the tone of offended dignity: you are appealing to us to discredit us, to put us in the pillory of public opinion. Us, who are deputies to the Sejm.

And among the dozen or so letters, two were ruthless, the most hostile, the most caustic. Those were the replies from the two doctors from the provinces.

---

* 1976 riots over the price of food.
† Stefan Żeromski (1864–1925), the most renowned Polish novelist of the first half of the twentieth century.

In the lines, people swear. They swear something terrible, and that river of curses could poison the fish swimming to the holiday dinners of our government leaders. In the evening, listening to the Premier's speech (his face always reminds me of a rotten pear) and seeing the deputies on their benches, my deputy-correspondents, applauding the plan that had ruined the economy, I thought about their letters of two years ago and their unanimous refusals. It's always unanimous! And it is true that the Sejm of the Polish People's Republic is not like the parliaments of Western democracies ... So then, just what is it?

When my brother was receiving several threatening phone calls a day from hoarse-sounding anonymous callers (it was in connection with his wife Halina's activity in KOR), Jerzy Markuszewski, who was present at one such call, advised him not to set the receiver down next time but to answer calmly, "Sir, if you have so much time on your hands, then teach your grandmother to piss in a bottle." Markuszewski always had a feel for the real spirit of the language.

■ JANUARY
1979

I was going to write more about various literary affairs, but the elements have provided us with a real-life calamity. Snow.

On the first night of 1979 we were already snowed under. That night the palace,* with a lantern above its entrance and lights in its tall covered windows, emerged from the white darkness like a fluorescent apparition. We were cut off from the world. The New

---

* At Obory, a former private country estate and now a retreat for members of the Polish Writers' Union.

Year's guests who had to drive from Warsaw couldn't make it through the blizzard. We were cut off from time, imprisoned in the last century. Zanussi's film crew, filming here in November and early December, had transformed the interiors into a nostalgic vision of the last century: brocade curtains hung everywhere; an old-fashioned yellow grand piano stood by the door to the card room, creating the illusion that Chopin had just left it a moment before; and in a side drawing room, directly across from a mirror, they had set up an enormous table with a red tablecloth, armchairs, and a glass bookcase in which the spines of *Brockhaus* German editions gleamed with gold. Outside, on the decorated gable, an armorial cartouche with lances and a shield (an extremely skillful imitation), some spheres made of plaster of Paris, and urns on the balustrade along the pond. It seemed that any second a merry sleighing party would be leaving here, jingling sleighs would bear us away into that whiteness to our neighbors' manors, for dancing and diversion . . . But, no. We sit in a chilly television room staring at the screen from which a frightened announcer with a concave nose and what looks like a stitched upper lip cries out to us: Warsaw is short of coal; there are breakdowns in the heat and power-generating plants; municipal transportation is at a standstill; people are freezing in hospitals and apartments. Pipes are bursting, and snow had paralyzed the main downtown arteries. Trains are running ten to fifteen hours late, and many runs have been suspended; the roads are impassable; there is a shortage of snowplows; the army is clearing the railroad tracks of ice and snow. The government has declared a weather emergency. The campaign against winter's onslaught is being directed by the Council of Ministers headed up by the Premier. Several cities have been without light, heat, and water for two days. The flow of gas has been reduced. The ports and shipyards are not operating. Domestic flights have been canceled.

The announcers are clearly under great stress. Their funereal faces are frightening. Especially the one with the little indented nose. He used to have a merry wink in his eye, and now he speaks like Starszyński* from the besieged capital; he calls on people to persevere, to tough it through. What has happened to him? Well, what has happened is that a bad dream that had been oppressing him for years in the early morning hours has come true—the dream of the day when he would have to tell the truth. To tell the truth using real words. To speak of what everybody knows: to say "the roads are impassable" instead of "the landscape is covered in white down"; to say "a lack of coal reserves" instead of "our heat and power generating plants have overfulfilled their plans." That's what has happened to him. He cannot wink merrily anymore; he cannot chat on in his warm tenor about the miners' New Year's Eve balls, about the children invited to the Belvedere Palace for cocoa, about Snow White and decorated Christmas trees. The streetcars are at a standstill; the radiators aren't giving any heat. The commentator's showmanship is to no avail. This cannot be put into pleasant images and this cannot be didactically misrepresented as Poles consuming too much heat in their apartments or using the streetcar system too often. The streetcars are at a standstill. The trains are stuck. Municipal services have failed. Once again the administration has demonstrated its incompetence: it has let winter take it by surprise. Today the announcer has to talk about what everybody can see with their own eyes, about what is actually happening. And that is why he is afraid.

And what is actually happening? The Polish winter has arrived with its snow and ice. Not in May; at the end of December. It might have been expected that after a few mild winters, we were due for a severe one. They gave no thought to that. They did not lay in reserves of coal; they did not have their equipment ready. Factories are at a standstill (the paper factory right near us at Mirków is still not in operation). The rolling stock that hadn't been repaired for years went to pieces at the blizzard's first blow.

Disorganization. How easy to subdue this country, constantly

---

* Mayor of Warsaw at the time of the 1939 siege of the city by the Germans.

warned of domestic and foreign conspiracies. All that's required is 20 degrees of frost and 50 centimeters of snow, and after a week, there are already problems with bread. And where are the causes for all this to be sought? Who is to be held accountable? The government? The system? We ourselves? This winter has revealed something—not only the weakness of the economy and the administration but something considerably more important, namely, the unclear state of affairs that blurs society's identity. For some years now, we have not known what our capabilities are and who we really are: an enslaved nation or a nation of alcoholics; in the industrial forefront of the world or else the age-old *Polnische Wirtschaft;* martyrs, anti-Semites, or a society ill-adapted to modern civilization. Since the war—that is, since the time when we still knew who we were, for we had affirmed our identity—we have been experiencing our fate outside of real experience, knowing less and less about ourselves as a collective all the time. Gombrowicz would have said that we had not matured into form. We no longer know what we project and what is falling on our heads. We have lost our bearings as to our share in accounts that have been falsified—what is happening at our expense and what is to our advantage. We can see the lie, but it is increasingly difficult to sort out the truth. In such cases people reach out to the past; forty years ago we were still ourselves, still living an authentic life. But the past is no longer the truth either; it is our image of the past. And so we exist between coercion and legend, in a something that goes on without regard for our refusal or consent and is constantly making us over. Until finally one winter we discover that it has snowed. Then we ask ourselves, Is this our snow? Are we under any obligation to shovel it? For there is some question as to whether this snow might not be *theirs,* imposed on us by the Russians in the framework of friendship, and so—shouldn't they remove it themselves? The authorities appeal to us to come to the aid of society. But one thing is not clear: Who is appealing to us—society or the authorities who cannot be replaced? Still, we look around for shovels; we have to dig ourselves out somehow, we have to leave. And then it turns out that there are no shovels. And then again we ask ourselves, Who is supposed to provide the shovels—the government or the people? *Them* or us? We stand in the snow deep in thought and, at the same time, are unable to draw any conclusions. The lack of shovels not only robs us of energy but renders our minds inert. I always laughed at the Prince in *The Doll*,* who at moments of patriotic impotence would say with a sigh, "An unlucky country . . ." Perhaps he repeated this phrase too often, but after all, at bottom, he was not being funny.

The frost has abated slightly. This morning it stood at 14 °C below zero. But it's snowing again. Yesterday an order was issued: all vacation and resort homes are to be closed until further notice. There is no coal; food is running out. The newspapers report that Warsaw has reserves of potatoes enough to last eight days. After reading this notice, people went rushing off for potatoes and bought them all up in a matter of hours. There are also problems with dairy products and butter. I had taken N. G. L. Hammond's *A History of Greece to 322 B.C.* in Anna Świderkówna's translation from the library. Hammond tells of the torments out of which Athenian democracy arose, how many battles, upheavals, and primitive instincts accompanied the maturation of that least easy of systems. Solon's poetical legislation has a beautiful ring to it. I recalled one passage: " 'I enacted laws in the spirit of equality for base-born and for high-born, according straight justice to each . . . I gave to the people the privilege sufficient unto the people, not diminishing its rights, nor demanding more . . . I stood holding my stout shield over both parties, and I did not allow either party to prevail in despite of justice.' " They challenged Persia, an empire that allowed them to make a living. They could have lived in peace ruled by Darius's satraps. But they loved the freedom of their city-states and so they resisted Persia. Everyone to Salamis!

The appeal to come to the aid of society issuing from the

---

* A novel of nineteenth-century Poland by Bolesław Prus (1847–1912).

radio, communiqués sounding almost direct from HQ on our battle with the elements, and the handful of us cut off from the world by the blizzard are a bit reminiscent of 1939 and the war. Then, we were called upon to dig antitank and antiaircraft ditches. I reported with two colleagues from the university to the assigned point, a long courtyard, on the even-numbered side of Nowy Świat, where, as I recall, there used to be a skating rink in the winter. Everyone got a shovel; we dug along strings stretched out as markers. It was a very warm day. A woman in a dressing gown and high-heeled slippers was working beside me. She was having a hard time of it—I, jamming my shovel into the ground, could see her out of the corner of my eye, her slender white feet sinking into the clayey earth. A woman who looked like a maid was digging alongside her. "You should rest, ma'am," she advised her when the sun grew stronger. The woman in the dressing gown took out a pack of cigarettes but didn't have a light. She bent toward me when I brought a lit match over to her cigarette and I could see two black trickles of sweat running alongside her nose. It was then that I recognized her. A year and a half before I graduated from the Gymnasium she had solicited me as I was walking down Nowy Świat, somewhere between Warecka and Chmielna Streets. I had heard about her before: my classmates Andrzej Rudnicki and Jurek Lichtenstein knew her. Her name was Zosia Bergy. Her real name was Gadomska or Gostyńska; her father was a respectable doctor. She solicited me in a passageway, whispering a few words in French.

1939–1979 . . . Forty years, a mere trifle! Yesterday, over tea and jam at Seweryn Pollak's house, we were discussing the odd way in which time seemed to be flowing, creating a simultaneous twofold impression of a protracted present and a past that was cut off, as if every "yesterday" were at the same time a "once upon a time" in which our reflections and shadows remain imprisoned. In memory we seem to be our own ancestors, and not such distant ancestors either, from two years, twenty years back. How do we differ from the émigrés—probably only in that their memory of the past is identified with Poland; they have not only been dispossessed of time but of place as well. When feeling nostalgia for a weeping willow by the road, what they are longing for is themselves under a willow before 1939 or 1945 or 1968—for the landscapes of their youth, and not for the countryside or the cityscape itself. After all, we have that landscape, every day, and don't we long for it too? One longs for what is absent. And it is we who are not here, we who are gone: we as we were in the past, in 1922 or 1957, during our childhood, when we had teeth, hair . . . But perhaps we are longing for the old system? Perhaps it was better then, more just? To be frank, I am not certain what it is that I am longing for, but one thing does seem indisputable to me: that a system in which I lose my teeth and my thick dark hair is not a just system.

Today, at daybreak, my wife and I awoke at the same time in a dull gray darkness and M. told me her dream. Could it have been that which had woken us up? In her dream she was with herself as she was at twenty, beautiful, with smiling eyes, and she held herself closely, making certain that it was she. She was very moved. Her younger self said to her, I beg you to remember that we are both you, think of that when you are dying. Your illness, your wrinkles, none of that has any meaning; don't worry. No one knows which one of us people will remember after death; we exist together, both together, remember. She embraced her. The young Maria embraced the old Maria, stroking her face with the palm of her hand. After she had described the dream, we lay together side by side in silence. Then she continued, "I was wearing a light-blue suit and a dark-blue beret—you must remember it, just the way I look in that photograph of me standing by the entrance to the museum."

I hadn't had any dreams. But I remembered that blue suit. The first time I saw her wearing it I said, "It's not fair how pretty you are today."

A day in Warsaw. The city gives the impression of having been devastated by the winter. There are snowbanks everywhere, a dirty, disfiguring white. Along the sides of the streets, immobilized cars; some, completely buried in white tapering caps, look like abandoned bunkers. Weary people shuffle along the sidewalks, their faces gray, as if unwashed. One feels a stifled fury in that weariness, that shuffling. Someone in a store says, "When it warms up, the authorities will melt away." At home quite a few letters with New Year's wishes and an invitation to a literary symposium in Vienna. Its theme: historical consciousness in contemporary literature.

It is mostly placards from the May Day parade that are being used to shovel the snow. A stick with a square board nailed to it and held upside down becomes a shovel; only first you have to remove the image of one of the leaders of the working class. There was a shortage of shovels in Obory, and I had asked Staś, the stoker at the boiler room there, if there were any placards like those at the state farm. Staś thought for a moment. "There were," he said, "but they got sent over to Mirków to demonstrate solidarity with Angola." Soldiers are shoveling snow in Warsaw, and shovels are distributed to office workers on their days off. On January 17, banners were hung up over the icicles and snowdrifts: to mark the anniversary of Warsaw's liberation from the Germans.

In spite of the fact that I haven't been reading newspapers for a few years, every once in a while magazines—literary, sociocultural, or illustrated—end up in my hands. They contain articles, reviews, why, even debates. They print a multitude of authors, discuss books and premiers; they even create great writers . . . Someone from the outside, who came here from, say, Venezuela, might have the feeling that Poland's cultural life was on fire. What could possibly be lacking here! There's everything, and everything in its proper place: creative work produced here, translations of literature from the three worlds, analyses of contemporary civilization, sociological polls, structuralism, human rights, civil rights, new terms—paradigm, trauma, trends . . .

Everything, the entire spectrum! How many years would a person have to live here before he could decipher this system of shams and smell the hovering stench. Here everything conceals the corpses hidden under the floor. A book that is being written up is supposed to drive the book that is not published even further down. Buried between the lines of every text printed are the names one is not allowed to mention, the facts about which one remains silent. The places and dates blotted from history create a dead zone whose silence is filled with the noise of artificial polemics and where semipoets give interviews to semijournalists and express their semitruths to their semireaders. There is no lack of anything here except for the half that has been amputated.

And what's happening with that amputated half?

When *Zapis* was founded three years ago, I had my doubts about whether we could afford to publish a literary periodical that depended on a small group of writers who had rejected a semiexistence in our society. I was afraid that after a couple of issues, we would start running out of reserve material. I was not alone in these fears. And, curiously, the reservations expressed by others made me resist my own doubts, summon up counterarguments. I remember one such conversation (the first issue of *Zapis* was already in preparation—I had contributed a fragment from *A Question of Reality*), the discussion that finally made me aware of the meaning of *Zapis*'s existence. The following arguments had been made: "We are deviating from our years of being on the defensive, from the game we have been playing with our own creative work. By employing tactics to deceive the tyrant, we were defending the last living values in our culture, we were ensuring their endurance, albeit in the form of allusions and subtexts. In choosing open battle, we deprive ourselves of that possibility."

One might have also added that in publishing *Zapis* we were putting our own personal safety at risk: increased repression was in the interest of the police. But that argument was not advanced. Clearly, we had no wish to frighten ourselves.

I spoke up a couple of times, essentially to reply to myself. I was quite familiar with that way of thinking; it was, after all, almost literally the way I had formulated things myself. For many years it had been my view that all that remained for us was to squeeze our way in through the chinks, to exploit every last weak spot in the system, every relaxation of the censorship, to smuggle in what we had to say through the cracks. I cited examples, especially from the second half of the nineteenth century, when writers had to play a similar game with censorship, and I cited various books. I went further, asserting that limitations and prohibitions and the need to elude them, the quest for a canon, all make for ingenuity; new allegories and metaphors are born, which, in deceiving the censor's eye, create new means of expression. And once again I reached out for examples—from church art.

But now I was struck by the minimalism of that line of thought, felt the coercion and the narrowness in it. For what actually is culture? Can the idea of culture be reduced to works of art and thought? If the answer is yes, then we really have no other path but that of "deceiving the tyrant." But are we deceiving the tyrant or is he deceiving us? It is not true that in exchange for the chance to publish poetry, we give up on stating the values that that poetry conceals, from which it arose, and to which it makes reference . . . If that is the case, then one may suspect that we are paying too high a price. We are paying for the written with the unwritten. There are moments when the unwritten values create the culture. Perhaps those are only the moments of tension and crisis, situations in which the boundaries of everyday endurance must be overstepped and the rules of the game broken. Then the majority of examples from the history of literature become useless and one must appeal to other ones. To the unwritten ones. To acts and attitudes that have not been anthologized but are a part of the collective imagination, impregnating it with their gestures, scenes, faces.

With a certain embarrassment I admit that during the discussion, I mentioned side by side the November night of the Belvederists (1831)* and the general meeting of the Writers' Union in February after the cancellation of *Forefathers' Eve†* as two examples of unwritten facts creating culture.

The problem could have been stated as follows: we had taken a certain intelligent step out of a situation that was hard to bear; we had created a new situation, unknown to ourselves, one that was open and dependent on circumstances different from those that had existed thus far. *Zapis* had come into being. We didn't know what it would be, how many issues would appear; we only knew what it wouldn't be. *Zapis* had arisen for several reasons, from a variety of needs. Certainly the need for freedom was among them. But also from shame at the thought that we would leave nothing behind us but the stories and poems that had been published, nothing more than that. But to utter the word "culture" is to make reference to greater things. And that is why I consider this above all to be an intelligent decision. Today *Zapis* is self-evident: its copy undergoes critical evaluation (there are already other independent journals besides *Zapis*); it is genuine, that is, results from authentic materials, from the experience of things as they are. Is it a good journal? Probably no better and no worse than the people who produce it and who write for it. It is like them. But it *is* like them. If a journal becomes like its authors, that means something different than authors becoming like a journal. In that regard as well, the founding of *Zapis* seems intelligent to me.

All this occurred quite recently. How long can it last? Three or four years ago there was still practically nothing. And it had barely started when friendly warnings were heard. Well-grounded warnings of the consequences. When KOR was founded, there were warnings about the dangers of its becoming

---

* The start of the first armed uprising against Russia, when a group of Polish officers from the army cadet corps in Warsaw occupied the Belvedere Palace, home of the Grand Duke Constantine, brother of the Russian tsar and the tsar's proxy in Poland.
† A play by the poet Adam Mickiewicz (1798–1855), a production of which was canceled by the government authorities in January 1968 because of its embarrassing anti-Russian sentiments.

a political organization. After the first issues of *Zapis* were published, the naïve were warned against the people who had founded it, ex-Communists and former socialist realists. Writers were warned against losing their existence as citizens, against losing contact with their readers, and of a new dependence of literature on politics. The worst auguries, ominous forecasts . . . And it had just come into existence. It had barely bounced off the bottom. Today the idea of "bottom" is having its moment of glory: in saying that word we create an alibi for ourselves; everything is at bottom, everyone is on the bottom. As soon as someone tries to rebound off the bottom, the alibi is undermined. Then the damned bestir themselves: "How long can it last?" I suspect that this is a question that should not be asked, and if it is, it is better left unanswered, even to oneself.

How are the birds withstanding this severe winter? There are many sparrows here, numerous blackbirds, and a flock of coal tits. Yesterday I saw a woodpecker. These are birds that do not fly off to the warm countries. Storks and swallows migrate. To this day, no one has explained to me why some birds are unable to live the whole year in Poland and why it never enters the mind of others to fly off abroad. My sympathy is for the domestic birds. Those unsung resident starlings that do not emigrate. I never understood completely people's joy at the sight of a stork returning or that myth of the stork as the venerable bearer of newborn babies, the stork that devours field mice and frogs. But perhaps that's just it; perhaps one has to fly away and be gone for some time to increase in value. I recall my return from France seven years ago, when there was a rumor circulating that I had emigrated. I was greeted like a stork. How much warm gratitude could be read in people's eyes back then! But the error didn't persist for long, and soon enough people realized that I was a domestic sparrow. My foreign shoes didn't matter. They only fooled the beginners at black marketeering at the market for three days: "Yoovont Polish munee?" On the fourth day, they saw me out with my shopping bag.

Back in Warsaw. No new events. People are talking only about the snow. Hundreds of roofs have collapsed; many apartments have been flooded; icicles are crashing to the sidewalks. An icicle killed a dog on Piwna Street. Thousands of people are shoveling snow, and this is no longer a "volunteer effort"; a ruling has made worker mobilization obligatory. There are still too few plows and dump trucks. Masses of university students and schoolchildren, people from institutions and ministries, are out shoveling. The Market is buried under three feet; only two black catch basins protrude from the snow.

Yesterday at the Kijowskis there was talk of the paper shortage, so far advanced now that, apparently, certain publications have to appear less frequently and books are coming out in printings several times smaller. Certain facts pointed out by filmmakers are also pertinent here: the shortage of color film, poor copying facilities—moves made to limit the distribution of the better films. I realized that I was indifferent to the conversation, as if it didn't concern me. I basically write for one reader and in an edition of one and everything beyond that I consider a piece of good fortune on which I had not counted in advance. The only reader I have for certain is M., for whom my reading the manuscript aloud is enough. Perhaps this is absurd, but it's not so far from the truth. As the chance of my books being published grows slimmer, my need for publication apparently decreases. Fifteen or twenty years ago I could not have imagined that I would be able to live and work in such circumstances. And the biggest surprise is that, overall, my life isn't much changed by these circumstances. I often recall what P. said about his conversation with the Russian poet Anna Akhmatova, who in the last years of her life had bestowed her friendship on him. Once, when he complained to her of his difficult situation (he had been forbidden to publish), she interrupted him: "Are you in danger of arrest?" P. said that he was not. "Are they kicking you out of the Writers' Union?" P. answered in the negative again. "So what are you talking about then?" P. claims that Akhmatova had been genuinely puzzled.

Such are the Russian consolations. Nothing should seem so terrible in comparison with the fate of Russia. That's not how things work, however. Russia's fate is not a part of our consciousness. It is alien to us; we feel no kinship with it or responsibility for it. It weighs on us, but it is not our heritage. I have always felt that way about Russian literature. I was afraid of it. To this day I am still afraid of some of Gogol's stories and of all of Saltykov-Shchedrin. I would prefer not to know their world, not to know it exists. One has to be a Frenchman to feel safe with that literature. Reading Dostoevsky, I have to remind myself that I will emerge in one piece from this illness, that I will somehow escape it, for to allow oneself to be gripped by it and to succumb to it means a spiritual death sentence, and I am not sufficiently submissive to accept that.

But meanwhile, that literature is drawing nearer to us, becoming disturbingly close. We have started using it to think; we see scenes and situations from our own lives in it. On the Monday television theater they showed an adaptation of Gogol's "The Overcoat." I couldn't watch more than fifteen minutes. There was already something of ours in that grinding down of small souls, that degrading burlesque of despair. The distance between them and us has decreased; what was formerly a concept, an idea of Russia, is now becoming our flesh and blood. It may have been Herzen who somewhere compared Russia to a peasant

woman who had been clubbed black and blue and was lying at
the feet of Tsar Nicholas I. A comparison like that isn't difficult
to remember. As a rule, it's only the winter that reminds Warsaw
that it's an East European city. This time winter has pushed us
back a century. The people standing for an hour in dirty, trampled snow at a bus stop look like poor, beaten peasant women.
"There exists a Northern imagination, as there exists a Southern one. The latter is made of sun and wine; the former, of vodka
and snow." Tadeusz Boy wrote that nearly half a century ago
when reviewing the works of the Russian writer Valentin Ka-
taev.

Snow and vodka . . . Let's also add lines in front of stores and
thick-headed officials. Why does all this seem so familiar? Only
because of Russian literature? No, it's today's Polish reality that
increasingly brings Russian literature to mind. Today Russia is
infiltrating us in a different way than thirty-five and one hundred
and fifty years ago; it comes in via vodka, via corruption and
bribery, and not necessarily as it did before, via uniformed Rus-
sifiers. Forget Gogol! They are doing scenes from Dostoevsky's
The Possessed in Żoliborz.* Kuroń's† apartment was invaded
during a session of the "Flying University" (the Society for
Scholarly Studies).‡ A lecture was about to begin when a band of
about thirty-five men forced their way in, passing themselves off
as "a debating society." The lecture was cut short. The gang
broke up into smaller groups, going about the apartment yelling,
arguing, and raising hell. It was perfectly clear that they were
looking for a fight. Bands of such "debaters" appear in nearly all
of Dostoevsky's novels, and they always stink of provocation.
Dostoevsky is a master in describing those scenes. He pursues

* A section of Warsaw.
† Jacek Kuroń is a leading figure in the Polish opposition movement and a
co-founder of KOR. He was to become a key adviser to Solidarity.
‡ A system of informal educational courses set up by a group of independent
scholars in 1978. Held in private apartments, the classes gave students and
lecturers the opportunity to discuss subjects which were forbidden for political reasons in the universities.

them, he bends the bow string of his plot to them as if aware that the arrow of his genius attains its highest, truest flight in those moments (is that an apt metaphor—"the arrow of his genius"?). We've known such scenes in real life for about ten years now. In the spring of 1968 I made the following note: a revolution of *szmalcowniks** directed by the Minister of Police.† It is significant that it occurred to me to use a term from the time of the German occupation. And no accident either. In the winter of 1940, shortly after the ruling that Jews had to wear armbands, I saw a gang of armed hoodlums walking across Marszałkowska Street led by a woman in a long man's overcoat and beret. They threw themselves, howling, at all passersby with armbands, hitting them in the face and often mauling them bloodily. The woman was shot later on; she was a drunkard and an informer for the prewar police. This took place during the German occupation, but the word "pogrom" came immediately to mind, and it was probably then that I first realized how the pogroms in Russia had worked, how they work in general. It's simple. The populace doesn't have to take part in them; a mass of hired lowlife is sufficient. After March 1968, policemen in Warsaw would hold quick morning briefings on city squares with small groups of adolescent hoodlums, which would immediately go off to the addresses they had been given. Those were not pogroms; rather, it was a matter of mental terror, of frightening the Jews out of Poland. The populace took no part in that either. After all these years, I get everything mixed up, and now, hearing that someone's apartment has been invaded or that a student was beaten in the streets by persons unknown while, by some strange coincidence, there was not a single peacekeeper in sight, or when learning of similar or even

---

* A derogatory slang word coined during the German occupation for people who spotted Jewish-looking Poles on the streets and blackmailed them, demanding money in exchange for not betraying them to the Germans.
† An anti-intellectual, antiliberal, and anti-Semitic campaign was unleashed in Poland in 1968 by a raging factional struggle within the Polish Communist Party. The campaign resulted in the exodus of almost all of the remaining Jewish community in Poland.

more ominous events, I invariably have the same thought: *szmalcowniks,* pogroms, Russia, occupation.

Those days when you wake up without a glimmer of hope are painful days. You have to tough your way through them, control them somehow with words or actions. What gives people hope in Poland today? Or, to put it more modestly, what arouses their interest? Timeless human affairs, of course, like love for a woman, raising children, and, let's say, the results of work, study, and so forth. What else? After that, the view flattens out. Love, raising children, work—in my thoughts all that encounters a sunless, gray plane; everything is cut off and bounded by a horizon that is close by and beyond which there is no light. But let's accept that that's how life is. Let's even assume that it's possible that all life's brilliance is only the result of our illusions and that real truth is one stripped of all illusion. Then what? What does a person wake up to then?

The morning paper. The news that something has happened in the world that is transforming life and resurrecting hope . . .

Poetry, philosophy, art. Tales and accounts of fate from an imagination or intellect, which reach higher and deeper than the average experience . . .

A stroke of luck, unexpected adventures, tomorrow, the coming week . . .

This is as far as I go, for next comes the sphere of religious experience, faith in redemption and salvation, and I am speaking here of people's earthly hopes, that is, of their interest in life. After due reflection, I came to the conclusion that our present existence lacks all incentive for an interest in life, since such incentives require a highly complex, a rich, and above all, an organic society, one that admits imagination and thought, that is open to art, politics, information, producing and absorbing substances for its own sustenance—everyday, ceaselessly, forever anew. Here, natural life has been reduced to a skeleton, and thus we ourselves have become skeletonlike. I wake up in the morning in a fog of something between recollection and sensation. It would be difficult to define it, but it doesn't have much in common with hope. Sometimes it's about the next line in something I'm writing, another time about some troubles, problems, and sometimes, when I'm half asleep, I think about the Pope, the Chinese . . . or about Stanisław August.* It varies. In any case, nothing about the taste of life tempts me to leap out of bed. Neither the morning paper nor a fresh, crisp roll. But, at the same time, I have no reason to feel any pathos or to complain and feel sorry for myself. It's no easier for other people to get out of bed, and others have it still worse. But we wake up in the same mood, with a vague sense that nothing awaits us. There is something cadaverous and spectral in it all.

And perhaps this too gives some indication of how close the Russians are.

■ MARCH
1979

As a young man, I was enrolled in the Łódź† Gymnasium for mathematics and natural sciences, which had been endowed by great industrialists. I felt suffocated in that Gymnasium's alien, cold atmosphere, stuck in a black uniform with a high collar and a hook-and-eye-type clasp. I was terrified by mathematical problems. I knew that I would fail and not graduate, especially since in the last two years of school there would be subjects with ominous names: business arithmetic, bookkeeping, the science of commodities . . . Year by year, I grew increasingly nostalgic for Warsaw, which I really only knew from legend—from history,

---

* Stanisław II August Poniatowski (1732-1798), the last Polish king.
† An industrial town west of Warsaw.

literature, and my father's recollections of it. When at last, in the summer of 1932, we moved to Warsaw, I walked the streets for the first few weeks in a trance. I had found myself within a myth, in a dream come true. In solitude, I retraced the walks of Wokulski*; sitting on a bench by the entrance gate to Łazienki Palace, I relived scenes from *November Night*† and *Early Spring*,‡ the white columns of the Belvedere's gallery to my left. It all became one—literature mixed with history, reality with painting, the past with the present. It was enchanting, mythic.

In no other great capital did I ever again experience any such entrance into an image, into the living stuff of concepts, ideas, and fantasies. New York reminded me of a gigantic Łódź, a hundred Łódźes bristling with skyscrapers. Paris revealed its charms gradually, different ones with each trip. But such a breathtaking confirmation of what I had imagined and such happy amazement at my own presence at the source of those fantasies as I felt that first summer in Warsaw—no, never again, and nowhere else.

Warsaw didn't dazzle foreigners in the twenty years between the wars. Gray, its layout chaotic, its back turned to the Vistula, it might have seemed a city of no interest. But for me, the world was interesting then. After smoky industrial Łódź, Warsaw was synonymous with worldly glamour. I was not one of the catastrophists. I learned Jan Lechoń's poetry by heart; I read Georges Duhamel's stories; the name of Franz Kafka barely reached my ears. Now I sometimes think that the world is small, stupid, and bloodstained. But less was known in those days. There can be no error cruder than to think that the more information we have about the world, the more comprehensible it becomes. On the contrary. The contemporary mass media only reveal the unpredictability of our planet, whose laws we do not know. Anything

---

* Main character in Bolesław Prus's novel *The Doll,* set in mid-nineteenth-century Warsaw.
† A play by Stanisław Wyspiański about the November Uprising of 1831 against Russia.
‡ A novel by Stefan Żeromski.

can happen; I can learn about it all, but that doesn't at all mean that I'll understand it. Back then, many of my friends' homes had no radios, television wasn't even dreamed of, and films were usually more sentimental than cruel. That summer, the Polish Theater premiered *Jim and Jill,* an English musical comedy. The Nazis had not yet taken power in Germany. War would not erupt in Spain for a few more years. Nothing was as yet known about the political trials in Moscow. Asia? Africa? The domains and colonies of the old powers were far away then. The world could be comprehended. To me it seemed far-flung and great, but normal. Poland, independence—these also seemed normal to us who had been born just after or just before November 1918.

In *Kuźnia Młodych* (Smithy of Youth)* I encountered for the first time people my own age who thought that this normal Poland of ours needed to be changed. They were Piłsudskiites; when they spoke of Piłsudski, however, they laid greater stress on his Socialist past than I did: a Polish revolution would fulfill Piłsudski's youthful ideals. Today that reminds me a little of people's attachment, after 1956, to the "young Marx" . . .

Days without writing. Correspondence, long-distance calls, a few unnecessary appointments with people, conversation tainted with gossip. I won't be going to Vienna for the symposium; I won't be going to Berlin. But all that requires letters, composing polite refusals, explanations, and then envelopes, stamps, trips to the post office, and so on. Everything takes time, and time is short. The days seem chopped up by a cleaver. At night I hear yodeling outside, then shrieks, "Police!" and voices babbling. Spring isn't far away. Some of the things the drunks say can be interesting. Yesterday one began roaring out a solitary rendition of "Poland Is Not Yet Lost."† Then he quieted down and added softly, to himself, "Goddammit, the Russians have come." Then it was quiet again. Later, a chanting, marchlike roar from the

---

* A bimonthly publication started in 1932.
† The Polish national anthem.

Barbakan:* "Gierek's a Jew, Brezhnev's a Jew, all Jews to Israel!" At daybreak, unable to sleep, I reach for my notebook to record at least those voices of darkness. On the whole, a bad night.

Berlin is a matter of finances. Six months without expenses at home plus the chance to set aside some money for next year. My earnings in Poland don't exceed 5,000 a year. The Department of Taxation considers me a "dead soul" and for three years now hasn't bothered calling on me to declare my income. There have been no reprintings of my books; *Rondo* has been locked away in the publisher's desk on Wiejska Street for two years now. Only from abroad do some royalties come in every once in a while. The press, television, and radio don't mention the forbidden names. Aside from me, there are at least another dozen or so condemned writers, infamous men (*infamis*) punished by expulsion from literature. Tadeusz Boy, Maria Dąbrowska, Julian Tuwim, or even Władysław Broniewski never knew the taste of internal banishment in the two decades before the war, though they would have had the ONR† seized power. The sentences are secret. "There has been no negative decision," I am informed in connection with *Rondo*, "and no positive one either. There is no decision."

It was under such circumstances that I decided to make the trip to Berlin. Blacklists, anonymous accusations, writers ousted from public life—it has been like this before; their solitude was greater back then and their personal situation a hundred times more dangerous. A few years after the war, when my books were appearing in large printings, the names of certain anathematized authors, like Zawieyski, Bąk, and Stawar, could not be mentioned in the press. Jerzy Zawieyski lived a life of poverty in a sublet room (with a prostitute right next door), supported by relief from priests. He had it worse than we do today, but Poland

---

* A reconstructed section of ancient medieval fortifications in Warsaw, currently situated in the part of town called the Old City.
† Obóz Narodowo-Radykalny (Nationalist-Radical Camp), a right-wing political party during the interwar period.

was a more dangerous country then. When I visited him, we would drink tea and joke, avoiding any conversation about what separated our lives. Only once did I take the risk of saying, "Jerzy, I can't pray; 'pray and work,' that's a commandment for two different people." But it was more than our views that separated us in those years; sometimes, after leaving his place, I would feel that I had been visiting a prisoner in his cell.

So, things were worse before. Today one often hears that truth being turned into a rebuke: "The present evil is the lesser one and so it shouldn't be provoked. Things were worse before." This argument is repeatedly advanced by people who were persecuted during the years of Stalinism.

Yes. But, in fact, a lesser evil can reach deeper and embrace more; it's easier to live with a lesser evil and that consequently means ... But to compare dimensions and types is beside the point here. And writers are not the main issue either. The main issue is how society will act toward those few thousand young people, that handful that has emerged from this society and that has been trying for five years to wrench it out of its passivity. Will society give them its support or encrust them in silence? No arguments can withstand the fact that a couple of thousand such people exist. None. Neither the argument that the substance of the nation must be preserved nor the fear of intervention from without. No warnings in regard to the past or the future, no historical analogies or political arguments, can cancel out the fact that for five years that handful of young people has created a living organism in an inert society, an antibody to the system: this small handful has created civic committees for self-defense and solidarity, social aid drives, independent publishing houses and periodicals, courses in science, printing houses, a distribution system, all the while displaying intelligence, courage, and character. And a good deal of sangfroid too: some of them have gone through the criminal courts and prisons, but the movement has resisted provocation. It is not a secret movement. Operating on the basis of constitutional rights, it makes a point of being open.

I am writing this today because I was thinking about it yesterday. These are not new discoveries, new observations. But sometimes things that are long familiar can appear in a new light, in a different perspective. I suddenly began wondering what that handful of people will mean to society in a year, two years, five. What will it mean to us? And do we realize that there is no more important issue in Poland today? For it is precisely what that handful will mean to us that will define us and determine in advance what our society will be.

A bearded young man told me of the latest methods for thwarting the activities of the "Flying University." Last week Adam Michnik* was to give a lecture in a housing development in Ursyn. A group, actually a squad of twenty-year-old roughnecks, was blocking the entrance to the building. Inside, another group kept watch on the stairs. They were all from an activist, government-sponsored youth group, which, all told, numbers around a hundred. The only way the students could penetrate the blockade was by force, which would have meant a clash. "I've never seen anything more horrible," said the bearded young man. "You see, all you could do is stand there and stare them in the face. You couldn't take one step. That would have been just what they wanted, a fight. You can be sure that the police would have arrived in a minute and made arrests for hooliganism. Us, not them!"

When Michnik arrived to deliver his lecture, the cordon let him pass, but he was attacked on the stairs. They dragged him upstairs to an apartment, pushed him against the glass doors in the foyer, breaking the glass, and then roughed him up, throwing him to the floor, picking him up, then throwing him back down again. Old Professor Szczypiorski was present at the scene. Saying goodbye to me, the young man added, "You know, they were students too. From the federation of youth groups. They shouted

---

* A historian, one of the founders of KOR, and a leading figure in the Polish opposition movement.

at us, 'You traitors, how much is the CIA paying you?' " Then, in a Wilno or Lwów accent he added, "The knife in my pocket is opening all by itself."

A week later, on Wednesday, March 21, a band of a dozen or so men attacked the Kurońs' apartment in Żoliborz. They used karate. Kuroń's wife and son were beaten, as were two friends who happened to be in the apartment. One of them (I know him, his name is Wujec) was beaten very severely. The other was Michnik, and he was roughed up again. Kuroń's son received a concussion. Kuroń's sick father was in bed in the next room during all this. After the attack, he was taken to the hospital by ambulance.

I heard detailed reports concerning these incidents on Sunday, the twenty-fifth, at a meeting of the Society for Scholarly Studies. The meeting took place at the Lipskis', in a building on Konopczyńska Street that was formerly the site of Mickiewicz High School. There were forty to fifty people there, mostly scholars—professors and docents, workers from research institutes, Catholic publicists, activists from the student solidarity committee, and a few writers. Other fields were represented by single individuals: one actress, one musician, and one postwar minister. Everyone was crammed onto the two couches and the few chairs and armchairs in a room bright with spring sun. The weather was exceptionally fine that Sunday. In the spring light I was struck by the uniform color of people's faces, haggard and furrowed with a sort of grayish tinge. Perhaps that is the coloring of independent intellectuals or the remains of the Polish intelligentsia. Or . . . There was, I recall, a similar sallowness in the faces at underground literary morning meetings during the Nazi occupation. Among those present were a number of interesting-looking people whom I did not know, people of uncommon appearance who seemed plucked from a crowd by a film director who needed to fill a number of character parts. A portrait of Jan Józef Lipski's father hung on the wall by the window; he had been the principal of Mickiewicz High School after the war. His grandson, a boy with close-cropped hair, bustled about the room and helped me with my chair when I got up to go out to the front hall for a cigarette. I remembered that this boy had already been arrested too, right after the riots in June 1976.

Adam Michnik, among others, spoke about what was happening to the "Flying University's" courses. He displayed a certain stylistic reticence in describing what had been done to him. In order to assure his audience that his was a reliable account, Michnik said, "I was an eyewitness." From this and other information that continues to reach me, it appears that these bands are organized and are operating on instructions. The larger squads of activists, such as the one in Ursyn, are composed of three groups, each with its task: the roughnecks, the choir, and the choirmasters. The first, mostly students from the Academy of Physical Education, are trained in beating up people; the second group cheers and yells; and the third consists of the instructors, who issue orders during an action—officials from police headquarters have been recognized among them. The students of the "Flying University" who were present at such actions are in agreement that it was young people from Warsaw student organizations directed by the party who were taking part in those attacks.

What this means is that, instead of employing police clubs, which would compromise the authorities too blatantly, the regime has sent its younger forces into action. It is organizing bands of students, teaching the young how to beat up people. At the meeting, someone said that the regime not only bears the responsibility for those who are beaten but for those who administer the beatings as well. It might also be added that to train someone in beating is the prelude to schooling him in murder. That has often been the case before, and it cannot be otherwise.

The "Flying University" is in a difficult position. The lectures have been broken off, the students intimidated. Moreover, the people in whose houses the classes had been held are now being accused of disturbing the peace. This method has proved effective. For that was the point—to isolate this group and make it feel itself a minority, cut off, ill at ease. Not only the Society for Scholarly Studies but the entire movement can find itself in a similar situation. Society hates the authorities, but it is weary. It still has its own skin to lose—salary, apartments, children getting into the university, trips, daily life. That's enough to make people afraid. It seems I was right when I wrote in *A Question of Reality* that ideas and ethical concepts seem beyond the mass of today's society and that society will not risk the little it possesses for them. And that is true not only for the new masses. Elżbieta S. told me about the confrontation she had with her parents when they found publications of the Independent Printing House in her room. They were terrified and wanted her to burn the books. They had both been in the Home Army during the war, and meetings of the Delegate Government had taken place in their apartment. "I've already done my part in the struggle," said the father. "Now I'm working and I don't want the police in my house." "What do you mean!" shouted Elżbieta. "Do you mean that history ended for you in 1945? Well for me it didn't!" Elżbieta then said to me, "Now their consciences aren't clear. I feel sorry for them. But I had to get the illegal stuff out."

There are no national minorities in Poland today, which has also placed the authorities in a difficult position; they can no longer blame the Jews for social injustices. But Jews can be created by isolating and persecuting a certain category of people. For the authorities this is now an even more favorable opportunity, for they can turn society's dissatisfaction against the people who defend the rights the authorities have themselves violated. A twofold advantage, a simple operation. So simple that society cannot get a grip on it. Or does not wish to. It sometimes happens that people who are inconvenient for the authorities in the end become inconvenient for society as well.

Not a very encouraging state of affairs. At times only one thought provides any consolation: things will change. In the past, when things have looked their worst, they sometimes took a completely unexpected turn, sometimes because of a single event. And life would probably be unbearable were it not for the thought that the future will be fantastic, unimaginable.

Yesterday, after I had read M. a few pages I had written recently, she remarked that I could be suspected of a certain aridity of feeling. She said that I write about desperate situations like a reporter. She doubted that my real experience was present in these accounts. "You create a false image of yourself."

I don't know how to write so as not to be suspect in any area. I tried to present the facts as they occurred. I would not have wanted, and would not have been able, to treat them otherwise. Why should I add in my own despair? Not to appear in a more favorable light, after all. Besides, despair and desperation have become obligatory in literature today, a species of stylistic material, almost like descriptions of nature were at one time. Meanwhile, in the life we lead here despair is becoming commonplace; our life is made of just such facts. We experience them every day, and they create everyday life. That strident Polish life of which we say, "Nothing new. Nothing happening." Nothing is ever happening here, except that you are constantly sitting down on glowing coals. And you have to pretend that you're in an armchair. You must always pretend a little, for decency's sake.

A young man in Polish studies came to see me. He is preparing his master's thesis and has chosen my film scripts as his subject. A nice young man, with a delicate face just sprouting its first growth, he had hitchhiked to Warsaw and removed his boots as soon as he came in so as not to track mud on the floor. In the course of our conversation, I realized that he reads everything that appears in *Zapis* and the other uncensored publications. I had the impression that this was, in fact, more important to him than my screenplays. At one point he asked me why I had dedicated so little space in *A Question of Reality* to the issue of writers who were politically active in the years of Stalinism, the former socialist realists who had later withdrawn from the party or were ousted from it.

What explains people having been able to have thought like that at the time? Then he mentioned several names, omitting mine; but the question was addressed to me, and we both knew that it concerned me as well. Why did they keep quiet? He told me that he and his friends were fascinated by this, precisely because it was enigmatic and shrouded in silence. (Not long ago, Tadeusz Konwicki* said to me, "These kids are fascinated by moral pornography; they're excited by the idea of digging some smut out of us.")

I attempted some reply, but after a few minutes, I realized that it was futile. I would not be able to re-create those issues, to reproduce them as a whole or break them down into their component parts. They seemed enigmatic to me too. Each time I attempt to arrive at some formulation, my thinking snaps in two, stopped by that "contradictory doubleness" I have written of elsewhere. For example, "I didn't know what was happening because I was deceived" provokes the immediate reply, "I was deceived because I didn't want to know what was really happening." But, at the same time, neither of those two sentences says everything. They would both require numerous addenda, references to the war years, the prewar years, to my own biography and that of other people, as well as to many ideas, like social reconstruction, revolution, socialism, and to still other ideas from another tradition, like organic work, making up for lost time in a civilization's development, reform, evolution. He wouldn't have understood any of it.

In the end, I told him that most likely that issue will remain an enigma, one of the enigmas of the past. There are many secrets and questions in the past, in history, for which there are no answers. Usually, years later, people attempt to solve those problems through the use of intelligence or imagination. Those

---

* Polish novelist.

attempts are the consequences of those enigmas, and they also create a nation's culture. Culture does not only arise from what is unambiguous; its current often flows from dark and damaged places, from the imagination, intuitions.

That did not satisfy him, of course. He was supposed to telephone me after the weekend. I promised to find the typescript of a few of my screenplays. I never heard from him again.

This evening, after the movies, a conversation with M., who launched into one of her passionate tirades, eyes and teeth flashing. Magnificent! She forgot about the water boiling in the kettle. We kept interrupting each other, walking back and forth from the kitchen to the living room, talking very loudly; no question that we could be heard on the stairs. And what was the argument about? Marriage. About the union of woman and man as a way of enduring life. About our nonmonogamous marriage, which might have fallen apart a number of times had we not been so linked by our differences that meshed so well, a mesh to which give and take were well fitted, as if the mutual contradictions of our natures had been aligned. This system functions well when the plus and minus signs correspond; for example, a marriage in which both people have similar anxieties is a worse match than one in which each of the partners suffers from different anxieties. It's better if she fears death and he's afraid of poverty, and bad if they're both afraid of the same thing. An ill-fated coincidence of similarities creates, in my opinion, a negative situation. M., on the other hand, believes that love is the fascination with otherness. Later on, that otherness becomes a source of conflict, and that is what marriage is about. Forty-five years ago, when we first met, we had no idea that a half-century-long struggle to create a third, joint, being out of the two of us was what lay ahead. Before our wedding, as I've told her more than once, I had a twofold vision of what would happen: the happiness of two people living under one roof and the unnaturalness of two organisms together inside four walls. Both visions have proved to be true. "Yes," says M., laughing, and reminds me of what someone once said: "I don't know if I love her, I only know that I can't refuse her anything and I don't like to be alone in the house." That third being that we have created was formed out of our ribs and in defiance of our instincts. It was born of our passions and quarrels, born while bombs fell and walls collapsed, born in the shadow of our errors, from our travels and our illnesses. We can say with perfect assurance that at some point it began to rear us, like a parent, and that today each of us is very different from the person we were forty, twenty, or even ten years ago. We have supported and resisted each other, and we have lasted. What should that being born of that union be called? "The union of souls," said M., a knife in her hand, slicing bread.

■ A P R I L
1 9 7 9

Easter. On the first day of the holiday we went to see the Rym-kiewiczes on Filtrowa Street with Julia and Artur. The city was nearly deserted but already free of winter's grime, the asphalt and the windows gleaming. In the Rymkiewiczes' bright and airy apartment we drank a strong rum concoction and then sat down at the table to eat and to talk. Ewa, Julia, and Maria looked like Chekhov's three sisters, wearing colors that ranged from white to gold to bronze. The evening was spent between the living room and the kitchen, between conversation and television. I spoke about an exhibition of photographs I had seen at the Museum of History, photographs of Warsaw at the end of the nineteenth century. Two photographs struck me in particular. One had been blown up very large and took up almost an entire wall. It showed the corner of Krakowskie and Koźa Streets, with the entrance to a pastry shop overgrown with grape vines. Two Russian officers in their summer whites are passing a woman in a dark skirt and light blouse, a parasol against the sun above her wide hat. A student wearing a Gymnasium cap is walking behind them, and farther back, a moustachioed Russian soldier carrying two bulging bags under his arms, and walking in the opposite direction, an elegant gentleman in a top hat. In the background a horse-drawn omnibus stands by a square. This photograph made a very strong impression on me, and I spent a long time in front of it. The amount of detail and signs of life seemed almost too much to grasp; both the substance and the movement, different from today's, had been caught in a moment of natural afternoon calm, the unhurried freedom of daily life. In comparison with that lively image, the streets nowadays seem dead, blind, filled with sound and fury, congested with crowds. The second picture was smaller than a postcard. At the bottom of its yellow border, a fine, faded caption in ink: "Exiled to Siberia." Two young men standing between two guards who wear visorless Russian caps. The exiles are in ragged frock coats, threadbare trousers, mud-covered boots. Both the soldiers are wearing greatcoats that are also soiled and muddy, and they are smiling at the photographer. But one of the exiles, who looks like a student—small, thin, bearded, with wire-rim glasses—has his head bent to one side and is looking at something with his sharp and sensitive eyes, the defiant intelligence of an excitable type. He has moved closer to the other exile, as if wanting to show him something, to tell him something of great importance, to warn him or perhaps only to keep the camera from somehow coming between them. The photograph was taken in 1864. I stared at it with a shudder. Those two bearded boys, the proud intellectual with the glasses ... Just whom does he want to warn, and of what?

Right after Easter, almost the day after, an explosive charge was set off in Nowa Huta, on the square that has the statue of Lenin stepping forward, one foot in the air. The radio report said that it had been done by "unknown culprits" and that a few people in nearby apartment buildings had been injured.

Lenin's statue lost a small piece of its rear leg. The explosion took place at night, on a Tuesday. Arrests began on Wednesday. Searches were made at the homes of people belonging to KOR and the Human Rights Movement: a few dozen people were detained. I hear about all this over the telephone. Kuroń, Chojecki, Macierewicz, the Czumow brothers, are in jail. As of today, no one has been released. "A really crude job," someone tells me by phone. No one has any doubt that the Security Forces were behind the explosion. The names keep coming in of people detained in Warsaw, Poznań, Gdańsk, Wrocław. The closer the city to the damaged statue of Ilyich, the smaller the roundup; only one person has been arrested in Kraków. And what does that prove? That this is not a matter of finding the culprits. Is it a factional struggle within the party? It could be. Or it could be machinations by the police, or it could have been stage-managed from without. Those are all possibilities. It is also possible that it was the work of a madman. In any case, it is startling that the explosion, the choice of target and time, had such an openly anti-Soviet character. It occurred on the eve of the anniversary of the treaty between Poland and the USSR. The calf of Lenin's leg blown off while the Tenth Congress of the Polish-Soviet Friendship Society opens! A great deal has been done in Poland for thirty-five years to prevent such things from happening. And so ... what was the point of these bombings? To compromise our No. 1 in Moscow's eyes and put a heavier hand in charge? That would explain the fires and the explosions. I've also heard another theory: they're afraid of the Pope's upcoming visit and want to inflame internal tensions to such a degree that the trip would have to be cancelled. It's also a possible explanation, but I don't think it probable.

Yesterday, talking on the phone with my brother Marian, I could hear a beetlelike scratching sound. A tap. The majority of the people I know have had their phones tapped, but Marian's had been installed by a young man who had come to his house to do repairs without having been called. "Your house is a broadcasting station," said a priest friend of Marian's smilingly, with a glance at the picture screws. The priest was a specialist in finding bugging devices in churches; when visiting friends, he always took great interest in their chandeliers and screws. A detective in a cassock ... But why does that sound familiar? Where have I heard something like that before? Oh, of course, the reverend Father Brown, you were the first! And so here we see an instance of the church modernizing itself in Poland.

There's been plenty to read in the recent issues of *Tygodnik Powszechny* (The Universal Weekly). Considerable space has been devoted to articles on John Paul II, including the text of the speech with which he greeted a delegation of Jews at the Vatican. He addressed them with wise and simple words, words I read with close attention and something more—a tremor like the hope and relief provided by light. It is no easy matter to be deaf to such words. After reading them, it is much harder to avoid thinking that there is some Providence that watches over us, that pure spirits of intelligence and goodness do exist. And then it becomes difficult not to believe in people's ability to purify themselves through love. What I wrote at the start of these pages, about the old Christian churches no longer burning with the fire of holy madness, may have been wrong. The holy fire of faith burns in this Pope. Is this faith in God or faith in man? At bottom, there is really no difference.

The smiling Vicar of Christ with a cross in one hand, a microphone in the other, blessing the faithful in thirty languages, certainly loves God and man: the God who allowed him to perform a great feat with his own humanity and the man in himself who had the strength to perform that deed. He certainly believes in the salvation of earth by heaven and that the intelligence of the church will deliver us from hatred; he is convinced, deeply and calmly convinced, that as long as man is alive, he can see the light at the end of the dark tunnel, but this act requires the courage of the heart. He has said, "My brothers and sisters, don't be afraid ..." He repeats the word *"paura"* very often. I think that what he has in mind here is the fear of doing good, the anxiety at the effort required to see God in another human being. This unusual Pope *è polacco* . . . One feels like asking, Holy Father, but how do you see the human being in a Pole?

On the day Karol Wojtyła's election to the Papacy was announced, people ran through the streets of Warsaw shouting with joy. A tearful old man put his arm around M. as she was crossing Świętojańska Street. "Did you hear? It's a miracle! A miracle!" It wasn't the Romantic poets who invented Polish messianism. Suddenly, in the course of an hour, everyone had become messianic, as if they had all been living for two hundred years in anticipation of The Coming. Only a nation that in the course of ten generations had lost faith in history's earthly justice could pass such an irrational reflex down through its genes. So many invasions, partitions, and betrayals were needed to transform what in other countries is political thought, social consciousness, or a sense of law into a thirst for a supernatural sign from the heavens. On that day, the word "miracle" was on the lips of both churchgoing old women and intellectuals. In an issue of *Więź* (The Bond) dedicated to John Paul II, that word runs through the statements of many of the writers, not all of whom are Catholics. I read that issue with a bit of trepidation. Thirty-odd articles, and nearly every second one was addressed to the man in Rome, directing, no, shifting their national expectations, everything that remains unfulfilled and unfinished, onto him. They have entrusted one Pole with all their Polishness, placing it on his head with thorns and brambles. Reading those articles, I asked myself if those feelings weren't too overblown. What was the Pope supposed to do with them? How was he to live up to those expectations? Today the man in every Pole cries to the Pope, Redeem us; return the dignity of a great nation to us; tell the world who we are! It is a moving voice. And again I ask myself, Is John Paul II capable of doing that, of doing that for us?

Something astonishing is taking place. On the one hand, a society of some 30 million people swollen with the dreams of the ages; on the other, a man with a universal mission and his own human concerns, a man who in his youth was an actor, a mountain climber, who wrote poetry and was called by his nickname by his friends in Kraków. Overnight, Karol Wojtyła has become the legendary emissary of Providence; he will appear here in a month, in Warsaw, and already 30 million people are possessed of the miraculous certainty that the arrival of this man will alter their fate. I have heard that John Paul II will fly over the city from Okęcie airport in a helicopter, then land on Victory Square (formerly Piłsudski Square, or, some say, "Piłsudski's Victory Square"). The Holy Father soaring in the heavens above Warsaw, the Polish Pope, who will descend from the clouds into the very heart of the capital . . . Don't tell me about the visions of the Romantics and the surrealists; no poet could have conceived that image. But still I wonder how he will experience all this and what he will think when seeing that hope-crazed Polishness rising up to him, that impassioned wave that wants to be purified by his hands.

A week ago, Andrzej Wajda came over for lunch, and he told me about his recent trip to Rome and the Papal audience to which he had been admitted on Palm Sunday. Wajda is more than a filmmaker; he is also an excellent storyteller. He had arrived here worried—the bureaucrats had been tampering with his already-approved new screenplay, which was on the verge of being shot. But as he talked, he gradually relaxed. One detail stuck in my memory—a description of his short conversation with the Pope. John Paul II asked him about *Man of Marble*. He mentioned that he had not seen the film and would be curious to. Wajda replied that screening the print that was there in Rome would present no problem (and indeed the Pope was shown the film soon after). "He is an exceptionally attentive listener," Wajda said. "He looks a little away from your eyes, somewhere past them, and all the while he is listening to you, holding your wrist firmly, very firmly, in an iron grip. You sense both Christian compassion in this and something of the healer's magnetic force. Great power. And, at the same time, no sense of being rushed. A few thousand people feel that he has come to see them all and will find time for each one of them."

* * *

Current events: the people arrested after the explosion in Nowa Huta have been released.

"Brothers, sisters, don't be afraid . . ." John Paul II's challenge sticks in my mind. The evenings are still chilly, and Małgorzata B. is wearing her long white sheepskin coat. One evening she told me what had happened to her brother, who had just gotten married. A zealous, believing Catholic, he had prepared himself for this wedding with all the earnestness of his faith. The couple was under the religious tutelage of a priest from the Church of St. Jakub, and both were going to him to discuss various matters. On the last Sunday before the wedding day, they went to church for morning mass. Their priest delivered a sermon; in a church that was full of young people, a sermon imbued with anti-Semitism. This happened quite recently. "The young couple ran out," said Małgorzata. "They didn't want to be married by him. They were terrified."

All reason founders before a fact such as this. Only words can liberate you from the nightmare: call it a mental illness or a virus and expel it from the world of the healthy. And do that for your own sake and peace of mind, for such things will not be expelled from reality. The priest at the Church of St. Jakub—is he a madman, a fool, an evil person? You do not have to belong to any of those categories to continue hating Jews in a country where there are no Jews. "There still are!" he would answer. "There were Jews here, and there still are!" He would advance arguments, refer to the years after the war. But I remember the war years and the year when the Jews were murdered. I was just another face then, a face that didn't look Jewish, and people talked in front of me without restraint. There were still Jews then, in the winter and spring of 1943. They were exterminated soon after. Today, on Western television, there are miniseries about the extermination of the Jews that depict Poles as assistants to the executioner, standing side by side with the Germans, their four-cornered hats in close company with the helmets and swastikas. It is difficult to extricate oneself from the mountain of falsehoods. The Jews who survived knew who was killing them—the Germans. But they also remember what people were saying. I consider myself one of the survivors, and I owe my life to many people, including both Poles and Jews; I too helped other people of various backgrounds and religions, and in doing so, several times nearly went under myself. At that time, not only were Jews in hiding turned in to the Germans, but sometimes even those who were being persecuted betrayed each other. It is no secret that there were voluntary informers everywhere.

These were known things, obvious, and in those degenerate years, natural—a result, I would say, of the very nature of life. But the air was filled with words. And if there is still something that I cannot explain to myself, apart from the crime that altered the very concept of mankind and was as blind as the violence of nature, that something is the words I heard spoken. The nice woman who weighed my meat in the grocery store said that Hitler had disinfected Poland of Jews (the Warsaw Ghetto was still in flames at that time); a certain intelligent lawyer declared, during afternoon tea, that he had to restrain himself from calling the police whenever he saw someone on the street who looked Jewish. Lieutenant W., who had been with the partisans in the forest, spoke one day at lunch about the monk who had absolved him for lacking compassion for the Jews dying in a small town ("My son, this is a punishment for the agonies of Jesus."). These words came from the lips of respectable people, good fathers, honest housewives. They did not know how to keep silent; they renounced compassion volubly, and in my opinion, it was not hatred that was speaking through them. They only wished to exorcise their anxiety, the unpleasant realization of their own indifference, by speaking of it. It wasn't they who killed the Jews. But the Jews who were in hiding heard what they said.

I try to think about all this as calmly as possible so as not to commit the error of accepting partial truths. The mountain of falsehood grew out of mutually inconsistent partial truths; the whole truth is clearly too complex ever to be grasped. Words continue to function, or, more precisely, words and silence. There are always those who keep silent. I said to M. recently that magical things are happening to the past that are sealing the lips of people of conscience. They often prefer to remain silent rather than to speak in simple phrases. The past cannot be recounted in simple phrases. Every receding reality eludes description and slips past comprehension, as if in its dying spasms it were divesting itself of the explicitness of words. Then it becomes part of the sphere of interpretation and is no longer the past; then it is history. And that was precisely what I was driving at with the student of Polish affairs who questioned me about the years of Stalinism . . .

The air is good, the climate healthy, the landscape pretty. And riddles everywhere.

This afternoon, over coffee, there was a discussion about the outbreak of the Warsaw Uprising (in connection with the book Jan Matłachowski has published in London) and the circumstances that led to the armed action taken by the underground on September 1, 1944. Nearly everyone was unanimous in thinking that that was a politically motivated decision—the outbreak of the uprising was to confront the Soviet command with the fact of Polish statehood. JMR maintained that the decision was a historically correct one: it appealed to the imponderables that are the cement of the nation's identity and that make it possible for us to endure. "But two hundred thousand casualties?" I asked. I was aware that this convinced no one. None of the people present would have sacrificed 200,000 people for a cause that was historically correct, and not one of them would have made a decision whose consequence would have been the murder of women in the Warsaw suburb of Wola or Staszic. But now such words are spoken, words that are used to endorse the correctness of other experiences and that touch on a reality different from the one the statistics contain. Uttering those simple words, a person incapable of hurting a cat justifies the deaths of 200,000 people who lived in apartment buildings and small houses with gardens. I want to say, "On the same street where you live today whole families were killed." And receive the reply, "That was the price." They should have been there and seen what that price looked like.

There is something wrong about understanding those graves too easily through the use of words, about that historical calculation of the losses and gains produced by people's deaths. O Lord, protect us from analogies; but some analogies obsess us. Respectable people who maintain that the death of 3 million was the price for national homogeneity, honest people who accept the price of a thousand or a million others shot dead in exchange for a nation with a classless society, and other good people who see the murder of 200,000 as the price paid for saving the nation's identity. It is the same mistake, the flaw at the very core. If the worth of another person's life is measured by any value other than life, one should check to see if the devil isn't lurking about somewhere.

No, let's change the subject! The air is good, the climate healthy, the landscape pretty . . .

A fire broke out on Thursday on Piwna Street in the nunnery at St. Marcin's Church, where the hunger strike took place two years ago. The flames and clouds of smoke burst from the attics, threatening an adjacent apartment building. In Warsaw these are called Russian fires. Mysterious fires broke out in Moscow and St. Petersburg even under the tsars; they are a police tradition there. Yesterday someone brought some news from the town of Laski. Church circles are taking the position that the fire was set. A man had come into the church that day, holding a small package in one hand. He asked to be baptized. Later on he disappeared, but apparently some nuns had seen him entering the attic. These days there are many such adults, the children of unreligious parents, who were not baptized and who now come into churches requesting baptism.

Yesterday, lunch at the Writers' Club. Two small rooms in a cellar, separated by an arcade and three small steps. The tables are crowded; seven people are waiting in line by the wall. Stuffy, airless. Tin forks and spoons, no tablecloths or napkins; when a chair becomes available, you have to sit with the remains of someone else's food. Prize-winning writers and poor poets come here for lunch, famous actors and older women living off translating and their memoirs, as well as a few popular lawyers. And quite a few striking, fashionably dressed girls. Standing in line, Andrzej Łapicki's daughter looked no different than the *Parisiennes* at the Café de Flore; her husband, the actor Daniel Olbrychski, beside her, wearing a rather exotic shirt *à la Russe,* with a medallion on his chest and with a light reddish beard, looked like someone out of Russian literature, Bazarov or Prince Myshkin . . . Well-known filmmakers, owners of foreign cars and villas on the Bay, rubbing shoulders with blacklisted writers and a mob of skinny critics, mixed in with a few literary informers. All together, eating their cabbage soup with tin spoons. At a small table far to the rear, Professor Maria Janion, surrounded by her assistant lecturers; the wise and splendid Professor Janion with the leonine head of a tribune of scholarship, her gaze sad and heavy beneath that mane. There is something monumentally Jacobin about her appearance, something of Marat in the tub.

People come here to eat lunch. They sit side by side as equals, avoiding the difficulties of eating in the city or cooking at home, fleeing the shortage of meat in the stores and the rudeness of salespeople and waiters. "Quiet!" shouts Joasia, the waitress. "I can't hear the orders!" She has been serving lunch at the club for more than a quarter of a century; she had been a beautiful, strong girl and remembers everyone here from the years of their youth, and her own.

After lunch, I set off for home. Approaching the Market, I can already hear the sounds of barrel organs. There are two new organ-grinders now. In addition to the old one with the black cap, sideburns, and caged parrot (people call it the parrot with the rank of lieutenant), who for seven years has been alternating between two tunes—"Cuba Drinks to Jakub" and "Tango Milonga"—they've hired a man with a cape that reaches the ground and another with a bowler. They represent the old Warsaw of

Bolesław Prus, the good old days, *la belle époque*. They have been stationed here with their barrel organs by the government of the peasants and workers, which always takes pains not to be suspected of having come out of nowhere. No, they have the shadows and the walls of the past behind them—a fake barrel organ from the days of Prus and a replica of the Royal Castle. Just as in those yellowed photographs ... But in those old photographs there were still policemen with long whiskers, and I feel like writing to the National Council to ask if a few worthy officials in four-cornered hats and summer whites couldn't be hired.

Mr. Pawlak, our superintendent and a former first-aid attendant, was washing down the hallway with a dish rag. He told me what he had said to a policeman. "This all comes from the Little Negro,* boss. They serve Neapolitan spaghetti there but have nothing to cook it with because the city hasn't run a gas line into their restaurant yet. So they put the dry pasta under hot tap water until it softens, pour on some sauce, and—Spaghetti Neapolitan. If a customer gets sick, he throws up in our hallway because there's no rest room in the Little Negro. The Department of Health should be informed, I think."

"To live apart, through oneself, exchanging ideas that vary little and that revolve around one's own idea, always the same, never changing; to read in the papers news devoid of any surprises ... to find there only claptrap about defeats, graced with the name offensive maneuvers; to be driven from the streets in the evening by the compulsory economizing on light, not to be able to enjoy the nightlife of a city that extinguishes its lights so early ... to no longer be able to rise to the pure realms of thought since the mind weakens from a lack of sustenance; to be deprived of everything that provides diversion for intelligent people; to feel the lack of anything new and refreshing; to vegetate in this monotonous crudity ... that is a boredom like that of a provincial town."

---

* A fashionable Warsaw restaurant.

I have only changed or deleted a few phrases in this description, which sounds so much like our lives here. But that was not a description of life in Warsaw in 1979. That was an account of Paris in 1870, a Paris under siege by the Prussians.

The papers are carrying a story with the headline "Arrests of Culprits in Warsaw Nunnery Fire:"

"The Procurator's Office of central Warsaw has announced the arrest of Robert K. on a charge of arson in connection with the fire in the Franciscan nunnery on Piwna Street. The arsonist gained entrance to the nunnery under the pretext of taking part in religious ceremonies. An investigation is under way."

■ MAY
1979

Summer has erupted. Women are bringing flowering branches back from the park and putting them in vases. Someone comes in from the city every day; they're immediately recognizable by their sweaty, pale faces. People are wilting from the heat in Warsaw, their eyes still frightened from the winter. The coming visit of the Pope is almost the sole topic of conversation. The first wave of tourists has already started arriving; people are coming in from the small towns, from every continent, from the Bug River and the Pacific, from Calcutta and Kielce, buying up accommodations and places at the windows in the houses along the Pope's route. Neither radio nor television has yet provided a detailed itinerary for his visit. No one knows anything for certain. They are apparently still making arrangements and wrangling over the ceremony, the homily, the mass. No one knows if the meeting with young people will in fact take place at St. Anna's, or whether there will be a solemn mass on Saxon Square. There's no more talk about the helicopter, but there is a rumor going around about a white boat from which the Pope is to dispense blessings as he travels, a white boat installed in an open car. The guesses, stories, predictions, bake in the sun, which hangs over people's heads like a bell. The nation waits. The government is frightened. A rumor circulated that the party was going to crowd 10,000 of its own roughnecks into the church when the Pope meets with the young people. Another rumor has it that the Premier's son got drunk at Spatif, the actors' club, and said to Daniel Olbrychski, "Are you going out to welcome that shepherd from Wadowice?" Olbrychski rose and knocked him under the table with one punch, then went to the men's room to wash his hands. Some people tell this story as if they had been eyewitnesses; others insist there's nothing to it. Some people say that they have heard with their own ears a bulletin about the 400 deaths that occurred during the Pope's second visit to Mexico; others are certain that the Western press has denied this story and that it was spread by UB* agents to cause fear. New information every day. The Primate is bedridden with illness . . . The Premier is in an oxygen tent . . . Cassocks are being made for the police . . . One is surrounded by a constant, passionate babble, and it is difficult to tell what is fiction and what is fact.

Webs are woven into this thicket; traps are set. Who is this Robert K. apprehended by the police as the culprit in the Franciscan nunnery fire? In Poland there are no madmen who set fire to convents. But perhaps—had the fire spread—someone would have been eager to announce that part of the old quarter had burned down because of negligence on the part of the church administration. And perhaps—another good custom—someone had been assigned to that pious act. But who is Tomasz M.? Because one column over there is an article about his arrest. The circumstances mentioned in the article indicate only that the arrested man was a photographer. But in the headline—another good habit—words are used that prejudice the result of any in-

---

* Urząd Bezpieczeństwa (Bureau of Security), the Polish intelligence agency.

vestigation: "A Factory for Forged Documents and Banknotes." The article ends with the question of whether anyone else was involved in this "criminal chain." Now we know who Tomasz M. is—one of the people detained after the bomb was set off in Nowa Huta.

Taking an afternoon drive to Wilga to see Andrzej Kijowski and his wife, we suddenly came out onto an overpass right past Góra Kalwaria with a view of the old Vistula Valley. Down below, to the right, a broad landscape sprinkled with orchards, a landscape that had still been bare and brown-gray in April but that was now in bloom. The overpass, the bridge, the broad Vistula overflowing its banks and swollen with light, the road descending smoothly until it was suddenly in among small houses, then the white veils of the orchards again, on our right and much closer now. We had not spoken all the time we were driving, but after the bridge and those orchards we both began talking at the same moment and together began naming all the children of people we knew who had left Poland in the past few years. The list went on and on like a litany. Children taken out of the country by their parents, sent to study, living in Paris and New York, staying with friends or relatives; children in Canada, Germany, Denmark; children studying or working as housecleaners or taking care of children. Children who will not return. We add more names to the list—Piotruś, who's at Harvard, little Ania with her pigtails in Geneva, Małgosia at Oxford, Jaś at Uppsala ... We exclaim each new name with surprise and excitement, and in the end, we start naming them more slowly and more slowly—and then there's Monisia and Witek in New Jersey says M., and Staś's daughter recently went to stay with them.

A church, a little town. Farther on, the road slips into a forest. We glide smoothly along the forest road, rooftops glinting between the trunks. The landscape changes again and is again beautiful. I think, In this lovely land there will be fewer and fewer children we know; we shall be left here with the peasants and the organ-grinders. Children who will be clerks or soldiers are growing up in those little houses, and there will be fewer and fewer children we know. But perhaps not all of them will leave. Some of them, after all, will be refused passports.

In his essay "The Crypt of St. Leonard," Andrzej Kijowski quotes a remark made by Tsar Alexander I in 1816, two sentences that can still give you the creeps. "In order to pacify the Poles, their love of nation must be indulged. In treating them thus at present, I will make Russians out of them while they go on thinking they are still Poles."

■ J U N E
1 9 7 9

June 8. Yesterday afternoon the mass performed by John Paul II at Auschwitz was broadcast on television.

I spent a few days after my return from Obory unpacking my bags and arranging various little objects about the living room, restoring our place to its former appearance, reaccustoming myself to normal Warsaw life—if it can be called normal. I didn't go out much, and there was no question of doing any work yet. On my second day back, I watched a discussion on contemporary literature on television: four men chatting and being unusually polite to one another, carefully sidestepping certain inconvenient names and, at the same time, taking care to keep the conversation on a high, free level. Their performance made me think of the pond in Obory, and I made a note on a scratch pad: "What is called literary life in Poland has for many years resembled a pond. Rotting duckweed on the surface, and deep beneath it carp swim unseen."

On Thursday, May 30, and on Friday, June 1, rumors by the score vied for attention, apocalyptic visions piling up left and right. Two million peasants will converge on Warsaw with their horses and wagons, trample the city, ruin the parks, loot the stores . . . Two million of them will be sleeping cheek by jowl in hallways, and they will leave disease, excrement, and corpses in their wake; at least 5,000 people will lose their lives, suffocated, attacked, crushed . . . The Premier is dead; his body is in cold storage for the duration of the Pope's visit. He died upon hearing of his son's behavior . . . Apartments will be robbed; valuables shouldn't be kept at home . . .

Usually, stories of this sort are fabricated for a definite purpose, but they also often mix with the spontaneous imagination of the street, which has its own sense of morality and the literary (the Premier in cold storage; the father punished for the sins of the son and for his own). I have learned not to treat such stories lightly, for the street does not always talk nonsense; at times its premonitions are closer to the mark than any intellectual speculation. On Friday evening, the eve of the Pope's visit, I went out to have a look at what was actually going on in the city. The scorching heat had eased up a little, but it was still a very warm evening. At the intersection of Krakowskie and Miodowa Streets, the cars were bumper to bumper, surrounded by crowds that inundated the road. A summer evening. Not a single man in a jacket; women in summer dresses, their arms bare. Young fathers carrying children up on their shoulders. I also noticed old married couples holding hands, and a few times familiar faces flashed past me, faces I knew from somewhere, that seemed to surface in memory from years back. The crowd was dense on Świętojańska and Piwna Streets, especially so in front of the churches, and less so on Castle Square. A podium was under construction by the altar in front of St. Anna's; workers were hammering away on the steps. The crowd was dense there as well. As I walked, I kept encountering more and more people I knew by sight but whose names I couldn't recall. It was only after a while that I realized that they were not people that I knew but simply people with the look of the old intelligentsia about them, people who disappear unseen into the masses every day. So, they still exist; whole families of them had turned out.

And it was precisely that, the family mood in the streets, that I found most attractive. A different way of walking, a change in style and rhythm. There was no sense of pressure in that enormous number of people: the crowd undulated slowly, people moved without bumping into each other, made way for each other. Little clusters of clergymen—priests and nuns—were threaded through the crowd at various points, their black cassocks and light-colored habits introducing a new accent in the image of the city, one reminiscent of Italian cities with their leisurely evening *corso* after the heat has subsided, when everyone comes outside and everything mingles. It was like that here too. For the first time in years I walked the streets observing people curiously, exchanging smiles with the people I passed. And I did not feel a single moment of danger, no twinge of fear or anger. I walked to Victory Square, where a cross several meters high had been erected, towering over the square from a point opposite the Tomb of the Unknown Soldier. A Catholic order guard was on duty there.

Walking around the square, I realized that during the entire way there from the Old City I had not only not seen a single drunk, but not a single policeman's face as well. Picking them out is no problem, and if I hadn't noticed any, that might have meant that Security had been ordered not to interfere. They were probably there somewhere, but they were concealed. Order was now being kept in the city by young people wearing light-blue caps. They were on guard on Victory Square, requesting through loudspeakers that the square be cleared; others stood in the alleys and directed the flow out of the area. The crowd moved away obediently. It was still light out. The square was slowly emptying, and the loudspeakers continued the polite announcements: the public's presence on the square is hindering the preparations and not much time remains before tomorrow's mass.

Returning through one of the alleys, between barricades made of metal pipes, I ran into a couple of painters I knew, and we exchanged our first impressions. It was clear to them and to me that something unusual had been happening in this city for the last couple of hours. I still couldn't define what it was. The image of that towering cross stayed in my mind. An enormous cross on whose arms a scarlet stole had been draped. Later that evening I spoke by phone with Andrzej Kijowski. He asked me if I had been in the city and how things looked there. I tried to describe the leisurely pace of the crowd, but I didn't succeed in conveying to him what had moved me the most deeply—the atmosphere, at once serious and free, and, more than anything, the inward bond uniting people. I only told him that things were calm and different and that nothing bad could happen. Hanging up the phone, I felt I hadn't said the most important thing. For what was most important was that difference, something rare and moving that we had not seen for years—the city living a real life.

A real life—that means one in accord with reality, the authentic life that, as a rule, is lived when the will of society is fulfilled, when what people have within them is expressed, and when people do not have to act counter to their social instincts and ideas. Then people come willingly, by themselves, and do not have to be coerced and lined up; police lines become superfluous. They go to the places that for them contain a truth as plain as day. That evening the police on Świętojańska and Krakowskie Streets and on Saxon Square had come to see the places the Pope would visit. And they had seen one another. A crowd of many thousands had beheld itself and been strengthened by feeling its own presence. A crowd of children and grandmothers, with ice-cream cones and dogs, not directed from without, a colorful, summer crowd that had come in from all the city's districts simply because it had wanted to be there, just to look and to see. The same reason I had gone there. Nevertheless, the very fact of thousands of people arriving in one place at the same time without having been convened was itself tremendously striking.

They had lost the habit of thinking of themselves as a living body, and great pains had been taken to convince them that they were a passive mass whose movements were steered from without. They had come there to have a look at the city on the eve of the Pope's visit with no other thought in their minds, unaware that their coming together would furnish them proof of their own existence.

What I am talking about here is not filmable; there are some things camera and film cannot capture. And it is precisely that sort of thing that I most wish to describe. How else to depict just how extraordinary that evening was? How else to depict its peculiar vividness and seriousness, its concentrated festivity? That is, without delving into the country's entire past, the nation's psyche. Later on, at home, I tried to determine what it was that evening had reminded me of. I racked my brains for quite some time until the simplest of answers occurred to me—some of the summer nights in Warsaw before the war. It was the first time in I don't know how many years, but many, a great many, that I had felt that so strongly. But that was not filmable either—time, as it exists within a person, can't be filmed.

Even amid all that is now happening in Warsaw, the fact that the church has assumed control of the city makes a special impression. There are practically no police around. Perfect calm reigns. All the scares have proved groundless. The streets are clean; even the commotion in the Old City has quieted down. We have not been trampled by horses or inundated by hordes of peasants. What is most interesting is that the general mood is free of all religious hysteria. There is a type I remember from the old processions, especially Corpus Christi—a fanatically religious woman, her cheeks feverish, embracing the edge of a portable altar, singing hysterically. It made you shudder. I don't see any of that now. Groups of students, girls and boys, often led by priests, frequently pass under my window during the night, talking loudly as they walk; but that sound doesn't bother me. I find its spontaneous cheerfulness contagious. Many such groups passed by my window at three o'clock in the morning before the Sunday mass at St. Anna's.

If I were to define in a single word what I experienced in watching all this for several days, that single word would be "amazement." I am not only amazed that a cross dominates Victory Square and that the authorities are keeping still, as if in hiding from the nation. I am most amazed by the thought that the nation had so ably protected and preserved its own truth. So ably and for so long a time. A certain serious suspicion arises. Have those masses been judged too harshly, seen as inert and weak? Has their subjugation been viewed as common stagnation, a lack of spiritual resources?

Automobiles, televisions, refrigerators . . . To call that a "little stabilization," to depict Poland as a society of neobourgeois, is to aid in the swindle without meaning to. It's certain that as soon as there was but half a chance of regaining an authentic existence, all the automobiles, refrigerators, and televisions would be tossed on the barricades. Yesterday someone said to me, "This is not an outbreak of religious feeling. This is a manifestation of patriotism, a national uprising without a shot being fired. He has come to lift us out of the mud."

How much of this could be understood by intellectuals in the West, those who organize demonstrations of homosexuals and feminists, even those like my wonderful friend from Berlin Oscar Callozos, who told me about the lesbian rallies in Barcelona? But do they have to understand us? They don't, just as we don't have to understand their problems and complexes. I have often maintained that we make ourselves ridiculous when we try to instruct the Americans or the French in how best to act and think. Our past is different from theirs; we have no part in their lives. We do not have to share their experience of Senegal and Vietnam, because our ancestors were not colonialists and it is not we who were sent to fight there. But they too have no basis for instructing us in how to think and to act, for they know even less about us. Shortly before the Pope's visit to Poland, I heard a report from someone who had just returned from Sweden. The intellectuals there are claiming that Poland has been seized by a relapse into religious fanaticism similar to the nationalistic outburst of Islam in modern-day Iran . . . At that moment, I felt a certain deference for the Americans. You have to appreciate a society that nicknames intellectuals eggheads.

On Saturday before noon, the P.E.N. Club office called: there's a ticket for me for the mass the Pope will celebrate on the sixteenth on Victory Square. I would have had a seat but I thanked them anyway, and it's probably just as well that I had refused: the television had close-ups, in particular of John Paul II, that were beyond the range of the spectators on the square.

A personality with a radiance I have never before encountered. His way of moving, his gestures, his intonation—all bespeak a simplicity that seems so ordinary you immediately think, A kind soul. And then, a moment later, you discover that with every move he makes he only augments his uncommonness. You sense the power of unrelenting spiritual and physical labor, a power that is frequently concealed behind a half-smile, silence, or the restraint of a gesture. Television captured the moment when he was greeting the bishops, and I understood then what Wajda had been talking about when he came back from Rome—the absence of haste, the Christian embrace. After exchanging embraces with the bishops, the Pope said, "My respects to you! But now I must go; I'm being hurried along." There was a playful humility in those words. The Pope moved away with the unhurried step of a gardener. Perhaps I have retained that moment in memory because the cameras framed his face in a closeup. I was struck by the way it had been sculpted out of a few large planes. The broad forehead and cheeks, the massive prominent jaw jutting powerfully forward. Set deeply beneath the fair, peasantlike eyebrows, the eyes have an expression difficult to catch—something between concern and swift, searching thought. I cannot define my associations exactly, but I was definitely struck by his resemblance to the stone busts from republican Rome with their broad heads and, at the same time, to the faces one sees here in the countryside—the same broad arch, the same strong simple planes. His entire form—burly, broad-shouldered—emanates a caution born of experience. Sometimes this is expressed in the way he offers his hand—never too quickly and keeping it close to his body—but it is also there in his entire bearing, in the way he inclines his head, in the rhythm of his gait, reminiscent, as I have already said, of a gardener's deliberation as he walks among his plants. It is difficult for me to recall a church painting of St. Peter, but I imagine that this is exactly what he looked like. I have learned the Pope's age from a biographical note in the papers: he was born in 1920. I would never have believed that the first person who would compel me to think of St. Peter would be younger than I am.

Description—communicating with words what the camera registers with an image—is for me a value or, better to say, an ambition; to confirm my faith in literature, in the meaning of literature. Literary description . . . Not much room has been left for it by the technological machines and political apparatus. Today the world is either shown or named. Writing—literature—is becoming an occupation that defies reality, an ever-more eccentric and solitary pursuit. It is precisely for that reason that this pursuit creates a need to resist the monitoring devices and stereos, a desire to wage war against the tubes, cassettes, and tapes. One begins to miss descriptions. Their arduousness, their solidity. In all likelihood, this is also a self-defense reflex against the tag line that is replacing description. A reaction against epithets and names. For we live in a world of names and tag lines created by various types of propaganda, and when we hear the word "agent" or phrase "brilliant leader," we should know that an attempt is being made to force a spell or slogan into our brains, a slogan that will liberate us from the obligation of describing things and relating them in all their complexity. Recently, during a dispute, I said, "Don't use names, describe." We were talking about someone we both knew, discussing his character. Description is more difficult and more just than tag lines and epithets. I have been convinced of that many times over. Fewer people can describe a thing or person than can name them.

Possibly when using the term "description," what I am really thinking about is literature in general, and when attaching special significance to description, I am speaking of the relationship between the written word and contemporary civilization. In our time, to be a writer demands not only faith in oneself but also faith in literature in defiance of contemporary civilization. An unremunerative but proud pursuit, a pursuit for Don Quixotes.

I've been doing some hard thinking about just how to define the unusual style of John Paul II's sermons, what makes them so out of the ordinary, which is not to say uncanonical. Their simplicity? The absence of both priestly and worldly rhetoric? I don't know. Yes, the Pope used simple words. It's often said that the truth is simple. I would add that the truth is also known. Known by people and so familiar that he seems to be speaking their thoughts. The Pope expressed the thoughts of those great crowds of Poles, the thoughts and memories that had been falsified; he spoke to them out of his own experience and expressed their own much-abused truth. Their best truth, I would say. These are dark years; this is an age of evil prophets. Using the words of a good prophet, the Pope gave people access to what is brightest in them and of which they had been aware from time immemorial. He cleansed them of everything that had been rendered opaque and stony by years of adversity and falsehood, preaching ideas that the church in Poland had not always expressed with such ardent conviction. And perhaps that is the source of the riveting individuality of John Paul II's style. It's as if with his words he had pointed to a locked door and then had flung it open, letting in the light. The words he spoke at Auschwitz about the Jewish people, the stress he keeps placing on tolerance for other religions and rites, the section of his homily that was devoted to the Russians . . . Had the church spoken like that when I was at school and in the university, how much less poison would I have imbibed.

Someone remarked to me, "I would like to kneel and pray along with him." And that confidence was imparted by a person with a secular world view. I tried to imagine what believing Catholics felt at those moments. Religious faith was never an area where I experienced any genuine emotion; rather, for me, it was an area of other people's experience, one that I avoided from a distance and not without a certain skeptical envy. But I tried and at times forced myself to understand what this means. The most difficult part was comprehending the feeling of love for God. What does that mean, to love God? I wondered if it were possible to love God at Auschwitz, that place of human suffering that in his sermon the Pope called "the Golgotha of modern times," where today it is impossible to defend oneself against the idea that we have been abandoned by Providence.

Asking myself what this means and what similar experiences might feel like, I always suffer moments of impotence. I can't see anything, I can't imagine anything. And what if that is the key to the truth—that perhaps only the gift of a love such as that can lead man out of his anguish and the pain of experience? I remember something from one of Juliusz Słowacki's poems or, rather, the sense of it, for I cannot quote it exactly: "You will die from a lack of love as from hunger." This phrase has two meanings: one dies from a lack of love from others and from not loving others. But is it only love for people, not love for the world, for God? I meant this more in the second sense of the quotation, which seems deeper and more significant to me and has more of the feel of contemporary consciousness about it. The source of depression, neurosis, and spiritual death, as we say today, is the alienation caused by civilization and by man's closing in egotistically on himself, death limited to the solitary, self-regarding ego.

But if a person is not graced with faith, if metaphysical experience is inaccessible to him since he is only a man of goodwill in whose mind the word "love" has been replaced by the idea of affection or decency, what is such a person to do? Behave decently toward God? Feel affection for God? No, here meaning crumbles. And so then perhaps what remains for him are exercises, mental gymnastics, spiritual workouts ... To learn faith by self-hypnosis, to practice loving the Creator, to pretend, to lie away the secular rationalism in oneself ...

In issue 11 of *Zapis* I found the following idea in something written by Wirpsz: "Lying, if it is conscious and, furthermore, is supported by the intellect and sensibility, constitutes difficult inner work and has a very high philosophical status."

I am visited at moments by the suspicion that many things that have at one point been seen as lies should not be lied about again, the things that were revealed as untrue by Voltaire and Marx, for example, as well as by the disciples of the thinkers who stripped mankind of its illusions and its received ideas. My generation grew up in an era when lies were overturned. The lies were stripped away from relations between women and men, from religion, love, history, and literature. A little while later, when the blows from the totalitarian beast beat down upon that generation, it turned out that a humanity freed from lies, in order to survive, had to fall back upon ideas and values that we had considered the noble platitudes of generations past, generations that had not been free of lies. A mind liberated from prejudice was not enough; one also had to recall the old mottoes about honor, sacrifice, and hope. And then still later ... Later came the cadres who used their own truths to strip bourgeois society of its lies, truths that already bore the seed of new lies. And these included freedom and brotherhood. And equality. Now, when reading, I come across the line "Inequality is a law of nature and equality the most horrible of injustices," I think that these words expose something that was once a truth stripped of lies and that was again covered over with lies.

Flee the new mystifications? Return to the old myths?

The consciousness of Poland's historical situation was present in everything the Pope said. He often referred to the fate of *this land,* pointing to its drama and sublimity. At those moments, I think that everyone had to see John Paul II as the spiritual personification of our nation's history. We know our own history, which does not mean, however, that we are always able to perceive its beauty. But it is beautiful. There has probably been no other country in the history of Europe that has committed so few blameworthy acts against the world. On either side of us are nations with dismal histories. Germany and Russia. Poland, in the middle, was a zone of law and of life. Between Germany's schizophrenic power and the deranged void that is Russia, Poland tried to live, a nation that for a long time took seriously mankind's noble ideas—Christianity, humanism, democracy, freedom, the human person, and faith—and that after eight centuries paid for its fantasies with its freedom and paid for its freedom with death. We never had the Englishman's practical turn of mind or the French passion for creating social states, be they absolutist or republican. But we allowed other peoples to live alongside us and among us. And that is sufficient reason not to feel degraded.

What does degrade us? The answer to that might be the contempt we have been shown. I am not thinking of any contempt from without; I am referring to degradation from within, from here, that which banks on people's lowness and their stupidity, thereby suggesting that we too are low and stupid. There are two main operations involved here. The first assumes that we have no memory. We are talked into believing a past that is untrue, a history that has undergone surgery and had tissue removed. This is the history of Poland minus the Polish-Russian war of 1920, minus Stalin's pact with Hitler in 1939, minus Katyń, and minus our betrayal at Yalta in 1945. The operation goes further, deeper—the massacre outside Warsaw at Praga in 1794* has also been amputated. On television, professors lecture on that surgically altered history with dignified equanimity, honest men who look us in the eye. But that wouldn't have sufficed. A second operation is performed simultaneously, which consists in switching

---

* In reprisal for the Polish insurrection against Russia, led by Kościuszko, Russian troops massacred the inhabitants of the Warsaw borough of Praga.

the target of our hatred. At least on one score the authorities have no illusions: they know who is hated in Poland today. Someone with that awareness and wishing to deflect that hatred from himself can either change his behavior or search for arguments with which to defend himself. But there exists yet a third possibility—to direct that hatred elsewhere, to provide it with a new target. For thirty-odd years television and the press have been employing the mental energy of their historians and publicists to invent a new target for Polish hatred: a Jewish conspiracy threatens us, our mortal enemy is the state of Israel. This mechanism runs on Polish anti-Semitism. We are with you, stop hating us, we'll hate together, rulers and nation, party and society . . . When this approach failed, it left only the Germans. Or, to be more precise, the West Germans. A couple of days ago I watched three television professors having a debate in connection with the upcoming fortieth anniversary of 1939. The principal dialogue was between two scholars and moved quickly toward its goal—to intensify Polish hatred for the only enemy it has, ever had, and ever will have, Germany west of the Elbe. East of the Bug we have the only friend who has always cared for us like a big brother.

This calculation of hatred contains a presupposition of evil, a nihilistic certainty that there are dark forces in the nation's soul that can never be allowed to rest. That faith in darkness does not stem from Poland's history and did not grow out of Polish soil. The Christian words spoken by the Pope in Warsaw and at Auschwitz seemed to reveal how shameless and alien such ideas in fact are.

In these pages I have written about miracles and myths, treating them more or less seriously, perhaps even ironically at times . . . But somewhere there was also a line expressing my confidence that life is fantastic and beyond any imagining. I have learned that it is always something other than what a person expects in his fears and premonitions and that fate operates on a logic different from that of the human mind, namely, the logic of paradox, surprise, dazzlement. Never what we expect. And this is what makes miracles possible. When the Pope's silver airplane appeared in the blue sky over the airport and began its descent, and later, when the figure in white appeared on the steps, that was, after all, the beginning of a miraculous tale, a myth. If someone had told me a year ago that a *Papa di Roma,* born in a small Polish town, would conduct a mass at the foot of a cross on Victory Square . . .

If the world were only "the tale of a madman," human existence would have no meaning. But, fortunately, we do not know the rules or the plot of the story, or the principle guiding it, and so we are interested in what happens next.

This morning I was awakened by the voice of an announcer on Polish Radio. M. was listening to the news. "We now belong to that small group of nations that has sent one of its citizens into space."

That had a great-power ring to it. We have outstripped England and France, and Switzerland lags far behind and beneath us.

While some of our citizens are in space, others are still on earth. Yesterday, in front of a grocery store in Gdynia, I saw two pensioners thrashing each other with their canes in a line of about thirty people waiting for butter. It reminded me of an idea that Stanisław Mrożek had for a play, which I don't think he ever got around to writing. It was to begin with a message from a general, the head of an African state, broadcast over color television: "Brothers, sharpen your spears and dig out your axes—three white faces have appeared on our coast."

■ *J U L Y*
1 9 7 9

The city seemed less crowded after our return from the seashore: many people had obviously left for vacation, and there was much less traffic. Apparently, there were heat waves in June. People were collapsing; the asphalt was melting. Now it has cooled off a bit. There's some breeze; the sky is a little on the gray side; the streets are getting a chance to cool off. Krakowskie Przedmieście in the afternoon, between Miodowa and Królewska Streets—wide, shaded by trees, running along the bright, curved facades of palaces and churches under a far-reaching sky ... The most beautiful urban panorama in the world. On Wednesday, M. and I took a walk to Łazienki. The park and the adjacent section of the Belvedere Palace, the ponds, footbridges, the island with its theater and fauns and even the people on the benches—all had an enchanting beauty, one that for me dates at least from the time I had first read *The Secrets of Łazienki Palace* by Zuzanna Rabska and from a later time, when I would go there with my lecture notes to cram for exams on Roman law. The Belvedere Palace is visible from behind and from below, its columns shining through the greenery, its terrace set high. One November night, students and journalists armed with rifles had to run up that hill.* I don't know if there is any other place in Poland where so many legends have grown up as beneath those trees between the statue of King Sobieski† on his small horse and the white palace that also seems small compared

---

* At the start of the 1831 armed uprising against Russia, Poles occupied the Belvedere Palace.
† Jan III Sobieski, king of Poland from 1674 to 1696, especially renowned for his liberation of Vienna in 1683 from the besieging Turkish forces.

to the role it has played. "A myth-making park," I said to M. "There are more ghosts here than live people."

There are a few lines from Artur Międzyrzecki's just-published volume of prose, *Age of the Mentors,* that have lodged in my memory: "A person knows and does not know. A person looks and does not see . . . Misery is close by, right outside your window. But it doesn't affect you directly. Sleep. So, a person hears and does not hear the cry for help. A person does not realize that violence is occurring. He realizes it when everything is over. Too late to do anything. Just in time to avoid being forced to take a personal risk."

"Heroism is first and foremost the courage to see in time."

Important lines. A person cannot avoid thinking about himself after reading them. What will they become, the people who saw but did not see, heard but did not hear the cry for help?

Reading those words, I remembered a meeting that took place years ago, in 1947 or 1948, a meeting of writers with a member of the party Central Committee. In his ardent speech he described the new situations and conflicts that people in our country were experiencing, moral conflicts and situations never before depicted by literature. "Comrades, imagine one of our boys from Security who's interrogating a fascist prisoner; imagine a simple, honest guy who knows he has a mortal enemy before him. And he must use all his strength to restrain himself. He clenches his fists, for he knows that he is not allowed to touch that man."

For years afterward, I wondered if that speaker with the burning eyes had known that he was not speaking the truth.

Five or six years ago, at a meeting with some of my readers (in Gdańsk), someone asked me from the floor, "When was the first time you sensed that what was happening in Poland was unjust?" I answered that I would not be able to furnish a precise date, but I did know that a decisive factor was my conversations with people who had been released from prison in the years 1954–1956. But the correct answer would have been different. I had my doubts from the beginning, but the stronger they were, the more

I repressed them and the more vociferous were my denials of them. Every doubt damaged the logic and the ethics of the basic assumptions I had come to accept, and burdened me with guilt. One was always on the lookout for signs of doubt in oneself and in others. In 1955 I was still trying to defend myself against the facts. At bottom, I was only defending myself from myself. It may be that the most essential mechanism in the system known as communism is this curious twofold one: the counterfeiting and the denying of the self.

"Too late to do anything . . ."

Yesterday evening, at dinner with the Konwickis at the Borowiczes,' the mood was good, amiable. First we looked at photos from Janka's trip to Greece, and later, at the table, conversation hopped from one topic to another, one epoch to another. Among other things, we talked about the Despot-Zenowicz family and M.'s paternal great-grandfather, Aleksander Zenowicz, who had been exiled and who later, as the governor of Tobolsk, became famous as the protector of the Poles who had been sent there (to Siberia) for their part in the January Uprising. Konwicki said that he had often come across Zenowicz's name when reading about his native Lithuania. Then we spoke of the first period after the war, which we had both spent in Kraków. Konwicki had been drunk on freedom; he remembers theatrical premieres when the sight of the curtain by Siemiradzki* made his heart beat faster. My memory of those times, on the other hand, is somehow dim, discolored. I found everything, the theater included, not very real; I felt that in comparison with the life that had existed before September 1939, something had been switched, displaced, duplicated. There was a sense of physical salvation, yes, and of hope, ambition, the desire to write, of course, and moreover a conviction that the remaking of society was a just task, an acceptance of the system's fundamental theses about the economy, education . . . But at the same

---

* A realist painter of the turn of the century.

time, there was a semiconscious melancholy at the passing of
time, the replacement of the stuff of a previous life with similar
forms but ones that were less fully rounded, less vivid, and did
not match the original. Even the Słowacki Theater seemed a
make-believe theater to me, a shell, and its curtain, a fake reproduction of the historical original. Konwicki shook his head in
surprise. "But back then," I explained, "I was ten years older
than you. Ten years is half the time between the wars. The war
destroyed our way of life, and afterward, everything smelled of
surrogates." I began listing the restaurants and little theaters in
prewar Warsaw, describing how racing fans used to meet in the
cafés on Marszałkowska, the ones near Mokotowski Field, to
pick their favorites over a glass of *café au lait.* I named the cafés
where members of the actors' guild used to congregate, the writers' and painters' bars, and others, with Chinese lanterns on their
terraces on Aleje Jerozolimskie, where crowds of people would
saunter on hot evenings until late in the night. And I recalled the
moment when I first became aware that all these colorful details
of daily life had been replaced by new backgrounds and props. It
happened in Lublin, where I spent a few days in mid-January
1945. We used to eat in a canteen patronized by many people
who had been well-known before the war and who had also been
friends of mine. They were all in officers' uniforms. Zaruba was
there in uniform, Lec was in uniform, Matuszewski was in uniform, and even Olga Siemaszków was wearing lieutenant's bars.
There was a theater there—the Polish Army Theater. They were
performing Wyspiański's *The Wedding.* I did not succeed in seeing a performance, but I imagined it with the Poet and Rachel
wearing uniforms. Later on, Kraków was an extension, a continuation, of that falling into line that had felt artificial and stage-
managed to me. The obvious reply was that the war had just
ended, but that would not have been explanation enough. Ten
years later, when Andrzej Nowicki, the poet who had been a
POW in a German camp for officers, returned to Warsaw after a
long absence from the country, he too racked his brains when
walking in the streets trying to define the change that had taken

place in the city. Finally, during his second week in Warsaw, he suddenly stopped on the sidewalk and said, "Now I know what it reminds me of! A POW officers' camp with women!"

It isn't easy, and back then it was especially hard, to specify the cause of the mental uneasiness people felt in that changed order. A sense of incompleteness, of being unable to grasp what was actually going on, a vague feeling of being "outside" of things, of things having been "switched." Many years later I was to call this "unreality," a term that was, in any case, already in circulation. But long before then, I had encountered an astounding manifestation of this phenomenon—during my 1948 trip to Russia, when the poet Konstanty Gałczyński and I were in the Polish delegation to the anniversary celebration of the October Revolution. Our plane was late in landing in Moscow, and thus we only had time to change our clothes in the hotel before we were taken to the Bolshoi Theater, where the anniversary commemoration was being held. As we were shown to our seats, flashbulbs started going off: Molotov had taken the podium. I remember the moment. On stage, behind the chairman's table, which was draped in red cloth, a few dozen people were sitting, arranged in four rows. Stalin was not there, but there was an enormous portrait of him at the rear of the stage, Malenkov was chairing the commemorative meeting, and I recognized a few other faces from the politburo in the first row (Mikoyan, Voroshilov . . .). Marshal Budenny's black moustache showed up prominently in the second row, while the third and fourth rows were filled with people whose faces were less familiar, people wearing dark suits and uniforms. I saw it all quite clearly with Molotov standing at the podium, lit by flashbulbs. He spoke for over an hour, stuttering each time he said Stalin's name: "St-St-Stalin." During the entire speech, the stage, the red table, and the four rows of the presidium were before my eyes . . . After the meeting, we were taken back to our hotel. We ate dinner; then Gałczyński and I fell asleep on the wide double bed. I was up first in the morning, awakened by a rustling sound at the door. Still sleepy, I jumped out of bed and noticed the edge of a newspaper that had been slipped under the door. It was a copy of *Pravda*, redolent of fresh ink. Most of the front page was taken up by a photo showing the opening of the commemorative meeting: Molotov at the podium, the presidium table with Malenkov in the middle . . . I scrutinized the photograph. There were only two rows of chairs behind the table; the third and fourth had vanished, replaced by a uniformly dark background. I was unable to grasp what the photograph was presenting. The truth? A fiction? Both? Or was I seeing things? I finally woke up Gałczyński and handed him the paper. Neither of us knew what to think.

The poet Adam Ważyk, however, who had spent the war in Russia, knew exactly what to think. When we returned to Poland, I showed him that copy of *Pravda* in the editorial offices of *Kuźnica* (The Forge). He looked at me with all the dignity of a Siamese cat and asked me just what I wanted to know and what did I find so surprising. I told him that there had been a third and a fourth row, and so why weren't they in the picture? "That's simple," said Ważyk. "The people in the third and fourth rows still don't deserve to be seen in an edition of several million copies." All right then, I persisted, but that means that the photograph isn't true. "Politically it is true," Ważyk cut me short dryly. That ended our conversation. One of my first lessons in dialectical thinking.

Certain wise observers in the last century maintained that the new source of human uncertainty is the multiplication of mental horizons around the mind of contemporary man. What to choose? Which of the philosophical criteria? In which direction should the mind advance? Marxism liberated people from doubt; it indicated a single direction, a single certainty. The Russians turned that capacity into an abomination by enthroning it at the pinnacle of a lie. They turned a West European doctrine into Potemkin villages. How easily dialectical thinking, with its retouched backgrounds, penetrated the weary postwar consciousness; how artfully it could replace reality with tiers of arguments and delineate the lines along which history would develop.

Along the idyllic facades of model villages that concealed the servitude of the countryside, a river of blood and lies flowed on toward the promised land of a classless society. The old Communists who had been released from the camps used to say that Stalin's dream was the day when bread would be given out for free.

Yesterday it occurred to me that many people, some of whom have been close to me for at least twenty years, have a mistaken notion of me as a "cunning" person. I had thought that no one could have any doubts as to my good faith. That's experience for you. It's a little bitter, but I don't regret it. "There are two things I don't regret," Staś Dygat, the writer, said to me when I saw him for the last time, "joining the party and leaving the party."

What else happened in July? We've been going to the cinema; the lines at the box office are shorter now. *The Death of a Chinese Bookie, Taxi Driver, An Unmarried Woman,* are not, of course, great films, but they are among the many American films I am mad about. How many have I seen? Dozens, maybe hundreds. Coppola's *The Conversation* and *The Godfather,* Altman's *Nashville, 3 Women,* and *The Wedding,* and *Easy Rider, They Shoot Horses, Don't They?, Vanishing Point,* and *Scarecrow.* I wouldn't be able to list them all—there are simply too many to remember. And probably there is another reason as well. All those films meld together, supplementing one another, and taken together, they create an image of a civilization and an era. There is no country besides the United States that shows the truth about itself with such force and, at the same time, expresses the truth of contemporary life. Sometimes, those American films, directed by a great many different directors working from different scripts, seem like one mighty work, a Balzacian *La Comédie humaine* of our times. Their cruel exposés and the yearning for innocence, the gangs and the loneliness, degenerate dreamers and electronically equipped police, the roar of hot jazz and high-octane gas, drugs, pastorals of pure love, home and bars—a reality bursting with real-life detail captured by masters of photography in psychedelic movement and color. A new system of montage: narration as a code, almost puzzlelike, sometimes starting in the middle of things in quick cuts, with everything coming together only later. As if this were the latest in the technology of fate. And they really can tell a story! Stories about what? About themselves. But they also show us how those stories could be told about us as well. You think that their actors are playing purely American roles? No, they are for everyone.

The television announcers are afraid again. The thirty-fifth anniversary of the Warsaw Uprising is approaching. The whole downtown area has been plastered with official posters showing an anchor formed of the first two letters of the Home Army slogan "Poland Fights." For a week now films from those days have been showing on television—boys in helmets, barricades, graves marked with crosses. Never before in People's Poland have the heroism of the soldiers in the uprising and the populace's self-sacrifice been venerated so ardently. What is the source of all that ardor?

With fear written all over their faces, the announcers report shortfalls in the production plans for agriculture, problems with rolling stock, difficulties in energy production ... It's not only the anniversary of the uprising that's approaching; fall and winter are coming, and with them, the dangers of shortages in food and coal. And that is why the announcers are afraid. And that is why the posters with the anchors on them are being put up; that is why the rebels' will to endure is being praised. Tearfully, the announcers beseech their audience, "Poles, you who have been able to endure so much adversity, you who know exhaustion and hunger, Poles, stand up to these new ordeals and display this time as well a heroic readiness to sacrifice—when standing in lines, when freezing in your apartments, when waiting at mobbed train stations—be as selfless and patriotic as they were in Mokotów and on the shores of the Vistula thirty-five years ago!"

▪ *AUGUST*
1979

Lanckorona. Different from what I had imagined. Wajda had said, "There are some small hills, but you can take your walks on flat ground." The land is in fact very steep and craggy everywhere; only 40 kilometers from Kraków, but the landscape is like that of the Tatra Highlands, like that in Rabka or Tylmanowa, where we spent the summer with the Stopeks and Lena Walicka. The trip from Warsaw was tiring, driving into the sun the whole way, passing trucks on a two-way road; and since August 1, the speed limit has been reduced to 90 kilometers. Past Głogoczow, I began looking for the sign to Wadowice and missed the turnoff. I had to get off at Bielsko.

I sent Joanna Guze a card from Lanckorona: "I can tell you that it's very lovely here. We are staying at a rather odd *pension*. There's a plaster bust of Piłsudski in the living room, and in the yard, a wooden car made by our host, Tadeusz. Two giant homosexual roosters live in it. An ultramodern swimming pool in the garden, swarming with tadpoles. In the house there are twelve dogs, fifteen children, and one bewhiskered old woman. Six televisions. Bathrooms like those in Obory, a good kitchen. Moreover, there's a large upright piano, quarries, billiards, a stuffed wood grouse, and an elk skull. I'll end with that."

We arrived for a late dinner. A long, dark dining room, trees outside the windows, the greenery so thick that that is all you see at first. Only Piłsudski emerged from the darkness: a white plaster bust, the head, shoulders, and torso almost life-size, in a recess in the wall. Souvenirs and photographs had been arranged around him and above him: someone's medals and crosses framed under glass, a large photograph of an officer wearing the jacket of Piłsudski's Legions, resting on his saber, and lower down, a picture of Kościuszko. And then more Piłsudski. A pencil drawing, a photograph, and a reproduction of a portrait of him wearing the Virtuti Militari ribbon. At the very top, a photograph taken shortly before his death. Gray, gaunt, beside his sister's coffin. Then, closer to the stove, Wojciech Kossak's paintings of various units in Piłsudski's Legions, and beneath them, a color postcard of Kościuszko and Prince Józef greeting Piłsudski after death at the threshold of the Wawel crypt. On the stove, a bouquet of dried flowers in a vase, an elk (or boar) skull with yellow teeth, a miniature windmill black with age, and a figurine of Piłsudski, standing erect, wearing a cap, holding his marshal's baton.

The overall impression was that of an altar emerging from the darkness of a nave. Girls served us. The table was enormous, covered with an oilcloth; the backs of the chairs were high, carved. The interior of the house was permeated with the smell of rotting wood and herbs; high on one wall, a dusty, beakless hawk with its wings spread, a wood grouse with gouged-out eyes, deer antlers, and over a dark credenza, a broken cuckoo clock. On the other side of the room, by the window, stood a walnut piano covered by a tablecloth and flower pots, a television set between them. Plus an Empire-style wardrobe from whose mirror a pale, older man looked at me. Naturally I recognized myself in him. I've described the details that revealed themselves only gradually. It took me a week to learn my way around that room. Besides, we decided to eat on the adjoining glassed-in veranda.

I wrote the card to Joanna toward the end of our stay, when I was already feeling rather good. The first few days I lived in fear. It's hard for me to say just what I was afraid of—it must have been the fear of a place whose essence I could not fathom. What kind of a house was this? Where did that strange smell come from? I stood and stared at that building that reminded me of a mushroom-shaped growth at the foot of a forest-covered mountain. I counted the outbuildings, the steps, the roofs, the turrets, the wooden balustrades with their railings. Wearing striped pajamas, a warm scarf around his neck, the rector of the Kraków Theater School walked around the terrace amid drying laundry warming up his voice, which had gone hoarse: "Mi . . . mi miii . . . mamma mia . . ." Then he vanished. A half-naked man walked silently past me, pushing a wheelbarrow full of stones and dirt. Two roosters jumped fighting from the covered parking area. I walked a little farther. A red-haired girl in a bikini passed me, leading a pair of black dachshunds on a leash, and disappeared in the brush. From somewhere down below came the sound of people talking, water splashing, barking. The pool . . . A pool set among spruce trees surrounded by an embankment of earth, tall causeways with paths on top. Looking down through the branches, I could see girls swimming. The man with the wheelbarrow walked by again. The roosters were crowing. A car with French plates came out of a forest ravine and pulled up in front of the main house. A curly-haired athletic type with a cap on his head and a cross on his hairy chest got out. He was carrying an eighteenth-century alabaster vase with a cupid on it. "Your roads are horrible," he said to me. "Do you know if Ala's in the kitchen?" Out past the parking area the man with the wheelbarrow was smashing sandstone on the mountainside with a pickax.

"This *pension* has existed for fifty-three years," Tadeusz told me. "My father began work on the old house in 1922." Tadeusz's father had been an officer in the First Brigade of Piłsudski's Legions. Mościcki, Colonel Sławek, and Foreign Minister Beck used to come there. Tadeusz bustled about in a blue-gray Legionnaire's cap pulled down over his right ear. Off the forest road leading to the house I noticed a sign nailed to the tree. The faded letters read, "Legionnaires' St." Ala, Tadeusz's younger daughter, was twenty. Good-looking, always with a cigarette in her mouth, she worked in the old house with three young girls as helpers, the radio playing nonstop. The new building stood near the old one, but a bit higher up. Our room was in the new house.

Designed in mountain-resort style (wood, stone, glass, corru-
gated iron), it had broad oak stairs, a solarium on the roof, and a
deserted bar on the ground floor. Paneling and parquet floors in
the rooms. Covered balconies. Bathrooms, electric stoves. A
radio in every room. Wrought-iron grillework, paper lanterns on
the landings. Cobwebs and dust everywhere. In the reading
room, piles of old mattresses. The bathtub was covered with rust
spots; the toilet seat was dirty. When, drying myself after my
shower, I rested my foot on the toilet seat, it fell off. I picked it up
and fastened it back on. Dashing back to my room, I came across
two white Tatra sheepdogs pulling a stout man, who shouted,
"Please, stop!" I shaved over a plugged-up sink. The water
wouldn't drain out: I stuck my finger down the drain and
plucked out an olive jammed into the top of a tube of toothpaste.
Meanwhile, the bed had collapsed while M. was resting on it. We
decided to return to Warsaw.

Had a Swede or a Dutchman been brought there, he would
have packed his bags after an hour. And during that hour he
would have asked the following questions: Why has the dining
room been turned into a mausoleum? Why is meat delivered at
night? Why aren't the cobwebs and dust cleaned from the new
house? Why is there not a single bench in one piece in the garden
when a trampoline is under construction by the pool? Why has
that solitary man been smashing rocks for fifteen years? Who
constructed that useless wooden automobile and to what end?
Why are the Tatra sheepdogs kept locked up? Why have those
two enormous roosters been condemned to a henless existence?
Are the elegant gray-haired gentlemen leaving the tadpole-filled
pool and the other gentleman, the one wearing the pajamas and
the woolen scarf who recites poetry among the underwear drying
on the line, mentally stable? And finally, why do people who
would appear to be cultured Europeans stay in an old building
that is creaking with age and has no amenities and why are the
parquet floors in the new building thick with filth?

Since none of the Swede's (or Dutchman's) questions would

have received an intelligent answer, he would have left there convinced that the *pension* in the woods had been established by some mentally deranged people. We, however, who are well grounded in the absurd, stayed there for four weeks.

■ **S E P T E M B E R**
1 9 7 9

As a rule, my energy and spirits fall just before the autumn. I usually sink into this state, which I call the "eclipse," a week after I return from vacation. My apartment feels stuffy, crowded with furniture, cut off from the landscape.

All conversations begin and end with predictions about the results of our economic debacle. Work stoppages in industrial production, public transportation in ruins, moribund investments, an increasing hard-currency debt, energy shortages, bad harvests. And what else? I think of the ditty Wilek Mach was fond of repeating: "Winter's coming, there's no boots, I think I better die. Don't, you silly hen, spring'll be here by and by."

Inefficiency and obtuseness everywhere you go. In July a new antiparasite chemical agent was sprayed in the forests of the northern provinces and destroyed the undergrowth. Two hundred cases of poisoning have been reported, fourteen of them fatal. But not a word about whose decision this was and whether or not anyone had been prosecuted. At enormous expense we import electronic computers from the West that cannot be used in our industry, and the latest machines for refining oil, which go to ruin because the chemical content of the crude oil arriving from the USSR wasn't analyzed first: it contains sulfur. The entire country is blossoming with private residences belonging to the ruling cadres: villas; parks; hunting grounds; complexes of buildings surrounded by walls with electric eyes; swimming pools; exquisite kitchens; the best servants. No one is bothered by this classless luxury, which was still kept secret from Gomułka* (in Łańsk, when they learned of his imminent arrival, an alarm would go off, and the delicacies, carpets, and some of the servants would vanish. Later, when the provincial politicos complained about the excesses at Łańsk, Gomułka would cry, "It isn't true, I was there! They serve you curdled milk with potatoes and kasha!") The food situation grows worse and worse. But on Marszałkowska, near the Square of the Savior, there was a line of about thirty people standing right by the road, in the midst of all the noise and exhaust, absolutely motionless. They were mostly old people, with an unhealthy, sick-room look to them, women with swollen legs. "What's the line for?" I ask. Grapes! Around the corner from the square, in the Delicatessen, the line for vodka has wound around twice, more than a hundred men, most of them the same age as People's Poland, including some drunks with the faces of exhausted sluts.

A girl brought me seven roses yesterday. She had come here from Gdańsk. Pretty, wearing pants, well spoken. She had spent a year hitchhiking through the West. She said that she could have stayed there. Her profession—she's a teacher—clashes with her idea of honesty. She changed her mind, however, and decided to return. "After I read your book," she said, blushing. I was beginning to feel uncomfortable. She had read *A Question of Reality* in the library of the Polish Club in Hamburg. She has very blue eyes and small, strong hands, with fingernails clipped short. We spent the next hour discussing Germany. She had worked there. She is afraid of Germans, scared by their petty, blind aggressiveness. "You know, they're the same on one side and on the other. And there are exceptions on both sides too."

---

* Władysław Gomułka, former first secretary of the Polish Communist Party.

Before her trip she had only been afraid of Russians. "But our cleaning women," she said, meaning at her school or dorm, "were more afraid of the Germans. After the occupation . . ." Then she asked me didn't I think that in Poland it was the intellectuals who are afraid of Russia, whereas for the simple people, especially the older ones, Germans are the very devil. "That's the breakdown." Some choice.

At the time I joined the Socialist movement during my third year at the university, Piłsudski had been dead for two years. Even before he died, after graduating from high school, I left the Society of the Lovers of Virtue and the Legion of Youth to which I had belonged for a few months. Many young Piłsudskiites had undergone a split: one faction went to the left, to the PPS;* the other began heading in the direction of totalitarianism. The camp at Bereza Kartuska was set up during that period. Piłsudski had received Göring, and later Goebbels, at the Belvedere Palace. The speeches and meetings of the Warsaw branch of the Legion of Youth did not differ in content from the slogans of the ONR's Falange. When one speaker came out against the anti-Semitism in the organization and said, "My mother is of Jewish descent," the response was a chorus of sneering laughter. I asked myself, What am I doing here? and the next day I turned in my membership card.

I was a law student. It was clear to me that the country was slipping into mental and social darkness. The legend had lost its luster. Every day I heard the shouts of hired thugs on the campus, and every week I read reports of our ruling dignitaries' visits to Berlin. The two things were connected. A horrifying specter was on the rise. I had never feared anything like the specter of a stupid, ignorant Poland. And it was coming from two sides. I knew what Nazism was and I also knew that the Falange and the other splinters of that movement were Poland's version of Nazism.

---

* Polska Partia Socjalistyczna (Polish Socialist Party).

After 1945 and 1956 those groups were quite frequently referred to as "agents." I don't know who was or who is an agent; I never knew my way around such questions, and I have no fondness for people who are expert in such matters. A few students in my high-school class at Rej belonged to the ONR. There were some good boys among them; their leader was one of the top students, an intelligent boy full of hatred. But certainly neither he nor they were agents. But I am certain that had they been ordered to, they would have burned Tuwim's and Boy's books without any hesitation. Later on, at the university, I was to encounter the ONR in action. The sight of stupidity mixed with fury, the roar of thugs disrupting seminars, a gang of goons with clubs chasing a student who looked Jewish across the campus—all that was hideous. They called one of their weeklies *Pod Pręgierz* (In Pillory). At that time, the chief of Hitler's police (Daluege) and the Third Reich's Minister of Justice (Frank) paid official visits to Warsaw. Had this only been a matter of Foreign Minister Beck's visits to Berchtesgaden, only a question of foreign policy . . . Foreign policy can be explained in terms of tactics, *raison d'état*, and so on. This was a hundred times worse. A significant portion of the intelligentsia had begun to believe in friendship with Hitler. Germany's growing strength was impressive; the young *Sanacja* activists and the radical nationalists, invited to lectures in Berlin, returned to Poland with ideological models. A couple of years before the war, the Polish associations of lawyers and doctors introduced an Aryan clause into their statutes. The same thing occurred in student groups in the institutions of higher learning; not in all of them—the Polish studies group and the art historians group at Warsaw University, to which M. belonged, did not pass that clause. But the general drift was unmistakable. The Ministry of Religions and Public Education authorized the rectors to segregate students in the classroom. Students' files were stamped "even-numbered rows" or "odd-numbered rows." The odd-numbered rows were a few separate benches at the back of the lecture hall. The first to assign segregated benches was Father Witwicki, the rector at Batory University in Wilno.

I was assigned an "even-numbered row"—the criterion was religion—but I stopped attending lectures. I was depressed, disgusted, not only because it was happening in my country but, more than anything, by the thought that my nation, one of the most intelligent societies in the world, would not be able to distinguish between the truth and mere words, as had already happened so many times in the past—most often its own truth from its own words.

When the future Governor-General Frank was in Warsaw three years before the war, he was invited to give a lecture in the university's Auditorium Maximum. The subject was to be law in the Third Reich. After a ceremonial opening address to the public, three young people—two girls and a boy—came forward with a bouquet of roses. They walked up to the lecturer and handed him the roses, requesting that he lay them on the graves of the freedom fighters who had been murdered in Hitler's concentration camps. There was a commotion; Frank was escorted from the auditorium, and to this day I do not know if that lecture ever took place. The male student was Leszek Raabe, the leader of the academic Union of Independent Socialist Youth (ZNMS). I knew him by sight. Slender, slightly stooped, with a beautiful face and bushy eyebrows, he reminded me of Piłsudski in photographs of him as a young man. A little while after this incident, a Falange gang beat him up with brass knuckles in front of the auditorium building.

Looking through the last few pages, I suddenly thought, The years before the war were pure years. What? Yes, they were pure. Just as there are pure colors in painting. Back then, I saw black and white, red and bronze, clearly differentiated. Light was separated from dark. Everything had definite contours, clean lines; no intermediate tones. Only the background was gray. And it was that gray background that I felt was menacing, the true source of trouble—the indifference of the majority. Blessedly pure years, when the left and the right were still separate and when only half the evil, one devil, fascism, was known. My convictions were clear. I was immune to all the pros and cons, to that state of mind where one is not certain of any reason, meaning, value, a state that I call the relative. There is a type of person, especially among intellectuals, who does not fare too badly in that state; the relative can be a rest home for the mind, a refuge from choice. It's not like that for me. I am only attracted by the relative from time to time, and that is always accompanied by depression—my "eclipse." Those two are old friends.

From my years in the ZNMS a few disconnected images remain. We were a handful fighting fascism in institutions of higher learning. We had an office consisting of three little rooms, two tables, a few rows of chairs, and a bookcase. Not a single portrait on the wall. We read Marx but didn't put up any images of him. There were no ceremonies apart from singing the "Internationale" or the "Red Banner" after our discussions were over. We met every week to hear a lecture. Scholars, politicians, activists, were invited to speak.

Today all that seems so good and noble. What did we want? A democratic Poland, the liberation of the proletariat, social justice. We believed that the left, in solidarity—Socialists along with Communists, the peasant movement and former Piłsudskiites—would fight together and win a Poland of that sort.

I was elected director of the university section and shortly after entered the organization's administrative ranks. I took part in various actions. We handed out leaflets in front of the university gates, stood against the wall during lectures as a protest against segregated seating, created an order guard for marches and meetings, and in the evenings sold antifascist periodicals on the streets downtown. Always a minority, always attacked by gangs. Sometimes people would return bloodied from that work. I carried a starter's pistol, a present from Marian, and a rubber tire from a baby carriage. The gangs used brass knuckles and ropes with iron balls on them. The police would arrive at the more heated disturbances, arresting a few of us as a rule. The

Falangists were not detained; at the time, some of them had joined the regime's OZON.* At the university, the Falange gangs were led by a tall, pale fanatic, Andrzej Świetlicki, who later on, during the first months of the war, founded NOR.† The Germans allocated them office space on Aleje Ujazdowskie but liquidated it soon after. I heard that Świetlicki had perished—hanged in a cell. I cannot forget his face—the sunken cheeks, the dark circles under his eyes—as he used his club to pick up my student cap, which had been knocked off in a fight.

The authorities disbanded the Warsaw branch of the ZNMS in June 1939.

I spent the next year preparing for examinations to earn my degree. Andrzej Minkowski—a friend and a former classmate from high school—and I crammed together. We studied at home, in the Botanical Gardens, or at Łazienki Park. It was the spring of 1939. Hitler was demanding Gdańsk and transit across Pomerania. Our friendship with the Third Reich had come to an end. But the ONR's couriers were still prowling around the parks thrusting copies of their weekly Pod Pręgierz (In Pillory) at passersby. In May a gang killed two Jewish students at Lwów University. That same month, the dean of the law school at Warsaw University, Professor Rybarski, refused to sign the records of students who stood during lectures as a protest against segregated seating. All this was going on, I repeat, in the spring of 1939, three months before a million Aryan Germans invaded Poland and a year and a half before the ghetto in Warsaw was walled off.

In those final years before the outbreak of the war, I encountered phenomena, on a reduced and, so to speak, experimental scale, that would only later demonstrate their true reach and weight. My first close contact with Communists came in the ZNMS. Some of them were seeking refuge in a legal organization, and the ZNMS was tolerant of them (Jan Krasicki was one of those camouflaged Communists in our group). Others turned

---

* Obóz Zjednoczenia Narodowego (Camp of National Unity).
† Narodowa Organizacja Radykalna (Radical Nationalist Organization).

up as delegates of the illegal Life group, the union of Communist youth. We often worked on joint leaflets, and the members of Life participated in our actions at the universities. They were uncomfortable with us, suspicious and wary from the start. Sometimes editing a leaflet would take until dawn. They would arrive with a prepared text and would not agree to any corrections. Nothing, not a single comma. We would go hoarse trying to persuade them. Whenever the political trials in Moscow were mentioned, they resorted to contemptuous silence. I think that they believed the accusations and considered the defendants to be traitors. But with us, in front of us, they never said a word about it. Their stubbornness infuriated us, but at the same time, it earned our respect. Some of them had spent a couple of years in prison; a few had been expelled from universities. And they seemed made of iron, unyielding, impermeable. We would argue late into the night about the wording of the leaflets. Once, I proposed a brief text for a leaflet with the title "To the Students of Warsaw University." The delegates from Life brought a disquisition freighted with quotations from Marx and insisted on their own title: "To the Polish Youth of Warsaw University." I felt there was something insincere about that, some semantic jockeying going on. I explained that this sounded like we were disassociating ourselves from the Ukrainian and Jewish students. They didn't say a word. I changed my suggestion to "To Polish Democratic Youth." No. Then perhaps "To the Youth Studying at Warsaw University." The purpose of the leaflet was to put an end to the brawls that were disrupting classes. No. No changes. Neither in the title nor in the content. A cold, dry refusal. They threatened to walk out of the meeting. Three days later I was distributing leaflets with their text in front of the university. Szczęsny Zamieński from Life, who differed from the other Communist students in his absentmindedness, delicacy, and normal human warmth, was standing beside me. He read the leaflet shaking his head. "Who wrote this—it's unreadable." I didn't reply.

People of that sort were also termed agents. Many of their

contemporaries did not appreciate them and shared that opinion of them. Now in retrospect, through the prism of subsequent events, I can see them entering white rooms, gospel in hand, not realizing that those rooms were the chambers of the inquisition. Some of them will perish at the hands of torturers; others will become torturers themselves. Szczęsny Zamieński's bones were broken during interrogation by one of his former comrades from Life. Some of them would end up in camps; others would become army officers and members of the party Central Committee, prosecutors at courts-martial and prisoners held in damp, dark cells. But it all began with an idea.

I knew ONR members and Communists who had the faces of visionaries. With their gospel and their real, secular power, totalitarian systems seem capable of realizing that highly romantic idea of pushing history forward. There is a certain type of person who comes into the world with a concept of history as divine incarnation, God as He exists in time; in the movement of history such a person sees an ethical goal and a road to the ideal. People of this type frequently fall under the totalitarian spell. They are attracted by the idea of separateness—separateness by nation, race, purity of tribal blood—or by universality—equality, internationalism, a just community of free earthlings. Romanticism's womb was fertile; both messianism and socialism emerged from it. The superman and the fighter in a worker's smock are two of Romanticism's children. Both of the totalitarian ideologies, the Communist and the Nationalist, arose out of them. And today we can count the graves of the victims.

OCTOBER
1979

In the Church of the Holy Cross, eleven people are on a hunger strike, among them Halina, Jerzy Markuszewski, and Adam Michnik. The strike has been in progress for three days and is an act of solidarity with the prisoners of conscience awaiting trial in Prague. I called up Marian and asked if he was worried. "Everything's all right." Before leaving the house, Halina had left him a note. He hadn't known about the strike earlier.

It's cold in the apartment; you need a coat to go out. I huddle in my coat and feel warmer and older. The city is gray, empty. I avoid meeting people. I'm not reading newspapers, not watching television. I'm reading a mystery by Erle Stanley Gardner.

A warm, sunny day. Warsaw's trees are completely bare; the leaves rustle underfoot. The streets look veiled. People's silhouettes and the outlines of buildings appear blurred in the diffused light; everything seems softer, drier. Traugutt Street, strewn with leaves, yellow, copper-red, and brown, is shot through with light. You enter the church through a little courtyard planted with flower beds resembling a small square. A couple of students are sitting on the benches with books and notebooks. A small group of people has gathered in front of the entrance to the building. Among them a few of the hunger strikers, recognizable by their warm clothing (some of them are wearing sheepskin jackets) and by their pale, sharp faces. There's a small crowd of soldiers in the vestibule; someone is explaining to them the purpose of the strike. The soldiers listen closely, nodding their heads that they understand; then a few questions asked in low voices, and expressions of thanks. I'm looking for Halina, squeezing my way in the door. Nearly the entire floor is covered with brightly colored inflatable mattresses. Someone with a gray nose protruding from the plaid blanket wrapped around him is lying on his back in one corner. Sitting on a table by the wall, a gaunt man with glasses and a long sheepskin coat. I recognize him. "No, no, I feel fine," he says, smiling sourly. "It's only a cold. A doctor examined everyone." Markuszewski is standing wrapped in a red quilt that looks like a chasuble or a burnoose, from which a round, close-cropped head emerges saying, "I read your *Diary* in *Zapis.*" He hasn't lost weight; his cheeks have color, but I can feel how cold they are when I hug him. I catch sight of Halina, her eyes large and dark as vellum, talking with him. Markuszewski in his quilt is still going on about the *Diary* with M. "You like all of us, but you only love her." M. and Halina both laugh, each in her own way, and I ask how many more days the strike will last and if people aren't becoming too weak. Markuszewski answers that they could get through it all right. I see an armful of flowers in a pail under a window, a huge amount of flowers. "People keep bringing them," says Halina. "We have two or three hundred visitors a day."

We go back out. The students are still sitting there with their notebooks; a young priest passes us, bowing courteously.

There was something narcotic about it all, a mass hypnosis. I am thinking not only of the fifteen people in the Church of the Holy Cross but also of all those who are now termed dissidents. Always in their group, close-knit, constantly raising their political consciousness. The question is whether they would be able to live any other sort of life now. Many questions. Are they so close-knit because there are so few of them? Probably. Considering the circumstances, they are doing what they can. And, no doubt, what they have to.

I don't know to what degree they realize how isolated they are. In a country that loves to talk, they are passed over in silence even more often than the authorities are. In his diary, Żeromski reviled a "Poland of just plain folks" and expressed hate for that listless republic that desired so little. And for the majority of the people in today's Poland, freedom is not the chief desire either. They fear the risk of a sudden breakthrough, open situations where they would have to decide things for themselves. The majority does not believe that such goals are real and wants material improvements. And the republic adds: to hell with making gestures for those Czechs! The opposition is a game that won't last one day longer than the government allows.

You can live the way the government permits, read what the government permits. In the end, that begins to be enough and that's all you want. At most you dream of comforts, paradise with a swimming pool in the yard. Still, those dreams do contain some vision of a higher standard. Except for the vision of soaring above those standards. The republic does not trust the wings of youth.

On Wednesday, before noon, a drunken man with a bluish face and a fixed stare was lying on a block of basalt inside the Barbakan, and above him, pencil and notepad in hand, stood a young policeman. A buddy of the first drunk was reeling as he said, "Officer, sir, I give you my word, he's a decent man!"

Half of me was on the side of the drunk lying there, and I almost believed his friend's assurances. The other half ... What side was the other half on? On the side of order, morality, moderation? I was certainly not on the side represented by the policeman but on a side not represented there.

The trial of the defenders of human rights in Prague has concluded with sentences of up to five years. A month before the trial, the Czechoslovak authorities gave two of the prisoners a choice: emigration, or trial and sentencing. They both chose to stand trial. The writer Vaclav Havel was one of the two.

I don't think the police were prepared for acts of heroism such as that. And how about literature? Literature that has been extolling the decline of man for the last two or three generations must also have been surprised by heroes appearing in Jaroslav Hasek's native land. Let us reflect on what this means. The Czech intellectuals who chose prison instead of passports to the West did not come out of a Romantic tradition—their national poetry did not teach them to die for freedom—and past experience has taught that country to draw conclusions based on compromise and common sense. Their state had twice been betrayed by its powerful allies and sold out to two varieties of totalitarianism, one after the other. So they have no illusions. Those were isolated people who were brought from their prison cells to the trial each day, without defense counsel by their own choice, without support in their own society outside of a handful of people who were hounded just as they had been (it is not even certain that they knew about the fifteen people on the hunger strike in Poland), people who, when they stood before the court, once again rejected the accusation against them in its entirety. I say, Let us reflect on what this means and on whether literature has not been too hasty in announcing the death and obsolescence of heroes.

Only the naïve imagine the police as thick-headed guards with whistles. In essence, the police is a philosophy and a view of human nature. The police is glad to note that for a long time now heroes have been reposing on the ash heap of burned-out ideas. Thus is the bureau of investigation's fundamental assumption confirmed, the assumption that man's spiritual value is doubtful at best, or at least is a relative thing that can be molded according to the amount or type of pressure applied. At the root of that assumption is the profoundest of certainties that people are cowardly, envious, and corruptible; the police's psychological knowledge is based on a presumption of man's evil.

I use the word "police" in the contemporary meaning of the term, in a broader sense, as a phenomenon of the totalitarian state. The ideal of all police is a society where everyone is an informer and every informer is supervised. None of the old police states ever achieved that ideal—neither Metternich's Austria nor the Second Empire in France. They lacked two elements: the elimination of the existing social structure and the development of a new language for power. In a word, they lacked ideology. Only Communist totalitarianism has come anywhere near this goal. The politburos made an epochal discovery: it is not enough for a state to have its own police; the state must be transformed into the police, become the police. If the police dreamed of a society composed of supervised informers, then such a society must be created. What were the obstacles preventing the old police from realizing that *idée fixe*? Institutions and principles, laws, and ethical concepts. So they had to be replaced by others. The old police, wanting to know about everything, kept silent. Ideological totalitarianism grasped the significance of words. It realized that language not only forms the way people think but also functions as a pattern that controls people's ideas, reflexes, laws, and institutions. The old police had a fond dream of everyone saying the same thing; if someone said something different, paid informers would report it at once. The authorities in ideological totalitarian states have attempted to turn that dream into reality, a republic of volunteer informers, each supervising the others, all of them together subject to the word guarded by the rulers. The police would then be less necessary than they were in the Hapsburg monarchy—the police would be everyone. Good old Fouché, with his agents in top hats . . . He didn't know that this ideal could not be realized without German dialectics (he hadn't even read Hegel) and without the aesthetic theory, derived from Plato, that art should not depict what actually exists but that which would be for the good of the state.

What has been saved if, on the whole, anything has been? What has humanity, smeared with filth and blood, become? Haven't the Germans and the Russians revealed new truths about man? Haven't the totalitarian systems demonstrated the correctness of their assumptions? These questions are still very much alive. And the answers? There are no general answers. The answers are always individual, and such individual human answers decide the sort of life we have on earth. As if the future of the world really did depend on us . . . This is good news; let us rejoice in it.

A totalitarian state frozen in terror gleams like a glacier from a distance. Today something is coming apart in the ice; the slab reveals its internal contours. You can see more clearly the shapes of frozen people—the torturers and the victims, the conformists and the deceived visionaries, can recognize each other now. Ideology? Today one is paid for one's services. A certain bright, well-informed observer recently explained to me the guiding principle behind Poland's cultural policy. The development of creativity is not the goal. The point is to have a group of people who have been bought off in every creative milieu and who will buy off others. It's all just a question of time—the others are human too. Only human.

The police's presumption of man's wretchedness is firmly fixed. Today, however, it becomes clear that human wretchedness is rewarded. Everything is in the open, as it was in the good old days. Every person can either accept or refuse, approve or deny. I don't think it necessary to demonstrate what this means. In the long run, everything always comes down to the way one lives; everyone has always had a wide range of choices, from utter sobriety to extreme mysticism. Or heroism. Or playing the fool, or disgrace (one of the characters in my novel *Rondo* quotes the line from Shakespeare "Disgrace makes a fool safe"). Saintliness is always a choice as well.

Except . . . who is this lecture for? Millions of people want to eat, to have a place to live, to have children, to work, to make a living. They weren't born to choose between heroism and disgrace. I was not prepared for it either. Perhaps every society has a certain percentage of saints, just as it has a certain percentage of anarchists, geniuses, and homosexuals. At the same time, I now catch myself being ready to reproach those people who dream of little houses with gardens, reproach them for not going off into the desert. For God's sake, come to your senses—after all, I admire those who are prisoners of their own consciences equally as much as I detest those who stand watch over other people's consciences. And I would like to see Poland have as many family homes with little gardens as possible.

I'm concerned with something else, however—with what will grow in those little houses with the gardens. A few years ago, we spent our vacation in one of those houses. It had been built by two hardworking people and had parquet floors, tiles, nickel inlays; everything shone with cleanliness, and the garden was full of vegetables and flowers. Their daughter was a spiritual monster; she knew foreign languages, scorned her classmates who lived in apartments, and respected nothing on this earth apart from my French automobile. A draft slammed shut the door in our room, breaking a glass door panel. I realized that a terrible thing had happened: the two people who owned the house looked at that broken glass as if it were the shattered meaning of their lives. I ordered a new pane from a glazier, but we never went back to the house.

There are other points at issue here as well. For example, the type of suspicions the wealthy or privileged majority employs to defend itself against a threatened minority that muddies its practical arguments. "Who's behind this? Where do they get the paper for *Zapis?* How much are they being paid?" I could reconcile myself to the fact that the practical mind considers certain causes to be lost in advance. I only blow up when people try to compromise these causes using the arguments of the practical mind. Even the disbelief that people can act unselfishly I could find bearable, but when it is said that that unselfishness has been bought and paid for, my hatred is aroused.

This has all happened before, only the names change. Soullessness, philistinism, the bourgeoisie, consumerism. Flaubert wrote in a letter that one time in Croisset he saw a bourgeois family out for a Sunday stroll from his window and he was sick from disgust the entire day.

■ *NOVEMBER*
1979

A street band is pumping away by the Little Negro, just like a year ago. There were arrests before and after November 11, just as there were a year ago. A crowd of several thousand came out of the Cathedral onto Victory Square on the day of the anniversary. Those arrested were released fairly soon after.

There was a commemorative meeting for the anniversary of the October Revolution and a Month of Soviet Films, just like a year ago. I found an invitation to the P.E.N. Club in my mailbox, just as I had a year ago. Just like last year . . .

Is everything the same as last year?

In the course of a month, around one hundred people have lost their lives in three consecutive mining accidents in Silesia. The accidents were the result of negligence in ensuring safe working conditions.

In Tehran a few hundred students with the support of their government are occupying the American Embassy and threatening to kill its personnel. The students are demanding that the United States extradite the former Shah of Iran, who has undergone surgery for cancer in a New York hospital. The Shah had already been sentenced to death *in absentia* by a people's tribunal.

This year a television commentator with sideburns was instructed to declare November 15 "Prepare for Winter Day in the Railroad System."

As a result of prolonged building repairs at the Writer's Union, lunches are still not being served in the Writers' Club.

For the most part, we go to SARP* on Foksal Street. Not like last year.

On Friday, before a long weekend, stale bread was delivered to the co-op: no fresh bread had been baked because the electricity had been turned off in the bakery. There was an uproar in the store. "Ladies, get a hold of yourselves," said the man who was bringing the bread in from a van. "You'll be kissing the ground for bread like this when winter comes." The store turned quiet. A year ago in November it had already snowed.

And it was only this autumn that that woman appeared in our neighborhood. I first heard her behind me. A priest carrying a briefcase and wearing a black hat was approaching from the opposite direction and I noticed him quickly lower his head. Someone was walking a few paces in back of me and imitating a howling dog. I stopped to let that person pass, certain it was some drunk's idea of a joke. What I saw was an older woman, a scarf on her head, walking down the street barking and snarling, her eyes bulging angrily. I felt a twinge of fear but started after her. At the sight of some pedestrians, she would stop, emitting disconnected hollow sounds; at the sight of others, she would jump to one side, away from them, as if bristling with fury. She was wearing a tan raincoat and high boots with fur tops, and was carrying a leather pocketbook in one hand. Respectably dressed, she was emitting inhuman sounds. And perhaps that was the most difficult thing to understand. She had been able to dress, to zip up her boots, to remember to take her pocketbook, and then she went outside to bark. Her face bore an expression of indescribable suffering. No doubt there was some psychiatric term for it, but what about her? What was going on in her heart and mind? What was that animalistic babble supposed to express? Hatred and fear. It occurred to me that this madwoman might be seeing something we were not able to see, something there was

---
* Stowarzyszenie Architektów Polskich (Association of Polish Architects).

no way of articulating. And what if that something were in us, among us? And what if it were our own madness that she feared? Her bulging eyes and yelping voice might have been expressing her despair, her knowledge of the essence of our lives that we ourselves fail to see and for which there are no words in human speech.

I saw her several times after that, most recently near the garbage dump behind Świętojańska Street. Always dressed the same: the tan raincoat, the wool scarf on her head, the pocketbook slung over her shoulder. Outwardly no different from the other women, the wives of officials and scholars, who live in our neighborhood.

Wind, rain . . . November. That's it for the news.

Sometimes I miss strong connections with people, collective situations animated by shared emotions where something new is created—people working together, interacting. I increasingly feel that I am in a little hole from which I only creep out to crawl over to someone else's hole, nearby. There is no light, only a space filled with words that I don't believe and with faces that are of no interest. I spoke to M. about nothingness and death. She doesn't like such talk, dismisses it with a flick of her hand. She is a little superstitious; she fears reckless words, just as some people fear thunder, and she prefers to pass over her worries in silence. That was how she was brought up; that seems to have been the attitude in her milieu. I ask her how long she will be able to endure these depressions of mine.

About fifteen years ago, during a discussion about the stifling role of censorship in public cultural life, I said that soon it might be necessary to lock oneself in one's room and write for oneself and ten friends. Someone remarked that would be the first step toward the sort of *samizdat* that already existed then in the USSR. Then P., who had a good understanding of what that term meant in practice, said, "Listen, it's terrible too; you pay in a different way." At that time, I was not yet able to understand what P. meant by that.

I quoted Lessing this autumn to a young acquaintance of mine as we were strolling in a ravine full of fallen leaves and chestnuts. She asked me if I regretted the books I had written earlier, regretted having written them. No, I explained, I did not. There's no reason to regret that things were different at some other time. It's more interesting like that. I don't regret my experience and I look back without horror and see myself "in the shadow of my errors." That's how I grew, how I learned—and continue to learn my portion of the truth. To grow and to learn. That's more interesting than finding the truth all at once. And I quoted something from Lessing that I had read in André Gide's adolescent diary: " 'If God held enclosed in his right hand all of Truth and in his left hand the eternal aspiration toward the Truth (with the certainty of never attaining it), and if he said to me: "Choose!" I should humbly seize his left hand, saying: "Give, Father, for pure Truth is intended only for thee." ' "

■ D E C E M B E R
1 9 7 9

The year is coming to an end. Plans for next year? Work on finishing this volume until the middle of January and then ... I don't know. I'd be perfectly glad to travel outside the country. I'll apply for a passport—two passports—and either we'll leave or we won't. Heads or tails. Heads means travel; tails means Warsaw. Both are frightfully attractive. Heads: formalities, packing, travel, borders, and then passage into a vision colored by the West. Tails: everyday life, winter, a misty black-and-white vision diluted by our native grayness. To sink into it, deeper and deeper, to walk on my own ground, to be here. Or to take off and see how our country looks today, from over there, at a civilized remove. Both are important, both rich in consequence. Which to choose—heads, or tails? Better let them choose for me. Fraulein Richter has written from Berlin that a research grant awaits my arrival. If they give us passports, we'll go. If they don't, we'll stay. The blessed bureaucracy saves me from the agony of choice. "It'll be wonderful, you'll see," says M. "We'll travel light and spend our vacation with the Piotrys in Chante-Mêle." She is certain that we will be given passports. "And if we aren't?" I asked from the couch. "Oh, then we'll reupholster the furniture and have the bureau refinished! That deaf and dumb carpenter can come; he's supposed to do very fine work!"

It'll be fine either way. I had underestimated our situation, not realizing we could win either way. But M.'s optimism is a little forced; I don't hear her old triumphant verve in it. We both feel this and do not look each other straight in the eye. She has decided to be the way she used to. Using her voice, her eyes, her gestures, she summons her own image to her aid, the image of how she was in years previous.

■ **A P R I L**
  1 9 8 0

Three weeks ago, on the first calendar day of spring, I sent a letter to the Executive Board of the Writers' Union. This is a transcription from the copy I kept.

Dear Colleagues:

I wish to inform the Executive Board of the following facts.

In the summer of 1977 I submitted a manuscript copy of my new novel, Rondo, *to the Czytelnik Publishing House as per our contract. The book was received favorably at the publisher's and caused no reservation as to its merits. Soon, however, I was informed that Czytelnik would not be printing the book owing to the objection of higher agencies whose opinion was binding on the publisher. Their objection was not based on the contents of my book but, as I was given to understand, on the very possibility of my book's being published by a state publisher. Moreover, the Czytelnik Publishing House had kept my manuscript for nearly three years without sending it to press and had not for two years found it necessary to pass on to me any information on this subject.*

At the end of February 1980, I submitted an application for a passport to travel to France at the Warsaw Headquarters of the Civic Militia. On March 20 I received a negative reply without being informed of the cause of the refusal. I appealed that decision in writing on the basis that my connection and contacts with artistic and intellectual circles in the West were useful to Polish culture and contributed to its dissemination abroad, as demonstrated by the numerous reviews of translations of my books in the foreign press, to take but one example. I am now waiting for a reply from the Passport Bureau.

I take the liberty of calling my esteemed colleagues' attention to the fact that both of the situations I describe here constitute a limitation of my rights as a writer and a citizen, and both decisions are in contradiction to Poland's legal principles. I further maintain that often writers expressing views similar to mine and publishing their works with the same publishers and in the same journals as I do are neither forbidden to publish at home nor to travel abroad. Thus there are no legally valid sanctions at work here, and so I must consider both of the above-mentioned decisions as no more than personal harassment. As we know, harassment of this exact same sort has already been used against several of our other colleagues.

I believe that my esteemed colleagues will not be indifferent to these matters, which do not only affect me personally but whose consequences strike at the interests of every member of the Writers' Union. It is my profound conviction that discrimination against authors who are deprived of their rights as writers and citizens diminishes the value of the literature that is published and not subjected to prohibition and causes it to lose value in the eyes of the reader. The creation of such divisions will harm our literature as a whole.

These considerations have induced me to pass on these facts and reflections to the Executive Board of the Writers' Union.

I received no reply.

I should mention that I was prepared to be refused a passport, and when I reported to Krucza Street for a reply on the appointed day, I had an appeal in writing with me. When M. and I entered room No. 12 and gave our names, the official rummaged a little through various pigeonholes and then told us that this matter would require a telephone call. He asked us to leave the room and assured us he would call us in again shortly. The door opened a few minutes later. The official informed M. that she had been given a passport. "Your application has been refused, sir." M. explained that she had no intention of traveling abroad without me, and I interrupted her, asking the official to whom I should submit my appeal. He directed me to a little window where passport application forms were kept. With the consent of those waiting, I went to the head of the line and was informed that I would receive an answer by mail within three weeks. The deadline passed yesterday and I have still heard nothing.

I was prepared for that as well. I'm not the first to whom this has happened. In such cases one can demand to speak with a supervisor. There's nothing appealing in that prospect. Even though I am not a violent person, I do lose my self-control in certain situations. A friend of mine, a writer, a man of the highest personal and literary integrity, recently told me of his conversation with a supervisor when his appeal, like mine, had remained unanswered. The supervisor began to lecture him: "Instead of traveling abroad, you'd be better off keeping an eye on your daughter." My friend's daughter is active in the Student Solidarity Committee.

I had foreseen this turn of events, and it would have been out of place to act like a martyr. Many people are refused passports nowadays, and no reasons are given. I know people who rack their brains over why this had happened to them. I, at least, know: because of the books I had published abroad and because of my role on the editorial staff of *Zapis*. One half of my mind tells me that nothing I've done or written is forbidden by law in our country, and the refusal to issue me a passport is a violation of the law. At the same time, the other half whispers that had I uttered aloud even one sentence from the book I had just published while Stalin was alive, I would have rotted in prison for years. And yet a third thought rises above these other two to tell me that a person who lives by such a double scale, with two clashing standards of reality, a person who feels that, in comparison with outright cannibalism, the authorities' nonviolent highhandedness is a form of tolerance and who at the same time cannot accept this as law, for the sense of law has been removed from his culture, such a person is not a full-fledged human being.

I have this awareness and so, as I calmly listened to the official communicate the refusal to me, as I obediently handed in my appeal at the little window, and later, on the way out, as I said to M. that that was just what I expected for that was the sort of system we live in, I saw myself in an unpleasant light; there was something suspect in my reaction. M., on the other hand, had a healthy reaction. "What stupid spite!" she cried. I answered that I had known the price I would be paying and was prepared for it. But had someone said that of me, I would have been furious and called that a slave mentality.

For two weeks now (news gets around), I have been reading

that same thought in certain people's eyes. "What did you expect, a present? Or maybe you were counting on getting away scot free with your little opposition game? You know the kind of society we live in. We drew the right conclusions."

Had I replied that in using such words, they become collaborators in the creation of that very society, they would have felt offended. But by some miraculous turn of events had that "little opposition game" achieved some lasting political success, they would have claimed that victory as their own. These are people who are neither vile nor stupid and who think as I do about many things. They do not want to participate in what is most important to them, for they have come to see it as a lost cause.

We were supposed to have traveled to France and then to West Germany, where the Academy of Art's stipend is still waiting for me. Now we'll be in Warsaw for a while.

I sent the letter to the Executive Board with no faith in its being effective. The board usually turns such letters over to the Committee of Intervention. The chairman of that committee is a party literary official who has no desire to make my life any easier. Nevertheless, I decided to write the letter and send it. In imposing that obligation on myself, I was guided by the conviction that in cases of injustice, silence is consent. If I passed over those two incidents in silence, I would be helping to strengthen and deepen the social passivity in which the abuses of the authorities take root. We often use the word "Sovietization" to mean shortages, dull bureaucratic autocracy, and the defilement of daily life. Uttering the word with disgust and contempt, we relate it to external reality: stores, trade unions, schools, and newspapers are becoming Sovietized while we have remained inwardly unscathed, as evidenced by our disgust and our contempt.

I am afraid that is not how things are. Sovietism is a spiritual phenomenon. It is not so much a machine spewing forth a mass society as it is, primarily, a loss of memory: it makes us forget who we are and what we wanted to be. Notions of dignity and justice endure, ragged and limp, in our minds, but if we encounter injustice or if our dignity is degraded, does a holy wrath really rise up in us? Or do we think, It's tough, that's the system we live in, that's reality ... Such thoughts keep us participating in the system and, at the same time, Sovietize us as individuals from within. The system depends on such thoughts; they are its cement. Every day, with millions of similar reactions, we ourselves strengthen the pyramid that we hate, and in the end, the boundary that separates us from what we hate will be effaced. Perhaps we will not notice that that moment has come, and we will go on maintaining that Nazism is rooted in the German soul and that Russians are born slaves. We will be able to find consolation in the higher parts of our minds and call the absurdity growing within us "they," until one day we realize that they have become us and we them. I don't know whether there'll be any hatred left after that point. I have no idea what goes on in the soul of a man who has allowed himself to be dispossessed of everything, a man with a totalitarianized mind. Does such a man still have his own reactions and opinions? Based on my past experience, I think he still does have them but no longer lives in any accord with them.

Here someone might say, You're joking. Years have passed; the old illness is no longer a threat. I'm not so sure of that. After thirty years, the illness that a poet called the "captive mind" is now manifesting less violent symptoms but is spreading more widely. Milder, it infects a greater number of people. I also know patients who are experiencing a covert recurrence. Looking around and observing various scenes from life, I see time and again mental and ethical erosion in people, a blurring of their sense of the boundary between good and evil. I'm speaking here of the limp tatters to which we have reduced those ideas and concepts that mankind used to call freedom, happiness, brotherhood. These, no doubt, are mankind's beautiful fictions, its "music of the spheres"—a reflection of celestial harmony. Without such illusions, the world would have to turn to stone, become mineral, and even though mankind cannot translate those ideas into life, it still does not wish to lose them. It knows no other way to live. Bereft of its ideas, it begins to fall ill. Then come the "dark ages." That's what historians call the period between the fifth and seventh centuries A.D. What was that darkness? Were the people of that era mentally ill? No, but Rome fell in every man, and the lights of the *Universum* were extinguished. It's not playing with words to say that the decadent West fell prostrate at the feet of the barbarians. The Lombards and the Goths broke in through the walls of ideas that had collapsed within people.

As I write this, I can see indulgent smiles on my readers' faces, a few of my friends among them. "But my dear man, it was just the other way around. It was precisely the concepts and ideas of which you speak that brought the darkness down onto the world; it is the madness of fixated universalists that plunges the world into blood and slavery every so often. So much has been written on this!"

Yes, true, a lot has been written. Nevertheless, your consciousness was formed by the ideas of Moses, Plato, and Christ; you still think with the ideas of the humanists and the Romantics; you are all descendants of the Declaration of the Rights of Man and of the Citizen; and it just seems to you that you have rid yourselves of Marx—he too is part of the way you think. Those ideas were mankind's energy and movement, signs of man's will to be transformed. It is only when they are imposed on you as a system of beliefs, rules, and laws that they begin to contradict one another. And then they are no longer ideas.

In his book *Religion and the Rise of Western Culture*, Christopher Dawson asks himself this question: "Why is it that Europe alone among the civilizations of the world has been continually shaken and transformed by an energy of spiritual unrest that refuses to be content with the unchanging law of social tradition which rules the oriental cultures? It is because its religious ideal has not been the worship of timeless and changeless perfection but a spirit that strives to incorporate itself in humanity and to change the world."

In the course of reading Dawson's book, I also read an interview given by the Soviet dissident Andrei Sinyavsky to French journalists. Sinyavsky speaks of the astonishing continuity and endurance in the structure of Western Europe, which impressed him. "I found this best exemplified by Italy, which everyone had thought dead and buried two years ago and which lives on in spite of terrorists and strikes. All of a sudden I discovered a culture of work, an interest in work. From that point of view, Western Europe is much closer to the Middle Ages, to the spirit of the guilds, the son following the father's profession, than is Russia today. Naturally, everyone is dissatisfied, but the foundations are lasting, unlike in Russia, where a person only works for a salary or to rise up a few grades in the bureaucracy. The Western system is constructed like a hive: honeycombs seem light and fragile, but their sound construction makes them resistant ... The structure of Soviet society is like a sack of sand, which only stands because it is tied up tightly. If that sack is punctured, everything will collapse and turn to dust."

I had thought that these two quotes would cross-fertilize, as if the second somehow supplemented the first. But which of them is about us? What are we? An incarnation of the spirit? A hive's industrious construct or a bound-up bag of sand? Are we still held together by what remains of the old adhesive or would we spill apart too if it weren't for the knot that chokes us from without?

In a certain way all this is connected with the letter that I sent to the Executive Board of the Writers' Union. I had to squeeze two typed pages out of myself, a man of the age of the masses, in order to act like an individual who has not lost his own reflexes. Even if my reactions are now growing weaker, I have, however, kept a memory of them, and I try at least to imitate them.

But, at the same time, I feel a certain tightening of the knot. Echoes from many quarters have reached me since fragments of *A Warsaw Diary* were printed in *Zapis*. On the whole, they are encouraging, but sometimes I wake up at dawn with a thought that I myself have cursed: How long can it last—*Zapis*, NOWA,* the little printing firms that reproduce our books in printings of

---

* Niezależna Oficyna Wydawnicza (Independent Publishing House).

how many ... 2,000 or 5,000 copies? It all hangs on the slenderest of threads. In the evening, over a telephone that I know is bugged, I learn of the arrest of one of the people who founded NOWA; in the morning I concentrate on blocking the news out of my mind while I write. I have only one method for this: to summon constantly the fleeting certainty that even if everything falls apart, I will continue to write and tap out my text and make those three additional carbon copies. A few dozen people will read those four copies; one or two people will save theirs. There was still nothing when I finished *A Question of Reality*—no *Zapis* or other publishing houses—and I would lend the typescript for a week to people I knew—all told, about fifty readers. Such thoughts keep you going when you write. Marian called yesterday and informed me that a woman he knew personally, a reader of *Zapis*, had pressed 1,000 złotys on him after reading *A Warsaw Diary*—for me. She had most likely concluded that as a writer barred from publication, I must have fallen on hard times. I had never before encountered such a direct and lovely gesture toward an author. Oh no, I would not exchange that for a large printing.

When someone told B. that the current situation, in comparison to the days of Stalinist prisons, has nevertheless created a social fabric that the opposition might only end up destroying, he said, "Yes, it's not a prison; it's a latrine. But not everyone has accepted that alternative."

On Saturday I waited for M. as she stood in a line forty people long. All around, ugly, poorly plastered apartment blocks on litter-strewn, muddy lawns. Across the street, a one-story shed with dirty windows where fruits and vegetables are sold, and in the rear, a sort of general store. The self-service food co-op, with its dark, dirty interior, feels like a PX in an army barracks. Outside, by the entrance, cans full of empty beer bottles. Drunken men sway along the street, their heads hanging down or bent back. At the street corners, little groups of young people in jackets and sneakers, waiting for something with an air of hostile boredom about them. This is new Jeziorna. Old Jeziorna begins a bit farther down the asphalt highway, in the direction of Warsaw.

The little bus that brings the newspapers was a long time in coming. The line kept growing. It was drizzling. Waiting at a distance of about 20 feet, I saw M. wedged between a woman holding a bag stuffed with potatoes and a man with no legs. The film director Rybkowski was behind him in line, having no doubt come in from Konstancin.

The dampness made my spine ache that day. Looking at the wet line, I wondered why it was worth it to those people to wait for a newspaper that contained information either irrelevant or distorted, and why they couldn't buy it in passing, from a newsboy, the way one does in a normal country. I told myself that these people want to read the *Express*, that they have grown used to an afternoon paper whose editing is on a higher level than that of the others, a paper not overloaded with stories about party congresses or with commentaries on the Sejm's resolutions (*Express* often prints summaries of them). They have also grown used to waiting. It does not enter their minds that waiting in front of a kiosk is an absurd thing to do. They are already used to a daily life composed of petty, tiring oppressions. But why do they have to wait? Why isn't the *Express* printed in larger numbers? Because an enormous percentage of the paper available goes to print material that no one reads. And why? So the country can provide as much employment as possible for obedient journalists. For who are the journalists of the unread press, of *Trybuna Mazowiecka* (The Mazowian Tribune) and the *Głos Listonosza* (Voice of the Mailman)? They are activists who perform propaganda instruction in the field, functionaries in the provincial machine. The central press has to be smaller because more paper is needed for the local propaganda cadres, and therefore lines for the *Express* form in front of kiosks so people can be informed about the five baby kangaroos in the Budapest Zoo.

The central press and the provincial press are based on the same principle—bending reality into lies—and for this task to be skillfully executed, professionals are required. For years it has been done by the same people or by younger replicas of them. There are no great Lucifers among them. These are little, ordinary people who go with the flow. Slogans, party lines, directorships all change, but they, they are ever present, their tongues greased and ready to serve new bosses using the latest passwords—the people, the working class, patriotism, anti-Zionism and internationalism, martyrology, jobs, police campaigns. Always on guard—in the press, on television . . . "He lies like TV!" Ewa R. exclaimed recently, upset about somebody. That already has the flavor of a folk saying about it. Yes, they were here, are here, will be here, must be here. So we can buy newspapers.

When I realized this, the line in front of the kiosk on Jeziorna suddenly struck me as something desperate, humiliating. I ran over and began pulling M. away, shouting that it was horrible, senseless. Frightened, M. cried, "But today's paper has the TV guide for the whole week!" And I shouted back that I had to protect her from Sovietization. The people in line stared at me with frightened eyes as at a man bitten by a snake. And just then the little bus with the *Express* pulled up.

Oh, I had behaved stupidly!

But . . .

The day before yesterday I broke off at the beginning of a sentence and today I can no longer reproduce my train of thought. I had begun a new paragraph; I had written "But" when someone knocked at my door with news about the unsuccessful American landing in Iran. The operation to free the fifty American prisoners in the U.S. Embassy had ended in a fiasco. The commandos did not make it to Tehran; they flew off, leaving eight of their men dead in the desert and the wreckage of two helicopters that had collided at takeoff for the return flight. There is still no detailed explanation of why the mission failed. All that is known is that three helicopters proved defective. Apparently the plan for the operation had been ready for a few months.

There was film coverage from Tehran on television. The

bodies of American marines set out for public view. In exchange, the Iranian government is demanding the return of Iranian money frozen in U.S. banks. It is still refusing to free the hostages, demanding that the dethroned Shah be extradited. The Shah had been a cruel monarch; his police tortured people. A blood debt.

For two days now, all we hear about on radio and television is the failed rescue mission. Several friends confessed to me that they were literally choked up at the news, feeling much as they did when they heard the communiqué about the fall of Paris in 1940.

There is speculation about sabotage (three helicopters out of eight break down?); there is talk about the ineptitude of the American leadership and the weakness of American democracy when faced with the crude insolence of totalitarian regimes. It is the bitterness of disillusionment after a defeat that is speaking here. The way you curse your country's soccer team after it loses a trophy match. Had they won, they would have been heaped with flowers at the airport; now they are burdened with the guilt of defeat. We don't like to see myths undone—that makes us feel swindled. But it is we who create them.

American civilization . . . American technology . . . American ingenuity. We know about all that. Of course, one may have one's doubts that American civilization is the ideal society. One may reflect on what civilization on the whole should be. I remember an idea expressed by Baudelaire that the mark of real civilization was not steam power or electricity but a reduction in the effects of original sin. No doubt, were the author of *Les Fleurs du mal* alive today, he would feel great distaste for the technetronic civilization the Americans have created. Western Europe makes good use of it and, at the same time, perceives its dangers. But from Poland, viewed from the perspective of Poland's overworked misfortune, American civilization seems perfection itself. It is idealized by distance and by expectation. How does the life of people in the West differ from ours? In a thousand ways. But primarily in one: they do not live in a state of waiting, they do not live their lives with a sense that there is another, better reality across the sea that may one day come to them. They just live. They have their own goals and their problems, their philosophies and their religions, and they go abroad not to see what real human life looks like but simply on business or as tourists. They work, they earn money, they buy things. Such is their daily life. Lived not in anticipation but in existence. I recall that when Janusz Minkiewicz returned to Warsaw shortly after the war from a few weeks of traveling in the West and was besieged by questions of what it was like there, he answered, "It's normal there." At the time, I didn't realize how wise an answer that was.

Probably since childhood, I have been used to thinking of American civilization as a precision machine that does not make mistakes. The American army is part of that machinery. In spite of their losing the Vietnam War, I had thought that an expedition to rescue the hostages, equipped with the latest in technology, could not fail . . . .

I had wanted good news, confirmation of my trust in the star-spangled banner, in the army of boy scouts landing on the shores of our hemisphere to save us from the flood, in the Americans who, in their own hemisphere, have for two hundred years been accepting people from our land fleeing poverty and fear. America. The Americans. To this day, saying those words, I see them enveloped in a romantic haze. I also see the landing craft touching ground on the beaches of Normandy and those boys in helmets, running in a dawn mist. I think I am like many people in Poland in my grandiloquent idea and vision of the United States. They associate America with high-minded convictions in spite of remembering that it was that very country that thirty-five years ago decided to abandon the Poles to Russian domination.

So that is the way it has to be. It makes me impatient sometimes. Does Warsaw always have to believe in the perfection of the West, which does not think about us? Why don't we realize what it really does think about? How long can one permit such self-deception?

But still . . . at the same time, somewhere, unconsciously, I too believed. All right, we're foolish to believe that the Quaker principles that keep watch over the world and, every twenty years or so, save it from the abyss, had endured in American society. Those principles were symbolized by the figures of noble, visionary presidents. Woodrow Wilson was such a figure; Jimmy Carter is that sort of president.

The evening news showed him speaking to Congress. His face was sad; it had aged. He was leaving for Texas the next day to visit the soldiers who had been wounded when the helicopters collided. The Secretary of State, one of his principal advisers, had been opposed to the rescue attempt and has now resigned. Looking closely at Carter's face on the television screen, I thought that he must be a righteous man and a slightly naïve one. Such Americans—the sons of Puritan preachers and farmers— have a deep-seated conviction that man is healthy by nature, and they believe in the social virtues that spring from that health. When they become politicians and statesmen, they think that their antagonists or partners on the other side of the world are like them in this respect. Later, when they come into contact with their moral nihilism, they are shocked. To us this is naïveté. Then we think, They don't understand anything because they have not had our experience; they don't know what man is because they have been spared the most severe trials to which man has been subjected. We feel superior to them in our heart of hearts, and we consider them more stupid than we, not realizing that we should put that unfortunate superiority of ours out of mind as quickly as possible. It is they who are superior to us precisely because they have no experience of our hells. Perhaps they are better than us because they have not known the evil to which we are subject. For them, witnesses are sufficient to demonstrate a truth; but here, victims are required. They have been living in a democracy for centuries now. Democracy means, among other things, that man is spared the cruelest ordeals. Correctly assuming that people do not need those ordeals and that knowledge of them is degrading, democracy avoids the state of affairs in which man would be exposed to them. Until the barbarian's cynicism triumphs.

Only in one sense are we somewhat superior to them. They have gained so much freedom (they don't know how much!) that they can exchange it only for its opposite. For us, on the other hand, freedom is only a mirage; we thirst for it, long for it, and therein, perhaps, lies our superiority. Neither of us realizes this.

■ MAY
1980

I have not noted everything that I have been doing, that has happened during the 150 days since I have finished the first volume of *A Warsaw Diary*.

March 25, Chojecki arrested. A week before, he discussed the publication of the *Diary* with me. Calm, with a smiling alertness in his eyes. A light-colored beard, his face haggard, dejected. "We'll send you galleys to proofread in six weeks." The courtesy and elegance, astounding in a man hounded for years by the police. His appearance neglected, his hands stained by ink, apparently.

In February the words of a taxi driver reviling the government when we were driving down Bem Street: "Hitler murdered people, killed people, but he let you live." If I hadn't heard this with my own ears, I would have thought it a macabre joke.

On a Saturday (in February, I don't recall the date), I recognized Piłsudski's granddaughter at a reception at the Wiktors', where Halina was reciting.

I am unable to recall the exact date, but it was probably toward the end of the month that my literary evening took place at the Society for Scholarly Courses (the "Flying University"). It was not a banal event. For many years I had been avoiding meeting readers in the Press and Book Clubs or in the Houses of Culture (now they no longer invite me), those organized meetings that are, in essence, a surrogate, an ersatz version of a real discussion between society and a writer. It's all predictable: the opening address, the content of the questions, the little bouquet of carnations handed to me by a cultured and worldly young lady. But my evening at the "Flying University" departed from the usual ritual.

Even that morning, leaving the house, I immediately felt my readers' eyes on me. I felt them on my back. They walked behind me on the other side of the street, keeping close to a group of Ukrainian tourists visiting Warsaw's oldest quarters. When I slowed my pace, they too began walking more slowly. There were three of them; one, with a merry little snub nose and wearing a quilted sweater, smiled at me. I stopped; they stopped too. They examined the souvenirs in a shop window, casting knowing, friendly glances at me. I realized that they wanted me to catch sight of them and to wonder why they were following me. My literary evening was scheduled for five in the afternoon. I was to be aware that my readers were informed and would be there without fail.

M. was in a store at the corner of Długa Street. I went in to get her; we had to go out to Żoliborz before noon. Near Świętojerska Street I looked casually behind me. Five of my readers were following me now. Glancing over at me, they were still walking behind the tourists from the kolkhoz. In their jackets and light overcoats, their heads bare (one had long hair and carried a blue denim zippered bag), they stood out from the short-legged Soviet peasants in their enormous fur caps. When M. turned onto Bonifraterska Street to buy a few things in the Delicatessen and I stayed waiting for her at the corner, the group of five broke up. Two of them followed M.; three stopped not far from me on the other side of the street.

Fifteen minutes later we got into the car. No one drove off after us.

The evening was to take place in the apartment of the B.'s on Bednarska Street, near the Marienszacki Market. M. decided to accompany me. She was worried. "If they're going to arrest you, I'd rather be there." It's four-thirty. We decide to walk. I've got my notes rolled up in one hand. Two of my readers are waiting for us by our front stairs, where the building residents are listed. Seeing us, they begin loudly discussing someone's cousin. They leave the building after us. I don't look back. We go down Piwna Street, then down Krakowskie Przedmieście near St. Anna's and the *Res Sacra Miser* building. It's after office hours. There's a lot of traffic, many people at the bus stops. The stores are crowded. I tell M. about Anaïs Nin and her bizarre relationship with Henry Miller. We turn onto Bednarska Street. In front of the gateway, from behind a grand building that had once been a brothel, a bunch of men who look like boxers are coming out onto the sidewalk, spewing curses. One of them is a thickset, bandy-legged blond, his entire face so pockmarked and scarred that his skin seems red; he is holding a German shepherd on a leash. We have to go out onto the street to get around them.

From a distance of 100 feet I can see the corner house at the end of the street, surrounded by admirers of my talent. They're here. Three private Fiats and a Nysa with a white Civic Militia plate. Young people with little two-way radios are standing in front of the house, a cadet order guard; girls with makeup on, their caps pulled down over their eyes, are milling about. We approach slowly. I spot Professors Amsterdamski and Geremek walking toward us from the square. From them I learn that the police are at the apartment of the B.'s. Just then Wiktor walks over with Ryszard Krynicki. He's wearing a beret, his face pale from anxiety. He calls to me, "It's all over! They're searching the apartment!" A married couple, the Sławińskis, both scientists, arrive; then journalist Jacek Bocheński with the timid poet Andrzej Szmidt, who had learned of my evening when lunching at the Writers' Club; then a tall, lanky historian wearing glasses, Docent Jedlicki.

We decide that no matter what, we have to go in. It's a couple of minutes to five. Two people will stay outside to warn the students and turn them away. We walk past the police cars, together as a group; the young people do not attempt to stop us. On the stairs, M. takes my manuscript from me and hides it in her bag.

Upstairs, in the apartment, our IDs are taken by a thirty-year-old civilian, with slender hands, light down on his face (a dark-blue turtleneck under a well-cut ash-gray jacket), and light-gray eyes, set close to his nose and at a bit of an angle to it. A radio with an antenna hangs at his side. His movements are easy, efficient. Observing him, I remember the description of a man "with the face of a fox who had betrayed his own species and hunted with men."

The search is still going on in the next room. We are kept in the larger room, which resembles a spacious attic. Lovely old furniture, an oval table by the wall, now covered with papers. A woman clerk from the National Council stands at that table taking down our personal data. Place of work? Profession? The names of schools and institutions issued in reply (Warsaw University, the Academy of Sciences, the Institute of Literary Research), as well as academic titles (professor, docent, lecturer). Two women who hold the rank of professor and whose personal data have been taken before our arrival are asked by the official conducting the operation to leave the premises. Our hosts, two members of the old intelligentsia, accompany them to the door guarded by a policeman wearing a cap with a chin strap. Someone asks if he can use the telephone. No, that's not allowed. Our host, a graying man who feels very ill at ease, offers us cigarettes. Every so often the walkie-talkies buzz with voices from the guards downstairs.

We both hand our IDs to the man with the radio at his side. There is a moment of hesitation at the table, as if something is being considered. The director of the operation walks over to me. He states that the premises are being inspected by order of the prosecutor, and if I wish, I can remain there as a witness. Then the woman clerk who is taking down our personal data speaks up, indicating a man with a moustache sitting at the table by the wall. A neighbor of the B.'s has agreed to be the witness. I ask if I can know the basis and the purpose of the search. "That is not possible," says the director, an officer from the Warsaw Headquarters of the Civic Militia (that was how he introduced himself). While speaking, he regards me intently, with a certain curiosity and a slight half-smile, or perhaps quarter-smile, in his vivid light-blue irises. I wouldn't describe him as a repulsive person. "Since you've come here on a social visit, you may return after the search is concluded." That surprised me. I ask if I have understood him correctly. "Come on, that's their idea of a joke," mutters Professor Geremek, standing beside me.

Our IDs are returned and we leave. Our hosts, Mr. and Mrs. B., say goodbye to us in the front hall.

During the entire course of the formalities, I could feel the eyes of the policeman stationed by the door fixed on me. He was very young and looked like a country boy: tall, thin, cheeks very ruddy, and dark eyes that seemed to have stopped moving in their effort to understand. He didn't take them off me. I was told later that Dr. Sławińska, who had left before us after her personal data had been taken, had asked him if he knew that it was my literary evening that was to have taken place, and did he know my books. He had blushed even more deeply. "Don't you think that policemen read, ma'am? I heard about Mr. Brandys's books in school."

"So you see, and today you're preventing him from meeting with his readers . . ."

"Excuse me," said the policeman nervously. "I'm here on official business. And you have to admit that I am being courteous, ma'am."

Downstairs, the guards let us through, feigning utter indifference. There too voices are rumbling in walkie-talkies. We wait on the square for the others. Jacek Bocheński walks over, followed by Andrzej Celiński and, finally, Dr. Jedlicki, grimacing ironically. We're only missing Dr. Geremek. He emerges after quite some time from behind the police Nysa, his little light-colored beard jutting forward. He had the university's official lecture with him and had not been willing to produce it for them. They had wanted to subject him to a body search. When he demanded that a separate record be drawn up, the woman clerk cried with despair, "I'll be writing here forever, Professor. Please, please leave me in peace!" Geremek took pity on her and handed over the lecture.

We return in the dusk along Krakowskie Przedmieście. Lights are being turned on in the buses. Waves of pedestrians are heading for the cafés and cinemas. A French psychological drama is playing at the Wars. The Old City gleams with the reddish interiors of bars. Only now do I feel the fatigue. On the way, M. pulls my manuscript out of her purse. "Here, it doesn't seem to have gotten crumpled."

Back home, Jacek and I down two cognacs apiece and discuss what happened to us. One might use the epithet, "Yet another of our adventures together." I can't get that policeman standing by the door out of my mind, the one whose eyes had been fixed on us like a pair of nails. He must have experienced some difficult moments because he had seen something he couldn't fathom: people who knew that Security had surrounded the building and that a search was under way in the apartment had entered instead of withdrawing. No doubt he had been terribly astounded by docents and professors acting so abnormally. (The next day I learned that Professors Janion and Żmigrodzka, who were a half-hour late, had acted in identical fashion: they too had gone upstairs.)

I wonder, What does he think now or what will he think tomorrow, that boy wearing the stiff cap who had been staring so intently at us? Yes, he stared intently at us, but his instructions had also been drummed intently into him at his briefing. How many years had he been "at school"? A year, two? Two years of having police newspeak drummed into his brain.

Around nine o'clock we call Bednarska Street. Mrs. B. answers the phone. The search has just been concluded. It had obviously been a pretext.

There is no doubt about that. The search had been ordered to keep the "Flying University" from meeting. The latest move in thwarting the "Flying University's" efforts at self-education. "Since you've come here on a social call ..." That my literary evening was to take place and when—the day, the place, the hour—had all been known: people talked about it at the university, the Institute of Literary Research, and the Writers' Club. A new way of preserving the appearance of legality and turning the "Flying University's" basic principle—its openness—against it. A good-sized squad had been mobilized, automobiles, technical equipment, and more—the operation had to have been thought out. Warsaw Headquarters, the Procurator, the National Council ... How much time, money, and energy had been used to face down a handful of scholars and students. When my apartment was searched before the war, there was only one plainclothesman and one policeman, plus the janitor. It is not only we who have gained experience and are learning new ways to live. Our police have too.

Chojecki was released from arrest on Saturday. This occurred a few days after a general meeting of the Warsaw Writers' Union, at which the majority of speakers demanded his release. Close to 150 writers sent a letter to the Executive Board demanding that the authorities take steps at once. Chojecki's release was undoubtedly a direct result of the letters, the meeting, and the rising wave of protests in other circles.

Four, five years ago, foreign journalists invariably asked me the same questions: What are the Polish independence movement's programs and objectives? What are its chances, its political intentions? My answers didn't satisfy them. This was shortly after KOR had been founded, in the days when collections were being taken up for the families of the workers from Ursus and Radom who had been imprisoned and beaten. The Student Solidarity Committee, the "Flying University," and NOWA had not come into existence yet. I recall that somewhat earlier, a dozen or so people had gathered in Professor Edward Lipiński's apartment. They discussed what to do next. I was not in favor of creating a permanent committee. In my judgment, actions taken on the spot, in response to changing situations, with something of a guerrilla nature, would be more effective. As had been done thus far in literary circles. I was, however, opposed by several young people, one of whom was Chojecki. That was the first time I had seen him. In a room full of antique furniture, goblets, and helmets (for years Lipiński had been a collector of antiques and old works of art), Chojecki gave his reasons. He insisted on creating an organizational body, maintaining that appeals and signatures were not enough. "Why not?" I asked. He rose and began to explain. The wives and mothers of the arrested workers are afraid to accept assistance when its source is unknown; their mistrust could be dispelled, however, by our being able to refer to a social committee founded for that purpose, with a name and a seal ... Three days later I learned that KOR had come into being.

What answer could I have or should I have given to the Norwegian and English journalists? The program, the political objective ... the chances. I had no answers. It would have been more proper to shrug my shoulders—the way the novelist Jerzy Andrzejewski reacted—or to explain that the students scrambling around for money for the families of the arrested workers, those boys whom the police have threatened with assassination, are precisely what constitutes our chance. No, I didn't have any program. I did, however, see what was happening in my own field, how the life was being sucked out of it by the censorship and the administration. I felt that I couldn't be more stupid than I in fact was; I couldn't write and think with half of my mind, the half allowed by the Bureau of Inspection. And that already meant that I belonged to the opposition. I think that the term "dissidents" was invented by Parisian journalists. And so I was a dissident, and like it or not, I was learning what a dissident's life was like.

Those were the first few months after KOR had been founded, a period of anonymous calls and threats. The secret agents and informers set to work. At my brother's, the phone was ringing like mad. "I understand Miss Mikołajska is paid in dollars; I'd be glad to buy them . . ." Metal filings were poured into the lock on his door, rotten eggs were thrown into his room, and one day a bunch of men burst into the apartment passing themselves off as a delegation from the working class. They stood by Halina's bed (she was ill that day) and threatened her.

Their methods were extremely diverse: a contraceptive sent through the mail to a venerable old lady; anonymous letters with obscene drawings; a package of vermin-infested rags labeled "Clothing for the Families from Ursus"; a friendly letter from a colonel in Warsaw who, fully respecting my books, tries to convince me not to trust agents of Adam Michnik's type who are fleeing to the West in order to profane Poland's name. The letter's arrival coincided with Michnik's return; he had flown back from Paris knowing he was in danger of being arrested. The airport was crawling with Security Forces, and he was arrested soon after. And another letter, from the town of Sosnowiec: "Mr. Brandys, here, near Sosnowiec, a Polish policeman shot and killed a certain Jew, Icek Brandys, in 1942. Was he perhaps a relative of yours?"

This was the program that had been worked out for me. I admit that I was greatly astonished. Clearly, in spite of everything, in spite of the events in March 1968, I still hadn't guessed how much filth and muck lay beneath the surface of the edifice that had been under construction for thirty years. I couldn't believe it. What intellectuals in the West had been prophesying since the beginning of the century—moral self-degradation, the destruction of human values, the rupture of the social contract— and what I had more willingly attributed to their part of the world had once again proved to be true in ours. Fortunately, I was not alone. But were it not for the handful of people who, without waiting for me, had founded KOR and those who are today on hunger strikes, in prisons and churches, I would still be locked in the dungeon of despair.

The program . . . actions . . . chances. The Western correspondents do not understand what the Polish "to be or not to be" means. They do not understand the nature of a country in which a hundred years ago the cause of national liberation was actively carried on by no more than a few hundred people with programs that were none too clear and had no chance for success. That was called the struggle for independence. I remember one of my brother's stories about his conversation with a French major, an aristocrat whom he had come to know in the Hammerstein POW camp for officers. The Frenchman praised Pétain and spoke of him as the savior of his country. That made my brother bristle, and he mentioned that in Poland the Germans had failed to find a single collaborator in the national government. "Yes," smiled the Frenchman, "but there is a difference between France and Poland. After losing the war, Poland ceased to exist, but France still exists." He would definitely not have been able to fathom how Poland has also continued to exist despite losing the war. And indeed it is difficult to understand the history of a nation that for nearly three hundred years, up until the present (I'm figuring conservatively, from the time of Peter the Great), has been in a hopeless position and whose only chance has been the stubbornness of people offering resistance to save the country from spiritual death.

When speaking or writing about such matters, it is easy to fall into exaltation and pathos, which always border on the ridiculous. I accept the risk of seeming ridiculous. Let it seem ridiculous that in today's world one can still believe in some sort of righteousness. Haven't people told me that I'm letting myself be taken in again. Wasn't once enough? I have no answer to that either. At best, I could assure them that no one was talking me into anything.

JUNE
1980

I am overcome by fear when I become aware of the monotonous rounds of my existence, its boring repetitiveness and invariable rhythm. I wonder if the calendar isn't taking revenge on me. The same dates in the same places, the same routes. Two or three landscapes, a single city. How long can such an existence be transformed into writing?

And from one year to the next, certain parts of my life are being confiscated. One piece at a time: the reprinting of my old books beginning with *The Invincible City;* then reviews; later on the chance to work in film; finally the right to be published; and now a document allowing me to cross the border. In the end, what will remain besides the view from my window and novels borrowed from the library? At times I feel that I am shrinking and shriveling with each passing day as if I were losing tissue. Fictions dry up on this plot of ground.

In the course of twenty-five years I have covered the distance between *The Citizens* and *A Warsaw Diary,* leaving flayed pieces of untrue skin along the way. Between 1954 and 1966 I quit the following: my function as chairman of the Warsaw committee of the National Unity Front, then my membership in the Warsaw committee of the PZPR* (I had been a member for a short time before and after October 1956) and in the party Executive Committee in the Writers' Union. At that same time, I did not agree to my publisher's proposal of a mass reprinting of *The Citizens;* I refused to participate in juries conferring state awards and in the

---

* Polska Zjednoczona Partia Robotnicza (Polish United Workers' Party).

ideological committee of the party Central Committee; I refused to join the presidium of the All-Polish Peace Committee or to sign its appeal; I also would not accede to a Central Committee secretary's wishes that I withdraw my novel *The Mother of Kings* from publishers in the West. At two successive congresses of the Writers' Union and at the expanded plenum of the Executive Board, I warned against bringing administrative pressures to bear on culture. I was summoned to the Central Committee three times and charged with antiparty activity, including once by phone by a member of the politburo (a face on which a smile seemed as unnatural as a nightingale's trill issuing from a vulture's gullet). A year later I turned in my party card.

Not all of it came easily to me, and I did not always think consistently. I still believed that the party would be able to purify itself, that the crimes could still be redeemed. In the spring of 1968, in a mountain health resort, I met a general whose death sentence had not been carried out† and a political columnist with twisted joints. The former had returned to the army from prison; the latter, upon leaving his cell, had demanded the return of his party card, taken from him at the time of his arrest. Neither man stinted in telling me what he had experienced. Along with the writer, whose bones had been cracked, I still had confidence that the party would extricate itself from the muck and blood. When I heard it said that the people who had ruined the machine could not repair it, I argued that it was precisely those who had constructed the machine who should repair it. At the same time, I was seeing some things all too clearly. New scum was rising to the surface. Out of irritation I published a plain little prose piece about two turds by the side of the road. One says to the other, "Do you feel it, it's thawing. Now we can really start stinking." The piece met with indignation, but there was a grain of truth in it that time has proved. The stories I wrote in those years, like

---

† In 1950–1952 a group of higher officers of the Polish army was arrested on false charges of conspiracy against the party.

"The Roman Hotel" or "Lest It Be Forgotten," blend a shaken consciousness and remnants of earlier convictions. I had also been unfair in judging those who had perceived the evil earlier than I and who had drawn bolder conclusions.

In the end, when I took the final, decisive step, I felt relieved. I was free. All the freer because I had no illusions about the delights that would flow from that freedom. I was able to prepare myself for the silence that would surround my books, published from then on in modest-sized printings; for being removed from school reading lists; and for my name being passed over in the press, on radio, and on television. Later I learned how to withstand attacks by the critics. I held up better at some times than at others. Two of my novels came out after 1970. Soon, however, I began to be disturbed by my fiction's veering away from present reality. More stubbornly, with more difficulty, I was constructing stories that seemed increasingly further from my experience, and finally the time came to wonder whether the story that was happening all around me was not more interesting than my own fictions. One day I stopped writing my novel in mid-sentence.

On Friday Radio Free Europe's evening program broadcast the speech made by Chojecki at his trial. The text had great dignity, a manifesto, really, about the moral state of society. He must have been counting on the maximum sentence to make such a declaration. A month before, he had still been on a hunger strike in Mokotów prison, and barely five weeks had passed since the meeting of the Warsaw Writers' Union. Chojecki had been released from arrest a few days after the meeting, and at his trial he defended himself as a free man. In the public eye, that was clearly the consequence of the speeches and the letter signed by 116 members of the Writers' Union. After his release, Chojecki sent out 116 letters thanking the signatories and requesting their aid for Bogdan Grzesiak, who was still being held under arrest.

If the November evening at the P.E.N. Club a year and a half ago was the anticipation of a miracle, then on May 5, in the

ZAIKS* auditorium, it was a test of strength and/or a provocation that were expected. For the literary silent majority, the existence of a liberation movement in Poland is a puzzle. The authorities are pretending they don't see, when all they need to do is . . . Puzzles are disturbing. Why are they closing their eyes to it since they could shut the entire opposition down in a day? For five years two thirds of the literary X's have been asking themselves the same question.

Answers that are too scrupulous and complicated weary those who ask the questions, scattering their attention before anything is explained. It is better to use examples, commonplace ideas, illustrations from life, and even slogans. I was taught this by one of my readers, a former Catholic clergyman. He was often asked what had motivated him to abandon the priesthood. Whenever he conscientiously explained the moral complications resulting from his duty to obey and to submit to a hierarchy, he met with disbelief and a lack of attention. One day he decided to answer differently: "A woman has come into my life; I want to have a family." He immediately caught a gleam of understanding in his listener's eye. "But, of course, that's clear . . ." Thus, to the question why the authorities tolerate the opposition since they could arrest everyone involved, it would be better, instead of arguing the complex economic, domestic, and international circumstances, better and fairer to answer, "Maybe, but evidently they have their reasons for not doing it. Apparently America could take Cuba in one day, but it too has its reasons for not doing it." An answer such as this bores no one; on the contrary, it evokes lively reflection.

I am certain that there are questions that one need not ask oneself, that are not worth the asking. I doubt that when David was standing before Goliath, he was figuring out the difference in their heights. He was thinking how best to aim his sling. He took

* Związek Autorów i Kompozytorów Scenicznych (Union of Stage Authors and Composers).

aim and hit the giant in the eye. To this day our collective memory continues to admire the daring youth who did not ask himself unnecessary questions.

At the May meeting in the ZAIKS auditorium, the principal subject under discussion was the letter concerning Chojecki's case. I felt that the majority of people there were on edge, fearing the moment when they would be forced to take a clear stand. Two hundred, three hundred people, each with his own dread and limitations. I have learned not to hold people's fear in contempt but to view it as a suffering that deserves respect. Heroes and cowards—I don't trust such divisions. I also cannot abide the division of people into those who sign collective protests and those who do not. Two intellectuals, a scientist and a film director, were once asked to sign a protest. One refused: "I can't. I have a son." The other one unscrewed the cap of his pen: "I have to sign, because I have a son." Those two answers express old alternatives in abbreviated form, two threads woven through the histories of many cultures. The idea of survival, the injunction to revolt. The preservation of one's existence, the legacy of honor. I think that two thirds of the people at those literary meetings in Warsaw are usually experiencing that set of alternatives. In the end, however, everyone must decide for himself what he fears more—life or himself. Everyone can come to fear losing his job and everyone has reasons to fear the loss of inner peace. You can curse those situations, but they have been with us forever, to a point where they are banal.

I went out for a cigarette and stood beside a group of people talking. Impressions were being exchanged and someone said, "I get a whiff of history here." As I returned to the auditorium, the words of one of the speakers from the rostrum reached me at the door: "The authorities do not tolerate the existence of an opposition because they are strong. The authorities are weak and so they have to tolerate the opposition!"

The authorities are weak ... They are strong enough to use their clubs. Sentences like that make the audience uneasy. It knows whose side right is on, but it also knows what threatens it from the side that crushes that right. Most of the audience is reluctant to hear such ideas. Here in connection with the case of a man imprisoned under a false charge, they are ready to side with him, but they are not ready for a political showdown, for an all-out battle with the authorities. If pushed in that direction, they will become horrified. They will waive responsibility and shift it onto those whose convictions are beyond any doubt with it; they will burden them with the responsibility for their own fear, and then, with uneasy conscience, they will seek arguments to justify themselves.

I did not sit in any of the rows of seats but by the wall, beside Professors Janion and Żmigrodzka. Three armchairs had been placed between the windows along the aisle, and I could observe the whole auditorium from there. Near me, in one of the rows in the middle, sat a man with a head of thick white hair who seemed not to be listening to the speeches. His chin resting heavily on his chest, his eyes closed, he was clearly dozing off. His profile looked familiar. Perhaps I had seen him in a film; he reminded me of American senators from the Midwest, vigorous old farmers and cattle breeders; an athletic, country sort of look. He did not open his baggy eyes throughout the proceedings, and only once did he twitch and raise his head. One of the speakers providing information about Chojecki's hunger strike said that the prison authorities were subjecting him to forced feeding through a tube. It was then that I caught that twitch, something probably well known to hunters: a quick, alert movement of the head. He leaned forward in his seat and cocked an ear; he was listening. Then I recognized him. I remembered hearing him once describe how, after six weeks of a hunger strike in which he had constantly, stubbornly spat out the tube, he once spat some fluid on a nurse's dress. She had burst into tears. "What have you done, now what will I wear on my date?" He had looked closely at her, considered the fact that he had spoiled a pretty young girl's summer afternoon in Łazienki Park or by the Vistula, and shrugged his shoulders. He agreed to break off the hunger strike.

He was a general whose death sentence had not been carried out and whom I had met in a mountain health resort in the spring of 1956. He had recently published a volume of memoirs and had been accepted into the Writers' Union.

I think that Jan Józef Lipski, a co-founder of KOR, was last on the list of speakers. He called the audience's attention to the fact that it was not too late to intercede for Chojecki, an innocent man. He warned them against being silent; protests should be made now, before it was too late. "Because, ladies and gentlemen," he said, "there may again come a time when people will be afraid to speak." And then he added, "And when I too will be silent."

From that entire meeting it was this moment that stuck most firmly in my memory.

"One hundred and sixteen signatures," said someone after the meeting. "That's a lot, and a little. It's more than the number of delegates that the Warsaw section elects for the general congress, but at the same time, it's only five percent of all the members in the Writers' Union."

The meeting lasted six hours. After leaving the building, trying to make my way back to the Old City, I got lost in the darkness of the square with the statue of Nike, and Andrzej Braun, who had left with me, led me by the arm like a blind man. I have not seen well in the dark for a long time; when there were blackouts during the occupation, I used to bump into people, horses, streetlights. It was also dark when we were leaving the ZAIKS building twelve years ago, after the meeting about the case of the play *Forefathers' Eve.** Word had suddenly spread that the Black Marias were on the way, that the Warsaw activists were going to club some sense into the writers' heads. I left with a dozen or so other people, including Paweł Jasienica. We hesitated at the doorway in front of the darkness; the Black Marias might already be waiting there. We went out. The square was empty. The

---

* See note on p. 44.

party activists only performed their task ten days later, instructing students at Warsaw University with their clubs. Chojecki was one of those students.

In a local library in Sopot, where I was taking out some books, the librarian returned my ID to me saying, "We don't need any deposit from you." She smiled at me. That's what it means to be at home. And to think that had they given me a passport, I would have gone abroad. Where else could I experience such a warm moment? To be at home . . . Even the drunks in the Old City recognize me: "Hello, Mr. B."

Returning from the library, I walked along the beach. Men and women sunning on beach chairs. Shortly before I left for Sopot, I heard someone arguing that the new masses in Poland were happy. They were aware of their class' victory and were reaping its fruits. I answered, "But at the same time they're aware that society is sick and they don't consider their life normal." Happy, unhappy? How an individual feels is also determined by how his society as a whole feels. The feeling of the normality or abnormality of collective life as experienced by the collective. A worker tanning on a beach in Sopot is thus perhaps experiencing the satisfactions of his class. But he also remembers what he is afraid of and what he hates. He fears and hates the same things I do. From the cramped lines in airless stores to the lies told in private and in public. ("Who tells you the truth today?" I heard a little reeling man say to a woman running a street scale. "Drunks or gypsies!") Miners, peasants, textile workers. Żeromski's yokels on the beach in front of the Grand Hotel. A class liberated from the yoke of exploitation and assured by the government that it likes living under Marxism-Leninism. I think, A duck likes to be baked with apples. And then I correct myself at once, An advance, social leveling . . . progress. Progress! I think it was in Sweden that before the seventeenth century, noblemen could not be tortured. That unfair privilege was rescinded in the seventeenth century, and from then on, all citizens without exception could be tortured. Progress.

* * *

Wednesday, as I was crossing Monte Cassino Street, I heard shouts and an uproar from the other side of the street. A commotion had suddenly erupted in a long line in front of the meat store. People shouted, squeezed together, pressing up against the door. I saw red faces, open mouths, bulging eyes. I thought something had collapsed or exploded. No. The line had spotted a van pulling up. Meat was being delivered.

Ewa Fiszer told me recently that when returning at two in the morning from playing bridge at some friend's place in Mokotów, she had finally found a taxi stand. The stand was located in front of a meat store. In a nearby gateway there were already some twenty people sitting on folding chairs and pillows. They invited her over to the gate, assuring her that the wait for a taxi would be quite long. They had various types of alcohol, little sandwiches, and cakes. Ewa, a poet and, in addition, a sociable and well-brought-up young lady, accepted the invitation. She spent half an hour in an atmosphere that was hospitable and garrulous, enjoying the treats. "Life at its fullest," she recalled somewhat wistfully.

■ NOVEMBER – DECEMBER 1980

Berlin. To Jan Stein in Venezuela:

My Dear Jan,
*   After we met by the sea in June, events have oc-*
curred in Poland about which you've read in the news-
papers. No doubt you were struck by the fact that the

first great eruption took place so close to where we had coffee with our wives. We didn't know that among the people strolling past us on the pier (I remember you saying that their clothing and appearance made you think of a crowd on a street in the West) were the future organizers and leaders of the strikes. At the time, I had argued that the masses in Poland were passive and in danger of being Sovietized. I was mistaken. I underestimated their hidden reserves. We awoke to a new society from one day to the next. As for me, it suddenly became possible to travel. I got a passport. We've been in West Berlin for two months. It was difficult to leave; Poland is probably the most interesting country in the world right now. I had my passport in my pocket for a month and a half, but I kept putting off leaving. In the end, however, we decided to travel. I don't know how long we'll be here. My grant runs through May. What do you think—will we get to see each other? I'd like to do some work here; I don't feel like doing any more traveling. But perhaps you could come to Berlin while I'm here. I'd like to hear again about your being shot down over France, how you parachuted out, and how you stabbed a Vichy policeman to death in the forest. And also about how, after the armistice, you stole that RAF plane from a hangar and flew to the concentration camp in Mauthausen for Michał, who was dying there of tuberculosis. You know how to tell a story; it's always a pleasure to listen to you. This letter is the first words I've written for four months. Too much was happening. I couldn't write.

Jan Stein, an RAF pilot during the war, was my first school chum.

Why didn't I send that letter? It's still lying in my desk drawer. I didn't send so many others too, composed in my head to people to whom I couldn't show friendship directly or from whom I was separated by distance or forgetfulness or laziness. There is little space or time to demonstrate the warmth at the core, where brotherly feelings dwell. We begrudge ourselves to others. What stupidity, what a shame.

* * *

There's no punishment fit for him, said the people from the area around Jeziorna about Gierek; he should just be buried alive. Simple people: women with pale-gray eyes, men whose expressions were indifferent rather than angry. Punishment! Revenge! A silence heavy with menace holds sway in the lines in the Old City. He made himself rich. He stole and let others steal. He deceived the nation. Poland? You'll help? A lie! He left behind a pile of dirty tricks, the country in ruins.

A man in a hospital gown, gaunt and treading uncertainly after a heart attack, out for a walk in the garden of the Cardiology Institute, repeated the same sentence to everyone who still had the desire or the courage to walk over to him and inquire about his health. "But my hands aren't soaked in blood . . ." It was principally that which distinguished him from his predecessor, Gomułka, who can also be met out walking these days. In the forest near Konstancin. Out walking his dog. He looks hale despite his 75 or 76 years. He is glad to strike up a conversation with people who greet him. "Agreements? In Szczecin? In Gdańsk? Those are no agreements; those are guns at their heads!" The locals also know him by sight. But no one says he should be buried alive. Have they forgiven and forgotten? No. They only feel less deceived by him. He didn't cheat them, didn't smile, and didn't deceive them. He snarled from the start, then shouted himself hoarse. He didn't make himself rich. He wanted a Poland without cars, with communal bathrooms in the halls. He kept the country in poverty. He choked it but he spared it. They know that he left 300 million in the state treasury. They also know that he allowed the shootings on the coast in 1970 and that he apparently requested Russian troops. That kind isn't loved. But he had been a tough man in his time—he had been in prison under Stalin, he had yelled at Khrushchev. He was like that from the beginning. Such people aren't buried alive. One just is sick of them forever.

A thirty-year-old man I know didn't talk about burying anyone alive. "Do you know what we need most now? A great wheelbarrow factory! So we can cart them out and put them behind the windows in the dairy bars and post offices. Just think of it: you're going to the post office with a registered letter or to a dairy bar by the Barbakan for some soured milk with buckwheat groats, and the vice-premier of planning gives you your receipt. Nice dream!"

Jokes are the most frequent form of redress in Poland. When dissolving the strike in Gdańsk, Lech Wałęsa said to the shipyard workers, "And now everybody's going home; make sure everything's the way you left it, and then to bed."

These words will probably not go down in history. But they should. There's a lovely, homey Polishness to them, emotion concealed in a joke. I do not know of another country where the leader of the working class, after a great victorious strike, would say to thousands of his comrades-in-arms, "And then to bed."

We're staying in Ravenna Haus. Morning and evening M. doesn't leave the radio. On Wednesday, local television broadcast a report from Warsaw. It showed the large meeting room at Ursus packed with people. Close-ups: a banner with the words "Free Janek Narożniak Now," the Polish eagle, and the national colors, the conference table. Behind it, a row of young Solidarity activists. I recognized a few of them: Bujak, Onyszkiewicz, another familiar face, and, at the edge of the screen, someone I must have seen at NOWA's evening in Żoliborz. The television is a small black-and-white one, and at times, from under the German reporter's voice flows the sound of Polish, murmuring like a familiar river. In another shot, young men in helmets against the background of a gate covered with enormous letters: STRAJK. A thin, dark young man smiling from the screen—Janek Narożniak, a doctoral candidate in mathematics and an associate of NOWA, released from arrest that morning. Between the German words I can hear his voice saying, "I'm glad that . . ."

There is a great emotion and seriousness in those crowd scenes, imperceptible to anyone not Polish. We have lumps in our throats, just as when we watched the moustachioed man brandish his enormous pen as he signed the agreement in Gdańsk. At that moment the camera had caught a young worker in glasses who, standing with some cable or tool in his hand, was trembling and crying. It was then that M. called out, "You are the son of two chosen peoples!"

People we hadn't known about for years, thinking we were an isolated island of intellectuals in an impassive society, suddenly emerged out of nowhere. "Do you know," I was told, "where the union movement in the theaters is coming from? From the upholstery shops, the costume shops, the shoemakers, the tailors. The actors too, naturally. Actors always find satisfaction in scenes and gestures. But the mainstream of the action is from the theatrical craftsmen, the workshops, the carpenters, the lighting technicians. And there's always some bearded sociologists debating with them in the hallways, experts, scholars."

The experts and consultants went to the shipyards in August. When the strikes were over, they spoke at Warsaw press conferences. You could recognize them by a certain expression in their eyes, by their intonation, and by something else, too, which Andrzej Kijowski has called their "distraction." Delivering a speech, Professor Geremek would bend backward a bit, his gaze fixed somewhere above the audience, as if wishing to recover the light and the color of those days at the shipyard. They returned from there, someone remarked, as from the altar after taking communion.

This is not understood in the West. People are afraid, especially in Germany. The headlines in liberal newspapers frighten people with reports of thirty Soviet divisions massed at the border. Fat, black letters: "GEFECHTSFERTIGKEIT. The Russian armored ring is closing around Poland."

They are afraid for us. This is what the *Frankfurter Allgemeine,* Miss von Doenhoff from *Die Zeit,* and our German friends say. One Bavarian journalist reported that the atmosphere in Poland and the increasing number of incidents are reminiscent of the period of aristocratic anarchy, when every Polish nobleman had the right of *liberum veto.* Our German friends are trying to frighten us, to frighten us with the eighteenth century. In Munich and Frankfurt, Poles are warned not to provoke Russia and not to encroach upon the bases of the system that gives them the only liberty they're capable of. The East Germans write more emphatically: counterrevolution financed from outside and the eternal *Polnische Wirtschaft*. Personally, I think it's that old rage at Poland that is rearing its head on both sides.

When I read the headlines here, which report that Russian tanks will invade Poland with the frosts, when the snow is hard-packed, I see a white square with a column, deserted, snowy, and dark footprints left by people who had gone inside to hide. But there had been no snow when we left Warsaw, the streets glistening in the autumn sunlight. The day before, I had given a talk at an electoral meeting of the Warsaw branch of the Writers' Union; I spoke about KOR. And two weeks earlier, in an apartment in Żoliborz, I had been signing newly printed copies of *A Warsaw Diary*, volume 1. NOWA had arranged an evening to celebrate its one hundred publications, and the *Diary* happened to be the hundredth. I sat in a chair against the wall surrounded by a crowd. There was no table, so they put another chair in front of me, and a friend lent me his pen. Young girls, students, the anonymous printers, and distributors of NOWA came over to me. I wrote, "For Mańka and Zdzich"; "For Miss Anna Walentynowicz"; "For NSZZ* Solidarity in Białystok, wishing you courage." Over 200 people had gathered in that old apartment in Żoliborz, several generations, a difference of seventy years between the oldest and the youngest there. There was singing after the speeches were over. The boys and girls sat on the floor in a circle around two young singers with guitars, while we, the beardless elders, stood in a second circle behind them. The musicians sang a song I didn't know, but with a refrain we all repeated: "The wall will fall, the wall will fall ... the chain will swing at the gate."

---

* Niezależny Samorządny Związek Zawodowy (Independent Self-Governing Trade Union).

* * *

Dostoevsky: "People will not find peace through intellectual progress and the law of necessity but through the moral acknowledgment of a higher beauty that is a universal ideal." Dostoevsky: "Constantinople is ours, it should be ours, period ... Anyone who does not acknowledge the necessity of taking Constantinople is no Russian."

In 1970–1971 I lectured at the university in Paris. We left for Warsaw when the academic year was over. The director of the department had invited me to continue lecturing in the following years, and I promised to return for the fall semester. Once again we drove through Czechoslovakia and crossed the Polish border at Kudowa, and there, in front of the red and white barrier gate, I was suddenly afraid. It made no sense: all I had in my trunk were personal belongings, a package of French books, and my old typewriter. So what had I to be afraid of? Had time away from the country spawned that nauseating anxiety? By the gate stood a soldier wearing a stiff hat that seemed too small for him, the visor pulled low over his forehead. He was staring at me. I got out of the car clutching my documents in one hand. He didn't take his eyes off me. I approached the gate slowly, weak in the knees. Suddenly, he started shouting. I stopped, not understanding what was going on. "Szurkowski won the fifth round!" he shouted again from behind the gate, more loudly now. "You're joking!" I roared with happiness. "I didn't hear anything about it."

I didn't know who Szurkowski was; I had forgotten all about the Peace Race. Waving my papers, I began shouting to M., who was still in the car, "Szurkowski won the fifth round!"

Our baggage was not inspected. The customs men were sitting in their little booth, their eyes glued to the television and on Szurkowski panting, a laurel wreath on his head. Without taking his eyes from the screen, the post commander explained how to get to the tourist hotel.

Motor coaches were parked in front of the hotel. An excursion party—hubbub, commotion, and an unfamiliar song coming from a loudspeaker: "Give me your love, my heart is in my hand!" Inside, I was enveloped by warmth and the smell of sausage and sauerkraut stew. I asked hesitantly if there was any coffee. "Gierek gives us everything!" said the waitress proudly. Fifteen minutes later Mr. Pasela, the hotel boiler-room man, opened a squeaking gate for me. I drove into the barn and a hen jumped onto the hood of my car. I was in Poland.

I am writing this in Ravenna Haus, on Bundesallee in West Berlin. On the cover of *Der Spiegel* beside me, a Soviet tank with a red star on it is crushing a white eagle with outstretched wings. The news is growing more ominous all the time. Forty armored divisions. Consultations in Moscow. Counterrevolution in Poland. Alarm in the Western press.

I realize that by writing about my 1971 return to Poland, I am engaging in a form of self-therapy, as if I were plunging my hand into memories that were still warm and applying them like a compress to my forehead. Moreover, the very act of writing, the hours spent writing, are a shield against the onslaught of the future. When you write, you don't think about tomorrow.

Since my arrival here, I have been sending postcards and letters to Warsaw almost every day. So far, in a period of three weeks, I've received only one card. I telephoned Marian. I can hear that their voices are calm. They had just finished dinner; Marian had been at the movies. "But how are you feeling?" I cried. "We never leave the radio here!" They say they're doing all right; it's hard on the nerves as usual, but things shouldn't be exaggerated—there are ups and downs. And of course food is a problem.

"Why did we leave?" I say. "Our nerves are completely frazzled, and in Warsaw my brother's going to the movies."

Paradoxical Warsaw, strange Warsaw . . . The daily, desperate grotesqueness of that deranged life. I miss it already. Yesterday, falling asleep, I remembered the "girdle" incident and had a good laugh in the dark. How many years ago was that? It must be more than twenty. M. was buying a French girdle with garters at the Różycki Market. The woman who ran the stand, a fat, gloomy peasant woman smoking a cigarette, agreed to let her try it on for size. M. was standing with her skirt off, the girdle pulled halfway up; I was holding a mirror in front of her; and the peasant woman, cigarette dangling from her mouth, was screening us from public view with an outstretched rug, all the while praising her merchandise. Suddenly, we heard a shout, "The wrench! Put the wrench under his head!" A man had fallen to the ground in an epileptic seizure right in front of the stand, almost at our feet. A crowd had immediately formed around him. M., fear in her eyes, her blond hair lightly coiffed, seems somehow perched right over him. I struggled with the rug. The peasant woman was screaming, and the crowd had become a throng, watching the epileptic lying on his back, a wrench under his head, in convulsions.

Here, people would not be able to imagine such phantasmagorias, even in their dreams. A surrealism formed from slapdash absurdities and poverty's impure colors, the incongruities between people and things, things and people—here they have absolutely no idea what this means.

They ... The Germans, the French, the Swiss; their colorful pyramids of food, the brightly lit aisles in the supermarkets, the dozens of brands of smoked meat, of coffee, chocolate, jam. Huge, blood-red steaks, the rosy hams coated in white fat, fish from oceans and rivers the world over, pineapples, mountains of pineapples. They, and their banks hushed like cathedrals, their new automobiles like enormous jewels behind the plate-glass showroom windows, the golden luster of their furniture stores in the fall, heaps of furs, couches, the regal footwear galleries ... An onslaught of quantity and quality, here food consumes man, the neon lights blinking, seducing. They live in a civilization; we live in a drama. In her black marble bathtub, a celebrity intellectual gives a telephone interview on the coming anarcho-Trotskyist revolution. We will never understand one another— these are dialogues between the overfed and the starving. Their sense of time has a different structure. Look outside, look how they walk. They walk, whereas in Warsaw we drag ourselves along or scurry about. Here they stroll, and we are driven or crushed. The only thing that connects them to us or, rather, hooks us slightly together is the fear that we will drag them into our mad convulsions, place our burdens on them, and plunge them into our hells. Because they stroll through life, and we crawl through history. It has to be this way. They arranged it all quite a while ago, once in Vienna and another time in Yalta.

"As has already occurred several times in the past," declared the commentator on Berlin television yesterday, "the Poles' lack of consciousness of their own situation may cause them a rude awakening." This he said with the fatuously wise look of an uncle warning children not to play with matches.

What? A lack of consciousness? A lack of consciousness of our own situation? We lack everything; we lack meat, sugar, potatoes, but unfortunately or fortunately, we do not lack any consciousness of our own situation. You can say what you like, but we have more than the Germans did in 1941 and 1943. "I feel like laughing when I look at them, those future corpses," my father said when they invaded in 1939. It is precisely that consciousness that produces our instinct of self-preservation, a deeper instinct for spiritual self-preservation; that consciousness of our situation forms our character and intellect, creating our sense of the meaning of life through the force of simple dreams. What do we dream about? Freedom and justice. What do we want and what do we refuse? We want to be human; we refuse to live like subhumans. Oh, those ideas, "naïve" because purged of doubt. It is they that have shaped our humanity. There is great power in that desire and in that refusal.

Poland is the lead story almost every day on Berlin's television news. The map of Europe appears on the screen. The gigantic body of the USSR, which seems to be sucking in a wafer-sized Poland. Biblical associations are impossible to avoid. David and Goliath. Jonah and the whale.

It is not only Poland that the eastern empire seems to be ingesting into its monstrously distended belly. All Western Europe seems diminished by it, as if shrinking in fear. If you listen and read carefully, you can hear the West's faint-hearted recognition of its own biological weakness; they know their fatigue, the exhaustion of an old race that has to preserve carefully what strength it has. They don't want to perish. They see no values in the world worth dedicating their lives to. Die, for what? For the fatherland, an idea, in defense of dignity? Whose? What sort? They have the Common Market and civilization. And one does not die for civilization.

Today the West is emitting cries of horror; the intellectuals are grumbling; the consciousness of impotence is everywhere. They know already and are preparing themselves to be raped. All that matters now is that that rape not be a sexual murder but that it happens calmly, in some comfortable French bed. What should this upcoming state of affairs be called? Finlandization? Scandinavization? . . . But what if it's Czechoslovakization?

In these preparations the French are, as always, in the intellectual vanguard. No one is able to spread their legs as aesthetically, to lie down for the act with such *esprit,* as the French intellectuals. An old suspicion of mine: How much money flows from the Soviet Embassy to editorial offices in Paris? A crude, trivial suspicion; let's not pursue it. There are still respectable people there who are not on the take. There are the Western leftists. The left with its scruples about the world's first Socialist country and its fear of providing grist for the right's mill.

The left, the right. In our part of the world self-respecting intellectuals realized long ago that this was an idiotic distinction. In Poland any sane person who does not wish to make a complete fool of himself keeps such ideas to himself. But they still have currency in the West. The left, belonging to the left, solidarity with the left, are articles of faith for them and are at the same time their alibi. The colossus should not be annoyed; in its barbarian skull slumbers the people's revolutionary soul. In the West, revolution is part of the catechism of the intellectual left.

Both attitudes annoy me; there's something evasive in them. But what, finally, am I left with then? In spite of everything, that distinction does contain some lasting meaning; the division of people into two types—the left-wingers and the right-wingers—is everlasting. How to define it? I have come across the following note: "The left: a consciousness of the bonds between people, the movement of a mind driven by a need for justice, the recognition of humanity in others. The right: the organization of collective life as against the individual, a dogma protecting a community of interests, order based on force."

What is that gigantic stain that has spread across the map? What does it conceal besides immense space, a richness of natural resources, landscapes, and a military superpower? A quarter of a billion people and the history of Russia. I once divided the world into countries with corpses buried under the floor and those like France and Poland, which have no corpses to hide. No country's history has more corpses beneath the floor than Russia's. Russia built its capital on corpses and murdered its intellectuals. And in the name of an idea, that higher beauty of which Dostoevsky wrote, "Anyone who does not acknowledge [this] is no Russian."

It used to be said sometimes that a bit of the Russian soul has lodged itself in Poles, that "Polishness" is colored by a nostalgia for Russia. That no doubt came from the borderlands, the lost Eastern Territories, where together with the loss of freedom came a curious coexistence of peoples and nationalities. That's probably the source of the nostalgia. People traveled to St. Petersburg and Moscow; children were sent off to school in Kiev. Exile too was a way of experiencing Russia. After the 1863 insurrection, three members of the Zenowicz family were exiled and their estates confiscated. Given that, the Zenowiczes' fond recollections of Russia were especially surprising to me. M.'s parents were in Moscow during World War I, and the outbreak of the Revolution found them there as well. Wacław Zenowicz was an engineer in the Lanz machine factory, which had been evacuated to Russia in 1914. They returned to Poland in 1919. Immediately upon his return, M.'s father volunteered for the Polish-Bolshevik war, along with his two brothers. Later on I was to hear them reminisce about their years in Moscow. But with what feeling! There had to have been something sweet about Russian life. After holiday dinners with *paskha* or *kut'ia* for dessert, they would sing Russian songs in the dining room: "So, Men of the Light Cavalry, Let's Drink the Wine," and in the end, someone would always strike up "Ochi Chornie" or "For This First Squadron." That was in the years between the wars, in independent Poland. I frequently encountered the assertion that after 1918 Poland's economy and administration had been rebuilt by "Russian" Poles—economists, bankers, lawyers, bridge and road builders. And during the twenty years of independence between the wars, there were lively reminiscences in Poland of that Russia. Postrevolutionary Russia, separated from Europe by a chain of watchtowers more hermetic than an iron curtain, seemed far away and enclosed in a world of its own. Dangerous things were happening there but not, it was believed, things that posed a danger to Poland. Exceptions were extremely rare. I remember hearing how a few years before September 1939, Szymon Aszkenazy was strolling with Paweł Hostowiec through Warsaw, a city whose days, Aszkenazy was convinced, were numbered. With a historian's eye he could see foreign armies in a Warsaw that would soon be invaded from two directions, west and east. He was surprised that this wasn't clear to people.

But these were truly exceptions. I noticed no deep traces or any psychological trauma after the annexations and the most recent invasion. The memory of Russian literature was more enduring. My father loved to recite Lermontov when taking his Sunday stroll: " *'Skazhi-ka, diadia, ved' ne darom/ Moskva, spalennaia pozharom,/ Frantsuzu otdana?'* " (" 'But tell me, uncle, why our men/ Let Moscow burn, yet fought again/ To drive the French away?' ") I felt a disturbing caress and softness in their language. "But is it real?" flashed through my mind. A melodious hypocrisy was concealed in its phonetics, its cadence.

Over time, news began to pass through the eastern cordon.

Strange, mysterious, contradictory reports. Magnitogorsk—and the purges. Mayakovsky's suicide—and the parks of culture and rest. NEP and collectivization. The Komsomol, the moral purity of the Komsomol ... I took turns reading André Gide's illusion-free *Return from the U.S.S.R.* and George Bernard Shaw's good-natured travel reflections. Emil Ludwig, the German writer, had a conversation with Stalin, and when Stalin made a remark about the features common to the USA and the USSR, Ludwig exclaimed, "You don't even suspect how right you are!" Stalin smiled and said, "Who knows, perhaps I do."

Finally the Moscow trials. Then, September 17, 1939, and Lwów.*

I had no direct contact with Russians. No experience of them. Yet something within me resisted the idea of leaving Warsaw and crossing the Bug River to Russia in September 1939. M. remembered that recently. At the time, I had said to her, "You don't flee eastward during a cataclysm." I have no idea where that instinct came from. When Warsaw was under bombardment, I lay in bed reading *War and Peace* and took breaks to do antiaircraft watches on the roof (I had reported to the draft office but had been sent away empty-handed: there were no more arms to go around). I accepted the news of the Soviet invasion with a heavy feeling of resignation, as the inevitable consequence of Hitler's pact with Stalin. I had first heard of that pact scarcely three weeks before, through a loudspeaker at the Legion swimming pool, and in the August heat had felt a chill go through me. No one stopped diving, the splashing and laughter continued, and none of the bridge players began to tremble at their little tables. Seeing how calmly the girls were sunning themselves on the chairs, I thought I must be exaggerating things, that I had panicked too easily.

The news from Lwów came in slowly and was not at all clear. Red Army soldiers with cords instead of straps on their rifles, of-

---

* The Soviets entered Lwów on September 17, 1939, in accord with the Secret Pact between Hitler and Stalin. This was a severe shock for Polish leftists.

ficers' wives buying up nightgowns thinking they were evening dresses. Ceremonies to honor Mickiewicz, and at the same time, volumes of national poetry confiscated from libraries. Talks at the Writers' Union. But what sort of union was it—Polish, Ukrainian, Soviet? It was difficult to form a meaningful image of life there from all the varying reports. News about the deportations and the jailing of Broniewski and Wat came in later. A few people said that those were diversionary moves made by the Ukrainian NKVD. I listened to the stories going around with mixed feelings. People lived on hope, and in anticipation of a German-Soviet war. A psychological mechanism was already in operation, one that I would come to know well ten years later: the subconscious filtered out any information that could cause doubt or despair. The time came when my only source of support in my dark hours, during the terror, was the millions of soldiers with red stars on their caps—the first army that had succeeded in checking Hitler's drive. There was only one devil—a death's head on his cap above the patent-leather visor.

So then when did it first occur to me that there was more than one devil? And where did I begin to suspect that there was in fact a pair of them? I know the exact time and place. There was a certain moment on the fifth or sixth day of the uprising against the Germans. I was on an antiaircraft watch again. From the attic of a house on Solec one could observe the overpass on the Poniatowski Bridge. We stared at that overpass for hours on end. On my fifth or sixth watch, I asked myself why it was taking so long for a tank with a red star to appear on that overpass. There were other tanks on it—German Tiger tanks with black and white crosses. When it came, the thought was as cold as the touch of a knife: we're in a trap ... Yes, that was the first time.

At times one hears phrases like "Readers expect novels about contemporary women" or "The public is waiting for a play about the young generation." It is a paltry artist who fulfills the public's expectations. And if he does so, it means he's in a bad way. An author should not fulfill anyone's expectations. It's just the other way around: everyone should be taken by surprise. He should never anticipate or even sense the need for any work he has written. It is best when everyone is unprepared for that work, amazed, almost frightened by it—everyone, the author included. Very few readers were prepared for Dostoevsky's works one hundred and twenty years ago. They still shock us today. And one feels in Dostoevsky's works the author's own bewilderment at the simple discovery he had made—that good and evil coexist within every individual.

Dostoevsky himself no doubt did not realize the enormity of his work or, to be more precise, its meaning and consequences. To be sure, he had a sense of his own power as a writer even though he said it bore no comparison with Victor Hugo's in *Les Misérables*. But he was not able to grasp the essence of the revelations that he communicated in his five great novels. And one thing, more than all else, he never realized—that in creating his works of genius he had committed a murder. He had killed a literary genre, the novel. Or, rather, he shattered it.

The eighteenth- and nineteenth-century novel was an exponent of European culture's profoundest contents, of its very identity—the struggle between good and evil. Good and evil were distinct from each other and in absolute opposition. Not only in *The Lives of the Saints*, read by generations contemporaneous with Dostoevsky, but in *Les Misérables* and even in *La Comédie humaine*. There was no essential intellectual or ethical difference between Plutarch and Sir Walter Scott or between the novel and stage play. The Elizabethan theater too: a Danish prince dedicates himself to preventing the triumph of evil. Polish literature as well—all of it, from Jan Kochanowski to Stefan Żeromski, through the Enlightenment, the Romantics, and the Positivists—accepted that religious canon. Poland's loss of freedom, with its eschatology and the intensifying of moral contrasts, consolidated that canon and swathed it in emotion.

The canon that opposed good to evil and separated man from beast created the spiritual equilibrium of the novel. Fyodor Dostoevsky smashed that equilibrium. He snarled and tangled the good and evil in man. And since that time, the novel has not been able to be what it once had been.

I avoided Dostoevsky for a long time, knowing that I would find his work inaccessible, too dark, and cellarlike. Work in which, at the same time, too much has been laid bare. During the occupation I used to say to Stefan Otwinowski, an admirer of Dostoevsky, "I can't read him; there's always some drunken staff captain under a table whining about God." Stefan would chuckle. It was only after the war that one day I picked up *The Possessed* and fell into it as into a fever. But what captivated me from the start was the humor. Wonderful, ridiculous, tragic old Verkhovensky! That was the bait, and I swallowed the hook.

The Possessed, Notes from the Underground, The Idiot, The Brothers Karamazov. I kept plunging into the depths and coming back up for air. When was it that I actually found the key to that literature? It must have been later on, in the postwar period, after 1950. It's difficult for me to fathom just how it came about, what caused it. Was it because by that time I already had the key to who the Russians were? Possibly. Evidently Russia, its shadow, which had drawn nearer to us, had begun imperceptibly to seep into us. Perhaps through the Byzantine rhetoric of the authorities, the atmosphere of hypocritical ideology charged with repentant acts of self-criticism and ubiquitous suspicion. It was then, presumably, that our certainty—our sense that evil was unambiguous—was shaken. Smerdyakovs swarmed about everywhere, with their shabby misery, acting in the name of an ideal good, as did Ivan Karamazovs, possessed by the dialectic of means and ends. And it was perhaps thanks to them that I began to understand Dostoevsky better. He had described them all a hundred years earlier. Their imbroglios, obsessions, their stains of fear and hatred, their degenerate virtue. After all, even Piotr Verkhovensky was an idealist, and we can be certain that he professed a belief in the "ideal of a higher beauty," just as the idealists in the Red and Black Brigades do today.

Various trends in literature originate from Dostoevsky— Kafka, Gide, perhaps Przybyszewski as well. Faulkner. Céline.

Brighter rays like Camus also emanated from him. Brilliant and distinguished works in prose were written after Dostoevsky, but the novel with God on the side of good and against evil had only epigones by then. The spiritual canon had been shaken. And if we pause a little longer here and reflect more deeply, we will reach the conclusion that the road to some other place begins here, to the future, to the millions of people, not the worst of them either, who will let themselves be taken and follow the beast.

I was fleeing down Berlinerstrasse at night. I had no right to be there. A helmeted policeman caught up with me and cocked his pistol. I screamed for him not to shoot and swore to him that if he let me go, I would pray for him and his children till the end of my days.

The policeman hesitated. A moment later he shrugged his shoulders and said that God did not hear my prayers. "Didn't you ask him to save your life? But I have orders to kill you. And so you see, your prayers are of no use."

I grabbed his hand and replied that if he didn't shoot me, that would mean that God had heard my plea and that my prayers were not useless. I repeated that if he didn't kill me, if he let me go, I would never cease imploring God to preserve his health, his wife's, his little son's. "If God," I said, "were to answer my prayer that my life be spared, why shouldn't he answer my other prayers too?"

The policeman grew thoughtful, silent. He put his pistol away. "Maybe you're right," he said. "Go. Pray for me and my family."

It was early dawn when I awoke, and I turned on the bedside lamp.

Poles do not know how to think about Russians and Russians do not know how to think about Poles. Instead of thinking, both sides engage in knee-jerk responses, the result of a mutual psychological conditioning. A psychology fashioned over the course of three centuries. For decades there have been blank spots in both literatures, and neither literature strives for the deeper layers. The theme of Poles and Russians seems to have ceased to exist. The psychic petrifactions would have to be broken open, the old accretions of guilt and crime hacked away, the sources reached. But it is either too late or too early for that. The last forty years have set things back a century and a half. Polish consciousness is still at the level expressed in *Forefathers' Eve*. And Russian consciousness is still on the level of Dostoevsky's "treacherous little Poles."

Poles and Russians have been bad neighbors, but we have to exist side by side, and we will. The future is ahead of us. But what sort of future? No one knows. No future can be seen. Nothing can be seen. There is darkness on both sides, and no way of spotting a course. No one seems to have a broader vision. And so, 35 million Poles and 250 million Russians separated by fear and contempt; thus it must be and thus it must remain, despite the fact that there are still of course people on both sides who do not wish to be poisoned with hatred. What is going to happen?

I think the effort is doomed and we'll never get out of this predicament. It is bad now, even worse than it was before. In the past there were some enduring spiritual affinities with the Russian intelligentsia, an admiration for Russian literature. We had friends among the Muscovites, a larger number than today's handful of dissidents; there were universities and technical institutes where young Poles came to know the enlightened side of Russia. What is there now? The flesh and bone have been ground up, the head cut off, the colossus is flat on its back. A computerized brain has been inserted into the densely compacted masses, and a utopia, the ideal robot-Metropolis, has been realized. Everything that the Soviet robot thinks about the Poles has been programmed into it, and its brain transmits replies in accordance with the information implanted.

I encountered the Soviet robot's program about Poles in a Moscow restaurant, the Ararat, in 1957.

M. and I had purchased two tickets for an Orbis excursion to the USSR. After visiting the museums and galleries, M. wanted to see a Moscow nightclub. A bearded doorman in red livery stood by the entrance; inside, a dining room and a band. We were shown to a table where a young couple was sitting. They both understood Polish. The girl—swarthy, dark-eyed—told us about her brother, who had lost his life while helping liberate Poland from the Nazis. The young man with her wept. They ordered a bottle of wine; the mood was warm, cordial. The young man proposed toasts to our health, to Polish literature. He wiped tears from his eyes. He was genuinely moved. As we were leaving, he proposed a last toast. "I drink to eternal friendship," he said with a lilt in his voice, "to our brotherly countries, and may the Poles never again stab us in the back the way they used to."

They phoned the hotel the next morning, no doubt wishing to clarify or correct what they had said. Or perhaps to convince us they were right and offer as proof the high-school textbook from which they had learned history. I declined to meet them, and we left the next day. Thus ended my third and last trip to the USSR.

There, textbooks with falsified history, while here, the dates of the partitions, the places of execution and exile, are drummed into our heads. A year ago, when I was walking through the Barbakan, a group of boys, high-school students, walked past me. They were singing, or, rather, shouting, in chorus, "The Soviet scum will pay for Kiev, Wilno, Katyń, Lwów!" Stupid, blind. What good is it? None of the passersby even glanced at them. Everyone had his own affairs on his mind. Rooted in each of us is an image of the Soviets or Russians, an amalgam of collective concepts and images. Siberia ... the camps ... Stalinism ... kolkhozes ... executions ... tyranny and misery. That is Russia in the Polish national experience. The Russians could have created new experience; any change in this state of affairs depends on them and would have to come from them.

But the Soviet Russians display an unwillingness to think about Poland that is similar to that of the tsarist Russians. Just as it could not before, the refurbished empire cannot abide Poland's aspiration for freedom. Only the terminology has changed: "betraying the Slavs" has now been replaced by "betraying socialism." There are additional similarities: Moscow's old complexes about Polish culture, the Russians' contempt mixed with envy, their bad conscience, which transforms Russian guilt into Polish faithlessness. Everything just as it was during the exemplary reign of Tsar Nicholas I. I sometimes wonder if Soviet communism is a violation of Russia or, just the reverse, the very perfection of "Russianness." Be that as it may, the outbreak of war with Russia in 1914 was greeted with fervor not only by Prussian chauvinists but even by the German democrats, including Thomas Mann. For them the Russia of their time meant savage autocracy, a prison of nations. Even back then, it was considered the land of total slavery.

What binds that Soviet sack Sinyavsky mentions? Nominally, it is Marxist-Leninist ideology. But Marxism-Leninism is not creating the spiritual stuff of society. Established as a rite of state, reduced to a liturgical language, it has been transformed into a symbol of authority and, for the peoples of the USSR, has a significance akin to that of the tsar of all the Russias before the Revolution. The sack is bound with the cord of the Russian government, except that now it is drawn more tightly, more efficiently.

And so what's inside the sack?

The question of the Russians' own responsibility interests me: the Russians' responsibility for Russia, the Soviet citizens' for the USSR. I wonder how that responsibility enters their consciousness and if any such awareness exists in them. Do they see a connection between their own individual psychology and their social existence or don't they? Do they feel themselves the architects of their own slavery or don't they? Do they submit to it out of choice or from compulsion? Do they like Soviet life or not? And further, if they don't like it, if they submit in hatred, then at what point does the chain linking their own consciousness with the will to resist break and is that break caused by fear alone? I wonder if there are values in their lives that create noncompulsory, unselfish links among people and between an individual and the state.

Those are the types of questions I would pose to contemporary Russians. I assume that they would not be able to answer them, for those are questions that Russians do not ask themselves. Russian self-knowledge does not seem to extend past certain boundaries that have been drawn in their psyche, and Russian self-criticism shrinks from what is hidden within them at the very source of Russian unfreedom. They can see the physical power of the authorities that afflicts them and afflicts Russia. I doubt if they can see the Russia that afflicts other nations, and I do not think that they can see the traits of that Russia in themselves.

In 1831 Pushkin's poem "To the Slanderers of Russia" condemned the outbreak of the uprising in Poland.

In 1863 all the liberal Russian intellectuals with the exception of Herzen condemned the January Uprising.

I would not be able to name one work of Russian literature that advocates an independent state in Lithuania or the Ukraine.

I am not sure if in 1918 the voice of any Russian poet spoke out to greet a Poland that was reborn and sovereign.

The Russians have not been able to see in themselves the seed of Russia's wrongdoing in relation to the world. The Russian mind defends itself against self-knowledge; it has no awareness of "cursed Russia." Neither in St. Petersburg nor in the Russian emigration did any Russian poet feel *himself* to be *full of guilt*. In that respect, Polish literature has been more resolute. Its criticism of its own nation achieves a sublime, sagacious tone. What Russian writer would consider indicting Russia by name, reviling it as mockingly as Słowacki reviled Poland and himself? Or as Cyprian Norwid did with what he wrote about the Poles' stunted humanity. A tone of critical self-knowledge has been heard in Polish literature since the publicists and preachers of the Golden Age,* much earlier than Piotr Skarga's sermons, and it continued

---

* The period of the Polish-Lithuanian Commonwealth (1492–1572).

right up to Stanisław Ignacy Witkiewicz's *Unwashed Souls* and Witold Gombrowicz's *Transatlantic*. It is present in Stanisław Brzozowski's work and Piłsudski's letters. Desperate, angry, it frequently exceeds a just measure and is not sparing in the most painful of epithets: "peacocks and parrots," "a nation of idiots," "Polish immaturity." But it is splendid. It is an unusual case of courage in self-analysis, and the absence or silence of that voice in Polish culture would have impoverished it. The Russians find it highly amazing. S., a serious Soviet literary scholar, heard that voice in several contemporary Polish plays and novels. *"Eto istinno pol'skoe"* ("That's truly Polish"), he marveled. *"U nas etogo net"* ("That we don't have").

And they never did. The Russian writers never addressed Russia directly, by name, in warning or accusation. I also doubt whether they related those warnings and accusations to themselves. Certain Russian types—Oblomov, Manilov—have been satirized; later they were to enter the language of ideas—"Oblomovism" and "Manilovism." But no direct judgments were made about the Russian character or history. Apart from Chaadaev's letter* and Gogol's invocation, Russian literature has none of that truly Polish tone of responsibility for the fate of one's country. Chaadaev was considered mentally ill, and in the second part of *Dead Souls*, Gogol wanted to create the antithesis of the first part.

A certain young Russian woman, a Soviet citizen, once cried out in an outburst of sincerity after a couple of drinks, "Russians need to be ruled by the whip; they love the whip!" That was ten years ago in a restaurant in the Grand Hotel in Łódź, during a congress of the Writers' Union. After her next drink, she began to talk about Poles, and she was breathing fire. Why did they hold the Russians in contempt? What was the origin, the cause, of that unfounded Polish sense of superiority? She had recently

---

* In a letter from *Letters on the Philosophy of History,* published in 1836, Petr Chaadaev expressed bitter dissatisfaction about Russia's alienation from the "universal education of mankind," and attacked Russia's national self-satisfaction and spiritual stagnation.

seen an American comedy at a Polish cinema. When at one point a Soviet sub surfaced, the audience had roared with laughter. The young woman's voice trembled as she recalled the Poles laughing senselessly at the Russians. There was only one thing she failed to mention. That the words *"Vsegda Vpered"* had been stenciled in bright red on the sub's armor. If a man who is being whipped on proudly writes the words "Forever Forward," the effect has to be comic. The audience caught that one right away. Poles have a sense of humor, and they have known about the Russians' relation to the whip for generations now. They weren't laughing at the submarine; they were laughing at what was written on it. They had a feeling for the grotesque relationship between the slogan and the reality behind it. Perhaps Russians are not aware of the comedy in such juxtapositions, and it is that unconsciousness of theirs that also amuses the Polish audience.

There seems to be some barrier in the Russian mind that bars them access to themselves. It was not communism that created the *domination of words* in Russia. They have always loved words—words about God, about love for man, and about the ideal mankind to come. But historically they seem seized by a collective will to push forward, in which all thought of internal transformation and a better humanity is lost. I have often maintained that the form that Russian humanity assumes is that of office and service, and I travestied a quote from one of Norwid's letters: "A Russian is a lord on the outside but a servant at heart." I am not certain that that line is altogether fair, although it is confirmed at times by what people tell me of their trips to the USSR. A Polish scientist who studied at Moscow University provided me with a curious description of the customs of young people in Soviet universities. Apparently, their life does not differ much from that of students in the West: sex, jazz, alcohol, frayed jeans and sweaters, a little anarchism and cynicism, and a disregard for official bureaucracy. The change occurs the moment they graduate. The young Soviet citizen goes to work in either an institute or an office. Then the Soviet collective, as directed by the Russian will, begins cutting him down to size, and the young Soviet citizen submits to the process. The Polish scientist called this "going on duty." I wonder if this is not the point at which the chain breaks, a point that might be defined as the place where responsibility is cast off.

There is yet another way of putting this. Russia is a nation onto which militant Mongol hordes forced themselves for three hundred years; which under Peter the Great began to be ruled by clans of German officials; whose positions were taken by Bolsheviks schooled on Hegel, Feuerbach, Marx, and Engels. The features of the Asiatic invaders, German bureaucrats, and dialecticians have by turns laid their deposits in Russia for seven centuries.

However, I ask myself a question: Russia, the Russian people, are they an instance of the failure to produce a social body, will they ever be able to produce a living society with a structure unlike that of a stone crushing them under its own weight? I am frequently inclined to the view that Russia is a country encoded with a tragedy that is reborn in generation after generation, through cyclical destruction. The instinct for self-destruction and a sense of their own nothingness are rooted deeply within them; at bottom, they have an unconscious contempt for life, both their own and that of others. But they feel this, and fear and hate themselves. And they conceal that flaw. That is the source of all Russian literature—the despair at flawed Russian humanity.

■ J A N U A R Y– F E B R U A R Y *1 9 8 1*

News from Poland arrives in various ways, and despite a lack of clarity about details, the reports agree on one point, namely, that the economic situation is still critical and the government is unable or unwilling to remedy it. People are unanimous about the need for renewal, but the necessary reforms are not being carried out. The dilettantes who have been discredited have not been replaced by specialists but by people with equally unsavory pasts—those discredited in 1968. The party press is attacking the opposition violently, especially Kuroń and Michnik. The top and middle levels of the administration, which do not wish to lose the "golden freedom" they obtained by ruining the country, shield themselves against change. But, at the same time, there is a growing awareness in society that only reforms can lift the economy out of its decline. Such is the news I receive from home.

Among the reports it broadcasts from Poland, German television recently did a feature from Solidarity headquarters. The building was packed with young people crowding around tables heaped with publications. Many bearded faces—you can't hear what they're saying, but you can feel the atmosphere of debate, the electricity in the air. An image in sharp contrast to the official view, to the image of *order*. A revolution.

New strikes have erupted in Poland. The government has issued a statement that speaks of special measures to preserve order. The strikes are a protest against the government's failure to abide by the social agreements concluded in Gdańsk. This the government does not mention. The Procurator's Office has also issued a communiqué threatening repressive measures. The words "anarchy" and "lawlessness" are used in the text. The office also warns that publishing outside the official censored channels is punishable by up to one year in prison.

I saw a white llama on Kurfürstendamm. A long-haired youth in blue jeans was standing beside it and it sniffed at the hands of people passing by. Its nostrils trembled. Gentle and obedient, it was kneeling down at the edge of the sidewalk, the crowd brushing by it. It raised its head, its ears down, neon reflecting in its widely spaced eyes. It was on Kurfürstendamm, a busy street vibrating with light. The llama had knelt down across from an immense shoe store. Looking at it, I recalled what a certain charming and intelligent young woman had once told me. After emigrating and finding herself in a large foreign city, she kept going to the zoo during the first few weeks. She would sit on a bench with a book and stare at the giraffe. It was the only creature she felt close to in that city. "The giraffe too had been brought here from its own land." But just why had she chosen a giraffe? One look at my friend would be enough to answer that question. She had sloping shoulders, a long, slender neck, and a smallish head, whose dark eyes had a look of neurotic wariness to them.

I walk down Kurfürstendamm; I look, I listen, I bump into people, I stare, I think a little, and sometimes I come to a stop.

But this is the agora, the place where people gather, flickering, garish, shimmering with all the hues of temptation ... Here the human swarm is amused in a thousand different ways, the pleasures of life laugh out from behind plate-glass windows, stand on street corners, slip softly along the asphalt. Good Lord, what don't they have here! Photos of naked girls invite you into sex cabarets; the red caverns of bars beckon with their warm interiors; the newsstands are plastered with publications from the world over and resemble many-colored bouquets; electronic gadgets move about in display windows. Nearby you can purchase hashish from boys in baggy sweaters and from dark-eyed ephebes with faces like the Pankrators on icons; a little farther on, movie theater marquees beckon you with their fiery ads for westerns. A girl with a gold band on her forehead and a purple dot between her eyebrows sits on a small rug selling amulets, while at the entrance to a passageway another girl, wearing a red wig, raises her thin arm, her hand covered by a felt puppet with painted cheeks and a turned-up nose. And right around the corner, a German family can be seen consuming pink lobsters in the glassed-in terrace of a restaurant, while an unshaven old man wearing sneakers treads the white line at an intersection like a tightrope walker, deranged, his arms outstretched, gibbering, shouting in fear that he might fall. High above him, at a height one really could take a fall from, glow enormous letters BERLIN SPIELT LOTTO, and the word PANOPTIKUM hangs motionless in the dark sky like the title of a work.

This is life, I think to myself; after all, this is life, the most authentic form of life that could be offered us. There are illnesses and calamities in this life, for they have always existed and always will, although today there are fewer of them than there were in the past. The dark specters of plague and hunger have left us; the state supports the unemployed; there is equality among the city crowds; they can provide themselves with everything they need. This is life, human life, with its good and its evil; this is the existence to which we are enjoined. The living marrow has not been broken here; the bone has not withered. Was life better at some other time? It might have been worse. The patterns and the rules are already worked out.

Standing by the Café Kranzler, I want to cry out to the West, "You talk about liberating yourselves from the inferno of civilization? Wake up, my friends. What is it you want to liberate yourselves from—life? From life, with its innate afflictions, insufficiencies, dissatisfactions, but life nevertheless, authentic existence. From what God has destined for man and called life. If you do not desire this sort of existence, if you have come to believe in your own solitude and traumas, as taught you by the philosophers, and the will to live has indeed slackened in you, then perish. But if, despite everything, you do not wish to perish, then I will find something else for you to do."

I continue addressing the European mentally, but by now I have reached Wittenbergplatz and I'm a bit calmer.

I explain to them that they lack something that I call the biosocial imagination. They have lost their instinct for the future, the gift of intuiting or seeing their own fate in collective terms, that high imagination that is really a creative force surpassing logic. I could have sworn to them that we will share a common future. They cannot avoid it; it will come sooner or later. They will not escape what we have already experienced. And if it is true that their cities, those automatons of production, consumption, psychosis, and amusement, now cease to suffice them, if they are sincerely seeking a new and still unknown polis, then I say to them, "Turn your face to us; we are new, we are unknown. We are close by, right at your side. Don't turn away from the countries of Europe that have been sold out for your well-being, peace, and mounting food surpluses. Turn to us, and you will learn some interesting things."

I walk a little farther. I watch. I wait for a light to change. And again I ask, Why don't they see that a fate like ours awaits them? Their philosophers, scientists, artists, what do they think when they look at the map of divided Europe? Do they have some game plan for coexistence between Western and Central Europe? Judging by what they say, they seem already spiritually under socialism. They just don't take too seriously our efforts to transform socialism into life.

They are fighting for women's liberation, for priests and homosexuals to have the right to marry; they write about the shackles of their civilization, and at the same time, they ponder whether or not Poles should be supplied with grain. Is it worth it or not? Perhaps for conquered countries to regain their freedom, they must make it on their own and will no doubt manage better when their population is hungry. And perhaps giving the people food helps strengthen the system of slavery . . .

This is poor reasoning. By sending us trainloads of grain, you affirm your own moral presence in the world. That grain makes you an integral part of our life and consciousness, those trains unite us; they forge real links between us, between us and you. Do you feel uncertain, threatened? So do we, but in a different way. Do you see your own decadence? Are you searching for a genuine idea? We have a genuine idea. Allow me to make you an ideological proposition.

Set up aid circles for the countries sold out to Russia. Form committees and associations. Clubs, unions. Create them, expand them. Join them in mass numbers. In that way you will give yourselves a shot of vitality. It will make you spiritually stronger. Instead of coming to us to hunt and fish, try to understand our countries and exert your minds to create if not a common existence, then at least the concept of one, its imagined shape. This will raise you in your own eyes. Refresh the world's memory about the nations that fought alongside you in saving Europe from Nazism and about those nations, betrayed earlier, handed over to the Third Reich as protectorates. Organize circles of this sort in all the countries of the West. Not honorary groups chaired by dignitaries. Then you will feel better, much better. Dust off those old phrases of yours about the brotherhood of nations. Remember Byron's death, Mazzini's faith, Michelet's righteousness, and Schiller's dreams. That will be good for you. Memory will bring you back to life and resurrect your dignity. And if those old words sound unrealistic to you, allow me to ask, What is realistic and what is not? Five years ago in Poland a few hundred young people discovered that the impossible could be possible. They made their discovery by blind feel. That had the imagination, the courage, to ignore necessity. They were guided by instincts from that high imagination that transforms reality. It is they who, after a century and a half, were fulfilling the program spelled out in a certain poetic work that I had memorized in school, a work that had been taught to the point of boredom. That ode, which you have not read and which was written by a provincial schoolteacher, has a naïve message—to strive beyond what you can see, to measure your strength by your aspirations. But what is naïve and what is sober-minded? Perhaps the least naïve thing of all is to push against this massive division of the world until it petrifies or breaks apart.

Thus I carried on inwardly. And I know that there was exaltation and overstatement in that shouting to the conscience of the West. I know that I have fallen into the pathos of the preacher and that a complex is speaking through me. And perhaps I do not know Westerners well enough. I look at them from the outside. I don't have a Western stomach, and so, of course, I do not feel the pain of its ulcers . . . But I hadn't carried on without reason. For it was here that, for the first time in my life, I had encountered the West's indifference in the flesh.

We mean nothing to the Westerners. The revolutionary intellectuals are as indifferent to us as the housewives and storekeepers. Ireland and Chile mean more to Poles than the events of the last six months in Poland mean to people in the West.

In the meantime, we get letters, such as the one from Andrzej Kijowski in Warsaw that arrived yesterday:

> *It's curious how Poland's way of life has changed. The sham, the facetiousness, the hamming it up, the irony, have disappeared. You practically don't hear any jokes! On the other hand, a new trait can be observed—the patience to organize. The meeting of the Writers' Union lasted until four in the morning and a hundred people stuck it out in the auditorium to that hour, and the discussion as to further action remained businesslike, painstaking, and detailed to the very last. That impressed me. Besides, it was the same at our general Solidarity meeting—even the typists and proofreaders stayed in their seats until the meeting was closed, for seven hours, until everything had been said and voted upon. Everyone is organizing. On Waryński Street, a Social Committee of Those Awaiting Imported Furniture has been formed. It's not a joke, since such behavior was dictated by necessity and common sense. This is no longer a Gogolesque, Kafkaesque, or Mrożekesque country but one with entirely new moral qualities and entirely new themes. I don't know what all this means, but I do know that for the first time in my life, I feel that I am in my own social element.*

Ewa and JMR also called yesterday from Warsaw. Jolly, in a chipper mood, they cheered me up over the phone, telling me not to worry, everything would be fine.

So that's how it is in Poland now. What will happen next? Will we manage all right, endure, or will we end up back under a boot, Polish or otherwise? Will things be dark and muffled, or bright and humming?

Here there is increasing talk about the danger of a return to the cold war. Of all the possibilities, few are worse than that. If the West were to turn its back on us and if we were to turn away from the West, an iron curtain would fall not only between countries but within people as well. When I found myself in Amsterdam in 1954 after not having been in the West for eight years, I could no longer speak the language of the Europeans and they could not speak mine. I could not accept their way of thinking and they could not accept my experience. We were people half of whose minds had been amputated, people of the cold war. I remember how I stood in front of a store window with a display of household goods unable to imagine what most of them were actually used for.

But nowadays the cold war is spoken of here with something like quiet hope. The cold war was a period of prosperity in the West, and it was only the opening up to the East that upset that balance. And so perhaps everything will return to its former position, and Europe, judiciously divided, will again have ten years of rest. That, of course, would have to be preceded by a Russian military intervention in Poland, a subject topical in the press here.

Journalists are not the sort of people from whom you expect humanitarian compassion or an especially sensitive conscience. Their profession is to inform. At times, however, a short informational article can be more expressive than a literary account. When weighing the chances that Poland would be invaded by the Soviet army, a correspondent from a French newspaper had talks with representatives of the democratic movement in Warsaw and Gdańsk. One of the young activists calmly declared that he would not wait to be arrested; on the day the Soviet tanks broke the country's resistance, he would commit suicide.

My heart bled when I read that little article, but for the people here, if they noticed it at all, it was a piece of printed information about the state of affairs in a country that lies outside their ken—a country in the *Zone*. At one point, with an unpleasant sense of surprise, the people of the West received the news that a man from that country had been elected Pope. For it is not we but they who have a besieged-fortress mentality, and it is they who are drawing down the iron curtains within themselves. The very thought that in Poland today something has arisen that is newer and more important than the Western synthesis of Luxemburg-Marxism and anarchoterrorism, or the self-repairing regulators of the Western economies, infringes on their mental zone, for the young neo-Marxists, the bank directors, housewives, and the editors of *Le Figaro* and the *Frankfurter Allgemeine* all share a dislike for experiments conducted in an area of strategic importance to the Soviets. It is not we who are turning away from them, but they who are turning away from us.

■ M A R C H
1 9 8 1

Four months have passed since I left Warsaw. I have three months ahead of me here. For all this time I have been living in a caesura, an *entr'acte,* and I cannot rid myself of that feeling. My way of life has not undergone any great change—work, reading, conversation—yet at the same time I have a sense of having been snatched out of real time. A make-believe life. A pause. Sickening anxiety coupled with moral pangs. It reminds me of skipping school—after an hour of sitting on a bench in the park, I would be seized by a dislike for myself and by growing boredom. The boredom of sin. A small group of my classmates and I would shout that boredom down with jokes and pranks, but in our heart of hearts each of us knew that those hours were unreal and each of us could feel the emptiness of a freedom unearned. But the next day in school we learned, not without some disappointment, that our absence had not been noticed. Life had gone on without us; we had not really lost anything, but we had not gained anything either. Where had we been the day before? Nowhere.

After two rather quiet weeks, the march of events has again picked up speed in Poland. The radio and press have reported about a gathering at Warsaw University on the anniversary of March 1968, that is, thirteen years after the university campus was invaded by a group of party activists with billy clubs in their briefcases. On that day I had been standing on the sidewalk in front of the Church of the Holy Cross, a cordon of helmeted policemen barring me from the road, while across the street a group of students was chanting "De-moc-ra-cy, De-moc-ra-cy!" from the balcony of the Geographical Institute. That was, I think, the final group; the rest had all been dragged out in the roundup. Thirteen years later, on Sunday, March 8, several thousand young people gathered to mark that anniversary.

A counterdemonstration was held at the same time on Aleje Ujazdowskie. It had been preceded by the distribution of anti-Semitic leaflets written in a style that has not varied for years, the same style used by the press thirteen years ago and then eight years later, after the founding of KOR, when anonymous letters were sent to people active in or sympathetic to the opposition. The counterdemonstration drew a few hundred people, including chance spectators. People calling themselves "the veterans" were honoring the memory of the victims of the Stalinist-Zionist clique. There could be no doubt as to the point of the enterprise: to identify the police terror in the years 1950–1953 with the liberation movement of the present and to suggest that both were instances of a Jewish conspiracy.

A crude campaign that nevertheless breaks down people's psychological resistance. And it is occurring internationally. Today totalitarian nihilism does not shrink from the most trivial distortion of the truth, and by comparison, the racial theories of the first half of the century seem less perfidious. Hitler simply announced that the Jews must be exterminated. The modern anti-Semite contends that Nazism was initiated by Jewish financial circles, and thus it is Zionism that bears the true responsibility for the death camps. The Jews financed their own deaths—that seems to be the latest historical interpretation, one encountered not only in the ideology of nationalist Islam but in extremist groups of the left and the right in Europe as well. That method was adapted to Polish conditions for the counterdemonstration on Aleje Ujazdowskie: the Zionist-Stalinist clique that is today organizing the democratic movement of unions and students is financing counterrevolution in Poland. According to the new logic, those of KOR's founders who spent time in Stalinist prisons have been playing an active part in the Jewish mafia's plans for thirty years, both back then as prisoners and now as opponents of police methods . . .

Veterans, gentlemen! The fact that anti-Semitism is still so widespread in the world today has its political explanation in the propaganda fueling the Palestinian national movement and is directed at the state of Israel. But in Poland . . . In Poland anti-Semitism serves another cause. A disastrous reputation in the West has always been the price of Polish anti-Semitism, and if today someone cared to compromise those eager for Poland's freedom, to sully them in the eyes of the civilized world, to render them odious, isolated, and cut off from Western economic aid, then that desire could be most effectively realized by the founding of an anti-Jewish organization in Warsaw.

March 19: Three Solidarity activists severely beaten by the militia in Bydgoszcz.

March 24: A call for a general strike.

We were in France during April. After my return to Berlin, I found more than a dozen letters waiting for me at Ravenna Haus, as well as a telegram inviting me to a meeting organized by the Swedish P.E.N. Club between Swedish and Polish writers that would be held in Stockholm beginning May 17.

For a few days now, the date of our departure has been on our minds, and we speak of our return to Poland more and more often. We still have a month left, in the middle of which I will spend a week in Sweden, and then we'll have to pack, say good-bye, and buy food supplies. An image of devastation emerges from the Polish press and radio and from the debates in the Sejm. Poland today can be compared to an apartment where too many large objects have been placed for no good reason, which are causing the floor to collapse. The strands of the organizational and economic network that had maintained a passable equilibrium in Poland have no doubt been strained to the breaking point for a good while now. I remember a conversation from around 1964 with a member of the party's ruling elite who invited me for a walk around the Wał Miedzeszyński (he didn't like talking in rooms or offices). "Gomułka has a single obsession. He thinks about it day and night—how to feed thirty million Poles. It's his nightmare."

But now one has the impression that suddenly all the bonds have burst at once. And so what caused that to happen? Thieves and fools, people say. But, good Lord, how did they all get there? The party to which I had belonged has made truly historic achievements: the food stores have nothing but vinegar and tea for sale; people stand in lines for hours on end for meat, sugar, and other items—now rationed; and if they want bread, they have to make a couple of trips a day to a food co-op. Shortages of cigarettes and soap are frequent occurrences, as are shortages of powdered milk for children. Some patients are dying for lack of medication. And who is being accused? Party secretaries, premiers, ministers. The people's government formerly in power. A commission has been appointed to determine the responsibility of specific high-ranking officials, and special courts will try them. Who, what sort of people, will sit on that commission? People who themselves are part of the regime, who have been reared by it, and who bear as much responsibility as those to be tried.

When, and by whom, will judgment be passed on a system that is subject to no control and that blindly, despite the protests, has squandered the reforms made in 1944–1946 and has led to a social catastrophe unprecedented in Europe, a system not chosen by society and as life-destroying as a tumor?

Girls are exported to southern countries to perform in nightclubs. Their passage and passport are paid for, they work from ten at night to four in the morning, with no days off; they are also paid nine dollars for half an hour alone with a client. State institutions and enterprises like Pagart and Estrada have engaged in recruiting and exporting those girls, and in the provinces, Houses of Culture have also been supplying this merchandise. This living merchandise did not know what awaited it at the point of delivery; the consulates of the Polish People's Republic were reluctant about providing them any aid, since the state had a share in the nightly earnings of those Polish girls. As reported on the evening news, we were, at that time, one of the world's leading exporters.

People sometimes speak of flabby totalitarianism. But that was festering totalitarianism.

Counterrevolution, anti-Socialist forces ... Anti-Socialist forces are still being written about and spoken of from the highest tribunals. Hard, metallic voices bark down from above, from the summits of the party. I read one of those speeches, and it reminded me of the language used by the leaders of the Third Reich. Enemies in disguise, plots, Zionist intrigues. Every word a blow from a club.

Everything is before us. Unknown, unpredictable. I wake up in the morning and see M. sleeping and wonder how she will fare with her weak heart in Warsaw. How many times will she be able to conquer the two and a half flights of steep stairs to that apartment whose kitchen is without ventilation. Will she have the physical strength for it all. And will I have strength enough to write. For forty years now, from the first pages I ever wrote, cigarettes and coffee have been essential to my work. At certain times I was able to get along without a publisher but not without a few cigarettes and a cup of coffee. And so what will it be like now? I don't know. One way or the other, we have to go back. To a country where everything is possible—including hunger riots, as a political leader said recently to a group of intellectuals in Kraków. We have to return to life. Berlin was an intermission.

Looking at M. sleeping, a mass of graying hair falling over her arm, I feel a pang of guilt. She could have married an architect, a scholar, a doctor. Was our high-school meeting really so fortunate? Now and then I allow myself a risky joke. I tell her, "You married me to save my life, and I married you out of gratitude." She proposed to me one autumn, in an apple orchard. Vlasov's troops were combing the neighboring villages, rounding up suspicious-looking men. I had my doubts: Is this a wise step? "Please marry me," she said.

Now, as our departure approaches, M. is anxious about me again. We quarrel and haggle about the date. I want to go back as soon as possible; she, however, is afraid of certain dates. Better to wait it through—July isn't a safe time. To which I reply that September or November might not be safe either. And in the meantime, I'm losing my sense of the real picture, I'm gradually losing the threads, and after six months away from Poland, I no longer understand what is actually going on there. Wait it out? I might end up outwaiting myself. I remind her how old I am. She responds by saying that the years haven't changed me, I'm just as stubborn now as I was when I insisted that we remain in Warsaw before the uprising. Well, we lived through that one too, I remind her. I argue that instinct dictates my choice of direction. In September 1939 I did not want to go east, and now my instinct tells me to return to Warsaw.

Besides, I know, we both know, that our duels are pointless. We will go back; life has decided that for us. The only problem is that someone has to take upon himself the responsibility of choosing the date.

In the morning, over breakfast, during my ongoing debate with M., I succeeded in convincing her for a moment with a rather literary argument: since we first met, the two of us have always lived through everything together in Warsaw, as if our lives had been conceived in close conjunction with its fate, and in the end it would be absurd to accept any fate outside it. That would be an absurdity of composition. "I understand," she smiled. "You mean in the composition of your *Warsaw Diary*."

In conversation with Poles in Berlin, Paris, I can fill in some of the gaps. I have heard descriptions of the days preceding the general strike called for the end of May, for which thousands of people prepared with joy and cheerful excitement. A splendid mood. Someone said, "They were coming from all sides, as if they were going to an uprising." People were apparently bringing mattresses to their plants and offices; the large factories were to be turned into fortresses. When I said that it was fortunate that the strike did not have to occur, I was met with silence. The young woman I was talking with had not experienced the uprising in Warsaw. I, on the other hand, remembered the days preceding its outbreak, when it was apartments that were being turned into fortresses. Arms were being brought in. Then too the mood had been splendid.

It's no easy thing to hear about it all secondhand in foreign cities, to conjure up an image and make judgments at a distance. The maneuvers of the Warsaw Pact troops are being extended;

the Western press is again sounding the alarm about the danger of armed intervention. In Paris, where we were expected at the Centre du Dialogue at the Pallatine priests', I spent several weeks almost exclusively in conversation with Poles.

A moment ago I learned of the attempt on the life of John Paul II. Five shots from the crowd. Three bullets lodged in the Pope's body. It happened in Rome in front of St. Peter's Basilica. Wednesday, May 13.

The person who had resolved to murder the Pope was a Turk belonging to the international terrorist network that encircles the globe. Today a spider watches the world from its hiding place. We will probably never learn who directed this lost soul, where he got his money, documents, and deadly weapon—a fifteen-shot pistol used by professional organized killers. We will also never know if the moment was chosen deliberately. The Primate is dying in Warsaw. The press agencies and the radio have been reporting on Wyszyński's last days for nearly a week now. "You are a Pole," a French journalist said to me before I left. "It must have entered your mind what the Pope's death, the news of his murder, would mean in Poland today."

And here the mind forms the most abominable suspicions; here hatred enters the picture. At moments like these, it would be far wiser to say a prayer. As for hatred—those who do not wish to hate are impotent people.

"There is safety for man in Christianity." So I said in one of my Parisian conversations. "Protection against the sense of time that arises from the movement of history. Eternity has no developmental logic. It does not constitute a course of events, an advancing structure. Christian time is always fulfilled and closed, antidialectical. Prayer is salvation from the wheel of life and an activity fundamentally different from rational acts, which occur in open, historical time. The age of the Jewish prophets was a drama played out between a people and God; the age of the Galilean fishermen was the striving of man for God. The universal church created eternal time, which is neither a striving for

God nor an anticipation of God, but God himself, infinity. The church placed man in that time in order to tear him away from history's rational time, to raise him up from below."

At an author's evening in Paris, at the Centre du Dialogue, I read a fragment from the June section of *A Warsaw Diary* on John Paul II's visit to Warsaw. Many people had come—the auditorium was full. I autographed copies of the Parisian edition of volume 1, which was fresh from the printer's. On page 159 the book notes the moment when the Pope and the Primate prayed at the Tomb of the Unknown Soldier. I read the short description of that scene. The Pope and the Primate, who at that time were kneeling side by side, have now been struck down, both suffering—one critically wounded, the other dying. The two of them. The work composed by the Creator abounds in violent turns, and indeed, Providence cannot be reproached for any paresis in plot construction.

I had intended to write about Paris before my departure. About the meetings I had had in Paris, about Easter. Now, however, it is the Prussian plain that sweeps past the window of my compartment. Germany. East Germany. I have returned from the dining car, where there was nothing to eat besides a piece of cold, greasy sausage and a slice of stale bread. And to drink— warm lemonade or beer. At the buffet, a man wearing a none-too fresh white smock wrote out my check. The floor was littered with dry sausage skins.

After passing the wall, we return—instantly—to the mystery of grime, filth, peeling plaster, and uncollected garbage. Communism has deformed the Germans. Even in West Berlin their shapeless corporality made for a surprising contrast with the gleaming products of their technology. (Nowhere else is there such a glaring difference between the beauty of the automobiles and the people.) And here the external world intensifies their ugliness. TO GUARD AND SECURE OUR SOCIALIST GOVERNMENT IS THE DUTY OF EVERY RAILROAD WORKER. Then a dirty yard littered with tin cans. And right next to it, on a peeling wall: ORDER DISCIPLINE SECURITY. The train moves away leaving empty faces behind on the platform. The ugliness of capitulation. Sad, repulsive. Along the tracks, with their shopping bags, their bundles, their children, stand the sons of those who were conquered near the Volga and the Dnieper.

The wall ... it's behind me now. The barbed wire entanglements, the glassed-in watchtowers. A zone of harrowed earth and guard patrols with German shepherds. On a bridge, soldiers wearing stubby black boots and flared trousers—small, motionless, one with a pair of binoculars—are watching the train passing below them. The Berlin Wall. The second wall between people built by the Germans. I had a look at the first one forty years ago. When Germans build a wall, it's not easy to get to the other side. They know how to guard them religiously; *echt deutsche Spezialität kann man sagen.* In 1941 M. made her way through the court building.* "What are you doing here, child," an unknown gray-haired woman whispered to her on˘ Leśna Street. "You put your armband on wrong. Jews wear their star on the right arm. You better go home."

An East German customs official ordered me to open my suitcase. My briefcase and papers interested him. He glanced through them, and then my notebook caught his eye. He leafed through the pages for a minute and paused somewhat longer over the last page, as if trying to read it. Then he shrugged his shoulders, gave me back my briefcase, and left.

I was curious to see what was on that last page. It turned out that the idea I had written down had originated from someone who had been close to me and who is no longer alive. In Paris I had been given a Polish art magazine; part of the issue was dedicated to the memory of Stanisław Zamecznik. I copied down a couple of phrases discovered among his notes: "One must constantly, always, every day, morning and night, in summer, in winter, and in rain, in youth, in old age, and in between, when walking, standing, sitting at a café, on a veranda, in school, on a

---

* Before the Warsaw Ghetto was completely sealed off from the rest of the city, one could pass through the municipal court building, situated at the very edge, from one side to the other.

train, on the stairs, and elsewhere, against one's natural inclina-
tions, one must every day, constantly and always, begin everything anew. This is exhausting. Terribly. But this alone keeps us
from the end."

Those lines made an impression on me. I read them with an
odd feeling, as if I were hearing an old friend speaking to me
after death. Their meaning may be construed in a variety of
ways, depending on one's field: in relation to artistic work and
also to all of life, to oneself. I thought that in a narrower sense, in
my own way, I was living out that idea. In a narrower sense, as a
writer. Be that as it may, I do know what going back to the beginning means; many a time in my writing I have been able to
reject a self I had come to know and to reach out for my unknown reserves. Yes, to begin anew. That's the way it is in writing. But in life?

Our life, I think, has been subjected to other trials. Mine and
hers, always, constantly, in youth and old age. Trials afflicting us
from without. What to call them? They could be given various
names. The trials of ideology, politics, history ... We were in
their compass from the start, even when it seemed that we were
just ourselves and deciding our own fate. That wasn't true. We
were mistaken. We began anew; we made a choice and suddenly
it turned out that we were standing with our faces turned to that
same wall. Only the writing on the wall had changed. We felt a
loathing for *fascism* and we said *socialism.* And years later our
path was blocked by a wall engraved with slogans of hatred. The
same hatred. We had only one choice: to sell our souls or to
maintain them. It was not we who began anew—it was the darkness around us. In school, on the streets, in September, in March,
and in the rain. Constantly, always, despite our hopes, despite
our lives.

At the beginning of this diary I wrote that true calamities are
always personal. I should have then immediately written the following sentence: true calamities are always collective. Both of
these sentences may be recognized as accurate in spite of their
being contradictory and one seeming to cancel out the other. But

it is frequently, and perhaps most frequently, the case that two sentences, each of which sounds true by itself and which are mutually exclusive, create, when joined together, an idea that expresses a truth of life. That is often the case with proverbs: "Strike while the iron is hot"; "Fools rush in."

Tell me who is the more unfortunate—the one who dies alone in bed of lung cancer or the one who wastes away along with thousands of others behind barbed wire? I cannot answer that question.

The dates of our true calamities . . . those we know about and those of which we were not aware. One could make a political calendar of recent history from them. The symbols of what menaces us: jagged swords, a cluster of twigs, death's heads, black crosses, hammers, sickles, crescents, and stars . . . We were besieged from the beginning; there were always watchtowers on the horizon. To this day the spider's eye follows us.

My father, and I'm certain of this, was not aware of the forces I am writing about here; he never felt for a moment the part they played in our fate and his. He was a person full of virtues and faults but without definite convictions, like the majority of people in those far from stupid times. Ideology? Politics? He did not have a world view and he didn't need one. For fifty years he lived with a sense of satisfaction and the belief that, apart from financial losses, he was in no danger and that it was statesmen like Piłsudski and Clemenceau who engaged in politics. He loved life, loved earning and spending. Laughing, he told me that on the day of the assassination of Franz Ferdinand in Sarajevo he won a large sum from a lawyer, Piotr Kon, in a baccarat game. For him, ideas about countries and peoples took the place of a world view. By the way, he held both the French and the Germans in esteem—the French for their intelligence and gallantry, and the Germans, for their industriousness. He did not think highly of the Russians and six months before his death remarked that the Red Army was composed of streetcar conductors on horseback. Perhaps the movements of the beast that we had felt since childhood did not in fact have any great significance during his life. For a long time the spider watched him from afar. It overtook him suddenly, right at the very end, and devoured him in an instant. Today I am five years older than my father was when he was dying in Pawiak Prison.*

Precisely twenty-four years ago, at the beginning of June, a Soviet writer by the name of Aleksandr Chakovsky asked me what the Poles' real concern was in October 1956. He used the term "petit bourgeois revolt." I answered that the concern was for moral law. "Well, that's a provincial point of view," the literary representative of a great metropolis said, laughing indulgently. "Judea was a province too," I said, "a little province that gave the world the Old and the New Testaments." Chakovsky grimaced. That was in Moscow, during my Orbis excursion with M. to the USSR.

▪ J U L Y
1981

I am writing in Obory.

Two hundred and twenty-three days ... Bundesallee, Ravenna Haus, Berlin, and Germany are far behind us; those seven months seem a mirage to me now. I carried my manuscript into Poland on my back, between my shirt and my pants. The East German customs official gutted our overloaded car; I had to carry our suitcases and set them on his table. He rummaged through my sweaters, spent a good while leafing through the

---

* An old Warsaw prison used by Germans during World War II to hold Polish prisoners.

Paris edition of *A Warsaw Diary,* and ordered me to open up my typewriter, a fifty-year-old Olympia that I had bought in 1946 with money I had won playing poker. I declared in German that only the Gestapo had subjected me, during the occupation, to a similarly meticulous search. The customs official went to his booth and summoned an officer. Tall and thin, the officer arrived and rebuked me for insulting a customs official of the German Democratic Republic. "I'm not insulting anyone," I said. "I'm merely stating a fact—that the last time I was searched that thoroughly was by the Gestapo during the war." The officer glanced through the American edition of *A Question of Reality* and then read a bit of the introduction to the German edition of my short stories. *"Sie sind ein Schriftsteller"* ["You are a writer"], he said to me in the end, "and so all the more reason you should realize that this man is trying to do his duty well." "And he's doing it poorly," I answered, "because he can't tell the difference between a writer and a smuggler." The officer shook his head and walked off. The customs official returned my boxes of pow-dered detergent, which he had earlier pierced through with a screwdriver, and helped me replace my things in the car.

Polish officials had been following this scene from their win-dow. "You may pass," said a young Polish customs official with an eagle on his cap. "Have a good trip." He glanced knowingly at me with narrowed eyes. A half an hour later a cyclist drove right in front of my car at the intersection of the paved road and a side road. Going seventy, I slammed on the brakes and only the gravel on the side of the road prevented us from turning over. The cyclist hunched his shoulders and fled, pedaling hard. *"Ty baranie!"* ["You jackass!"], I shouted after him. O my native tongue, you have not forsaken me.

It was warm and crowded at the Zerwikaptur Inn; all the tables were taken by a group of noisy tourists from Poznań. I washed my face and hands in a muddy bathroom, where a sign had been posted with the price for using the facilities: two złotys. The towel was wet, streaked with dirt; the washstand was cracked and yellowed. As I was drying my hands, the cloakroom attendant, an older man, opened the door a little and, sticking his head in, asked if I had a few pfennigs on me. Just then someone shouted, "Miss Staszek, where the hell is Puchalski? He's not in the cloakroom!" I almost shouted back that Puchalski is here and had just been given fifty pfennigs. Back at the car, M. was talking to some children. Some Danes had just pulled in, and children were hanging around the foreign cars asking for candy and chewing gum. The foreigners, wearing glasses, smiled, ill at ease. I opened a can of Coca-Cola. Drinking it, I noticed a five-year-old boy, barefoot, with a mane of flaxen hair, staring at me. I gave him the rest. Delighted, he ran to show off to his friends. As we were backing up, I heard the boy shouting to us, "Your bag! Lady! You left your bag!" M.'s bag, with all our money in it, was lying on the ground. She had set it there when getting out of the car.

We drove straight through to Warsaw, arriving before dusk. It was still light as we carried our things across the courtyard. The woman who worked as a superintendent in our building was sitting outside on a bench. "So you're back. But why? There's nothing to eat here."

Letters had been arriving from Warsaw for many weeks: "Prepare yourself to return to a completely different country; the change is incredible, and sad."

I prepared myself, but nevertheless my first glimpse of Poland the day after my return was moving. The city beneath a warm, dim sky, the sidewalks full of people hurrying, the streets wide open. On Marszałkowska you could see almost the entire distance from the Saxon Garden to the Square of the Savior, which meant that there were fewer streetcars running. Only the little islands in the middle of the streets, where the streetcars stopped, were packed with crowds waiting patiently. In fact, there were practically no streetcars, and the wide artery of the Marszałkowska residential district appeared in a distant, surprisingly pure and exposed perspective. My first thought, This place is greater than Berlin. A certain monumentality about it. But what sort? A somewhat eerie one. A phantom capital to which something difficult to comprehend has happened. Vast, long roadways bordered with the dried greenery of small trees, and along the buildings that were now more exposed, as if more visible than ever before, lines of people hunched like strips of some congealed matter. From a distance, a line looked like an unhealthy growth clinging to the base of a wall, the way wild vegetation sometimes fastens on to the base of a tree. Lines adhering to walls, swelling out, tripling, quadrupling, their ends catching onto each other. Passing the intersection of Miodowa and Żurawia or Hoża, I noticed to my far right a large cluster of people pressing toward the entrance to a store that was probably at the corner of Poznańska Street. The line had already overflowed the sidewalk onto the street. At the same time, there are pedestrians everywhere, movement, haste. Suntanned girls in summer dresses, men in checked shirts, an ambulance waiting. Here and there, in the more easily visible spots, political inscriptions drawn by hand with indelible paint, and posters with slogans, some of them half ripped off.

It reminds me of something. No doubt something that I have experienced myself, something depressingly familiar. "It's like a city under siege," said M. "You just don't hear any bombs dropping."

That's probably it. It may not be so much any similarity but something that rouses memories, disconnected fragments of images from September 1939 and August 1944. Lines for water pressed against the walls . . . empty stores . . . handwritten death notices . . . nothing on the streets but the streetcar tracks. And on the sidewalks, confused movement, directionless haste.

The other day in the Old City I saw two tremendous lines, nearly all men, compacted in a furious, menacing silence—awful. Lines for cigarettes and vodka. Two monster lines chained in waiting, from which from time to time shouts would erupt. I hear it everywhere—there's nothing to buy. In May you could still get soap and vinegar; now there's nothing. "What do you mean nothing," I ask, "if the stores are open." They're open and they're empty; there's nothing to buy. The churches are full, but the stores are empty. A new stage in the development of socialism—the barter stage. People swap cigarettes for soap, vodka for cigarettes, and soap for vodka. Sugar, flour, kasha, meat, and butter are rationed. The waits are long. Children stand in the lines too. They secure a place for themselves, then run off to a nearby courtyard to play soccer or tag. A seven-year-old girl was interviewed on television: "Chocolate is a problem. One bar a month; that's awfully little, that's less than one bite a day." A new word is born: the women who sit on the front windowsills of stores from daybreak on are called sillers. Heroic women, granddaughters in direct descent from the Polish mothers whose praises were sung by the Bard. The nation has gritted its teeth. Millions of people have discovered in themselves deposits of superhuman patience; their resistance to daily affliction knows no bounds. Once again a culture of endurance is forming among Poles. Jokes still circulate. "When will they finally come," sighs a student delivering a monologue on stage. "When will they finally come." The audience is silent, stock still. "When will they finally come to understand us, those who have done this to us?" Frenchmen, Austrians, Swiss, participants in a world congress of architects, say, upon leaving Warsaw after the conference: the most peaceful city in the world . . .

Three days later, at the end of Królewska Street, as I recall, M. and I both suddenly cried out in wonder. The streets surging with life, loose, swarming crowds, a certain nonchalant undulation to their movements, free in all directions. A great city, splendid, alive. And once again in retrospect Berlin appears provincial, with its bucolic villas, parks, lakes, its secession style. *Ach, Berlin* . . .

My spirits are better here. Absolutely and totally contiguous with reality. After seven months, I'm back in my own boots again. But it didn't happen in a day.

I was missing 200 frames of film; there were breaks in the continuity. Before our departure, you could buy everything or nearly everything you needed in the stores: lines were a frequent occurrence but were not an absolute rule of life. Once a week we drove out to Siekierka to Madame Ch.'s for beef. All I remember was being unable to find any large envelopes in any of the stationary stores. Now, having returned, I rack my brains to understand how things have come to be stripped so bare and what people are living on here. Pure spirit? In the course of seven months, goods have almost disappeared and there is talk of hunger. But the crowds on the streets seem not to be aware of all that. They inundate the streets, gather in churches to sing "We Want God" and "Let Poland Be Poland," and wear ironic badges pinned to their summer shirts: "CCR—Creeping Counter-Revolutionary." These are the same crowds about which six years ago I wrote that they lacked faith, for they were under the sway of material desire and indifferent to the ideas of freedom and justice. Everything is so unexpected and arresting. "A worker with a crucifix," said M. "It's not what I had dreamed about, I who am an intellectual and practice no religion."

Seven days later we came back to Warsaw from Obory to turn in our passports and deal with a few other related matters. I spent the night in Warsaw. Before dawn, I awoke from a dream I could not recall. The clatter of a half-broken-off drainpipe reached me from below through the open window. It was still dark; a soft yelp could be heard near the market—probably some hungry dog looking for something to eat in a garbage can. I felt a chill coming in through the window and was aware of the feel of the fresh sheets on my body. I lay there with my eyes open, letting a stimulating current, a rush of thoughts and images, flow through me. I received them with gratitude, aware that I was experiencing a moment of happiness. Those moments, sudden and rare, usually come for no reason one can fathom. I could make out the door—a faint white in the darkness—but I could also see a multitude of faces and forms; I could hear my own voice and those of others. And I began a conversation. Not only with myself but with those other people as well. I continued unfinished dialogues that had been broken off at some earlier point, and felicitous replies now came to mind. I really was brilliant that night. I felt such inward strength that had those hours been able to last for the next few days or months, I would certainly have been able to accomplish remarkable things. I don't know why this happened to me on the seventh day after my return. But on the whole, what do we know of ourselves and of the life that so unexpectedly renews itself within us? Is there some wise and mysterious element coursing in our blood, some incorporeal substance that is kept wonderfully concealed from us?

I fell asleep in the morning to the scrape of Mr. Pawlak's broom sweeping the sidewalk in front of our windows. I awoke late. My arms and legs were trembling as after a wild party. It was only after that night, however, that the empty frames began to fill, and after ten days I already felt so much at home that it seemed I'd been there all the time and had never gone anywhere at all.

In my free moments I catch up on my reading of Polish publications, which I leaf through in bed. *Polityka* (Politics), *Sztandar Młodych* (The Banner of Youth), *Literatura* (Literature). And *Solidarność* (Solidarity).

In one of the back issues of *Solidarność* I came across Jan Walc's coverage of the incidents in Otwock, where an enraged crowd was on the verge of burning a red-haired policeman alive and might have done so if at the last minute it had not been addressed by a young man in a leather jacket who had been summoned by telephone from Warsaw and whose speech began with the words "My name is Adam Michnik. I am an anti-Socialist force."

The Otwock policemen's mouths fell open. They knew the name Michnik from directives from headquarters and the Procurator's Office. They had been dragging him into police stations for years; he had been assaulted and beaten in stairwells, shoved forcibly into police cars, interrogated, and searched. Attempts at persuasion would be made during the investigations: "Adam, where is it getting you?" Now the police were goggle-eyed, trying to understand one of life's ironies: Adam Michnik had come to Otwock to rescue one of their colleagues, who had been too quick with his club, from lynch law. The drunken, howling mob quieted down after he said his first words, and an hour later it began to disperse. The chief of the police station walked up to Michnik, his hand extended: "If you would accept my thanks . . ." Michnik did not refuse the handshake.

When officials of the Warsaw police station ask him "Where is it getting you?" they are expressing a thought widespread in this society. We owe our suspicion of words to the political ideologues and that is good; but, at the same time, they have instilled society with a disbelief in the compatibility of higher motives, unselfishness, and social action, and that is not so good—that is significantly worse. And this does not affect only policemen. Many people in my own milieu suspect Michnik of having other motives. They whack me on the back with sincere compassion when I assure them that Michnik is fighting for justice and freedom. Besides, he himself is well aware of what is said of him and has many a time summed up those same people with a certain term of abuse that he also used several times in his speech at Otwock.

A certain revelation of which I had no inkling has forced me to do some thinking. Over the years I had reconciled myself to the thought that the concept of a struggle for justice or freedom was beyond today's mass society and only put people on the defensive. That was, supposedly, the way things were. And indeed they were; but, at the same time, things were different. In one summer month an irresistible desire for freedom burst forth from the mass of humanity here, and suddenly it turned out that every other person was ready to fight for justice. Not all that long ago they had been silent; who does not recall the forest of hands rising in exemplary, unanimous elections. Three years ago, people smiled as they explained to me that of the one hundred signatures on the protest concerning the Constitution, ninety would have dropped out had the government taken more repressive measures. "None of this is serious." And perhaps not all of it was. Now, however, it becomes clear that in one respect it was serious, more serious than we had thought. We did not know, and we still do not know, to what degree human nature can hide from itself, how much it can deny itself. Perhaps any society, if skillfully trained with a stick, or a stick and a carrot, will renounce every truth. But a trace will remain in the depths of collective memory, a faint reflection of the ideal. I think that of all the things that have happened and come to pass, this is the most important.

The fifteenth day back. Today I refused to watch the evening news, and I haven't looked at a newspaper since yesterday.

The party commission that convened to examine the corrupt practices of the now-discredited party and government leaders is at work. The People's State Council has received motions that the members of the former ruling group be stripped of the state honors they had been awarded. At this moment, a person with the gift of making logical associations has to think, Will the medals be stripped only from those who were pinning them on themselves or also from those other people who received them from their hands? What will happen to the Virtuti Militari awarded to the leader of the USSR? Will the State Council request that it be sent back?

I ought to be curious about further developments. I'm not, however, and what I see and hear makes me sick. Duplicity is sprouting up everywhere again; such ambiguity and impurity hang in the air, such hypocrisy, that it makes you want to flee and hide in some forgotten corner of the world. Yesterday I read the lead article in a paper that has the reputation of speaking for the liberal center, an article written by an advocate of reform. The author commends the cause of renewal but immediately warns of the danger involved: a democracy that is extended too far threatens to weaken the state. This I read in a country where the idea of general democratic elections is sheer fantasy and where any schoolchild knows what in fact threatens to weaken this state. Everything has been painted with protective colors, concealed in civic-sounding phrases, but in every sentence you

can feel the arms and legs trembling. The same faces on television, the names in the newspapers unchanged. Concocted reviews of the foreign press, moronic reportage on the domestic
scene, and the more astute columnists already sniffing out the
new currents. Oh, those columnists who write for the weeklies . . .
One of them, a gray-haired young man who two years ago performed monologues on television with a parrot on his shoulder,
is today writing about the "need for disinterested beauty" and
says that we are being oppressed by stupidity: "Both anti-Semitic
and philo-Semitic stupidity, stupidity about renewal and hard-
line stupidity, stupidity about egalitarianism and about volun-
tarism." He further states that everything depends on the sort of
art we have, the way our artists behave, and says the writer, they
behave abominably: "The majority of them have made it a point
of honor to run panting after every little incident, to multiply its
echoes, to copy everything they read in the papers or hear at
meetings or in lines for cigarettes." In a word, says the columnist
and teacher of the nation, disinterested beauty, art, which should
outlast the theater of life and not stand in a servile relation to it,
is on the verge of being reduced once again to socialist realism.
That's the real danger. The rest is just oppressive stupidity from
which one should keep one's distance—anti-Semitic or philo-
Semitic stupidity, that's not the point.

I don't know if there are any philo-Semites in Poland today,
and if there are, what they are doing. I do, however, know that
over a period of a few months the country has been flooded with
publications and clubs whose slogans are straight out of *Der
Stürmer*. In printings numbering tens of thousands, on paper
which is in short supply, they castigate the Jews, which are in
even shorter supply. And thus does the state grow stronger.

Thirty-five years ago, a pogrom, instigated by the police,
erupted in Kielce. That same hand prepared the murders of several dozen Jews in 1946, and five years later, the execution of a
group of Polish army officers, falsely accused of conspiracy
against the party. The corpses in Kielce were Jewish. Again the
journalists in Paris had something to write about: *un pogrom po-*

lonais. In September of that year I traveled to France on a train packed with Jewish families fleeing Poland. An emigration center had been established in Paris, and Polish could be heard among those waiting there. Six weeks later we returned to Warsaw in an empty train, and M. asked me whether I was sure we were headed in the right direction. At the time, I shrugged my shoulders; today I would be able to answer that question—for me Poland is a necessity and that is why I return. Fine. But today, after my latest return home, I find my name in an anonymously published pamphlet that lists me as one of the members of a secret Zionist group whose aim is the destruction of the Polish nation. It's all too easy to guess who put this crap together and who picked up the tab for it. I only wonder if it's going to be like this for the rest of my life.

That's only one side of things, of course. There are others that keep you going. The realization that 10 million people have succeeded in organizing themselves, have their own publications, are operating at the workplace and in the schools, that corruption and lies can be brought to light and people cannot be trampled upon—that realization improves one's frame of mind. I am still unable to distinguish between the groupings and factions within the movement. I am not well informed about them now and I will not attempt to become better informed. The religious ceremonies, the Catholicism of the movement, the proclivity for church services and processions—I cannot feel very close to all that, but it's understandable. People had been given nothing for their spirit. The church, in its wisdom, was able to draw the right conclusions; it offered people what they had been deprived of. Where there is no hope for society, the church becomes an earthly force, a social body. It could not have been otherwise.

Thus far one can take considerable satisfaction in the political and organizational accomplishments, and in the strengthened condition of the nation as a whole, a nation that did not submit. That is a matter of psychology. In time, however, collective psychology is transformed into a real value and enters the equation of history on a par with reforms and rights wrested by force. And it is worth the effort regardless of any further developments. And regardless of what seems bad or laughable or brazen to us.

In the evening, on the terrace in Obory, a long conversation. "This is an abnormal country," someone says. "On the contrary," I answer. "It's a perfectly normal one between two abnormal ones."

Some Polish filmmakers were in a taxi in Havana. This was shortly after Fidel Castro had taken over and not much was known yet in Cuba about the fraternal Socialist countries of Europe. The filmmakers were talking among themselves, and the dark-skinned driver asked them what language they were speaking. They told him they were from Poland. *"Polonia?"* said the driver in surprise. "And where is that?" "Between Germany and Russia," answered one of the Poles. *"Santa Maria!"* exclaimed the Cuban, letting go of the steering wheel and grabbing his head. "How can you live there!"

The Cuban reacted correctly. The West, however, is fixated on an image of Poles ingrained in Europe since at least the end of the nineteenth century. Especially now, when we are making headlines, every other journalist has the honor of being an expert on Polish affairs. How to translate the French expression *lieu commun?* "Commonplace idea," "banality," "mental cliché." The West's knowledge of Poland consists of a few *lieux communs:* the Poles don't want to work; they are anarchistic, politically irresponsible, ready to stake their entire existence on nationalistic slogans . . .

Between the wars, Poland was a middle-ranking European state. From territories that had been subjected to three partitions it created a unified administrative system; it voted in a democratic constitution, repelled an invasion, and weathered the worldwide depression. And it achieved all that without economic assistance from the West. During the thirties it was militarily and economically weak and only in the last five years of that decade had it begun to rebuild its industry and modernize its army. Today one says of such countries that they are taking the road of civilized development. Between 1918 and 1939 there were no signs of instability in Polish society. Quite the reverse. In an epoch of dictatorships, Poland had rejected grafts from both of its neighboring systems: Hitlerism and communism. It had no mass exterminations or deportations on its conscience; opposition parties and independent trade unions existed in the Second Republic until the outbreak of the war. That particular Poland was not one of Europe's leading countries, but it was organically healthy and the majority of its society was immune to totalitarian madness. In one of his prewar comedies, Antoní Słonimski called Poland a "sanatorium for people weary of fascism."

I recall that three years before the war, after the peasant strikes, people who thought soberly had no doubts about the coming turn of events. Sooner or later the government of Poland had to be taken over by the Christian-Democratic center, along with a portion of the left and the moderate wing of the National Democratic Party. (It is significant that today, a half century later, free elections to the Sejm would no doubt produce similar results.) At that time, symptoms of madness began manifesting themselves to the east and to the west of Poland's borders.

To this day, we still have no new picture of Polish history. The Golden Age ... the Cossack and Swedish wars ... *liberum veto* ... the partitions ... the uprisings. The image is always the same—a progressive illness, a disintegrating body long in a state of decay. But it's possible to see things differently. For on what grounds can we be certain that modern European history was a manifestation of health while the Polish system was the product of a pathology? Perhaps it's just the other way around. It is not out of the question that the republic of nobles was a healthier organism than the absolute monarchies of the same period. Be that as it may, that organism—before it was ripe for reform—functioned for three hundred years without great disturbances, displaying a stability in its economic and social structures at a time when Europe was staggered by peasant revolts, the Inquisition, dynastic wars, religious wars, the Hundred Years' War—the Thirty Years' War. Who knows, perhaps it was Europe that was sick, all of Europe with the exception of Poland? No one knows what the history of the world would have been like had France, Russia, Prussia, and the Hapsburg Empire been transformed into constitutional monarchies in the seventeenth century and the necessary reforms been carried out in Poland. That is not what happened. But was what did happen for the best? The twentieth century, with its death camps and its 100 million corpses, does not seem to offer the most convincing proof of the normality of Europe's development. And it would not be in the least amiss to view that development as the history of an illness, a spiritual illness that afflicted Germany and Russia to the greatest extent and Poland to the least.

Playing the game of what might have been is not a bad way to pass the time on days when you stand in line for a box of matches. The present is not very encouraging. "Last week," said an old woman I know, "I cried three times for reasons of state."

On Sunday, for the first time since my arrival back here, I saw a person in despair for reasons having nothing to do with the state. He is ten years old. He had seen the conclusion of *Buddenbrooks* on television that evening and had been terror-stricken by the death of poor Hann. Standing by a bush, his fists clenched around the handlebars of his bicycle, he asked in despair, "What will I do when I die? Where will I be?" The grownups smiled. "What are you crying for; everybody has to die." And that none too tactful consolation made him aware of the menace in its entirety. He bawled at the top of his lungs. I was on his side. At last, someone shaken to his very soul by the essential injustice, the innate cruelty of life. Later I saw him walking with his head bowed, dragging his bicycle and sobbing: "Where will I be? What will I do?" The grownups were silent. For years each of them had been putting that same question to himself, and now they felt the weight of the moment: someone was asking himself that question for the first time.

I fell asleep after lunch by a wide-open window that faced onto a flower bed. We were in Warsaw. M. had gone to the hairdresser's, and I was waiting for her to return in an apartment that didn't resemble ours. Instead of a window, there was a vast arcade opening up to the sky through which squirrels and blackbirds came into the room. I fed them sitting on the floor. A young woman walked past me wrapped in a white bath towel, her back and legs bare, her hair wet and pushed back. She paid no attention to me as she walked by, but it was clear that she had noticed me. I felt uncomfortable and at that very moment realized I was dreaming. Of course, I had fallen asleep during a boring film at the Wars cinema, where I had decided to spend the time waiting for M. I awoke suddenly, with my head resting against the shoulder of a heavily perfumed old woman who was sitting beside me. Apologizing to her, I awoke again, but this time for real, for M. has come into the room saying that a new politburo had been selected at the party congress. The smell of damp grass floated in through the open window. It took me quite a while to leave that dream behind. I kept remembering details: the stale bread I had been feeding the birds on the floor, the fragrant lace shawl of the woman beside me in the theater. The squirrels had been no larger than field mice and had silvery tails, and I knew that the woman in the bath towel was a Russian (from a Bunin story I had been reading the day before).

Before lunch, I had walked down a treelined path in the park. There had been something soothing about my dream that accorded with the old trees and the whisper of light rain. I had felt a sudden fondness for nature, for its changes, and for the calm way it abided. It occurred to me that it would be wisest to live in a big family house full of children, aunts, and animals, amid conversation and meals taken together at the table. Perhaps houses of that sort still exist in the American South, but there are practically none left in Europe. Life brings death with it, and in time this park will vanish and something I cannot imagine will arise in its place. That, however, does not disturb me, because death also brings life with it. I thought of the lovely, ancient phrase that death is sleep's brother. It would sound better in Polish—sleep's sister.

■ *A U G U S T*
1 9 8 1

In Warsaw, toward the end of July, I noted down three types of rumors, three auguries.

The first prophecy concerns a lightning military and police action. The government declares martial law and 70,000 people are arrested in one night by specially trained Security squads. Rumor has given this action the name Operation Tent (I don't know why) and has it that the special squads are already billeted in Warsaw.

The second prognosis foresees a gradual infiltration and erosion of the independent union movement concomitant with the buildup of economic difficulties. And so, increasingly fewer goods on the market, increasing political tensions, conflicts, and splits within the opposition, the weariness of society. Finally, people will want peace and order. The stick will triumph, and everything will return to its proper place.

The third prophecy is optimistic. It defines the events in Poland as "the longest of the nation's uprisings," one that will lead to lasting change. The reform of the sociopolitical model will filter into other countries in the bloc, and the Soviet Union itself will be faced with the need to reform. During those transformations Poland will be independent for a third time.

It is also possible to imagine that the three auguries mentioned above are not mutually exclusive and that each of them could come true at some point.

I stood in line twenty minutes for bread and succeeded in buying half of the last loaf. I waited an hour and a half for gas in a long line of cars. In both cases the lines advanced efficiently.

Striking discipline, not a single quarrel. M. returned excited from the store this morning and said, "I got some rolls. A very interesting line today." Before leaving for Sopot, I saw Wajda's film *Man of Iron.* Now I am reading Friedenthal's monograph on Goethe, Orieux's on Voltaire, and Stendhal's *Charterhouse of Parma.*

There are generals in the government now. Throughout the country, marches and demonstrations protesting reductions in food rations. After 40,000 workers marched through the center of Łódź, an automobile demonstration was organized in Warsaw. For two days a great cavalcade of vehicles has been blocking Marszałkowska Street between Dzierżyński Square and the traffic circle. Further strikes have been announced. It is exceedingly difficult to isolate oneself in thought or writing from all that is happening here. The events of the day become one's inner life.

At the same time, I observe a certain constriction in private life. Everything—daily affairs, home, personal life, conversation—is absorbed by the stream of collective events. A single drama is occurring, a single story, and there is no room for individual experience. Even suicides have to be seen in a social, public context. A well-known doctor hanged himself from a tree in Konstancin, incurable cancer the probable motive. No credence is given to that explanation, however; shortly before the doctor's suicide, two former ministers had hanged themselves, and so the prevailing opinion is that the doctor was "involved in the affair." Everything, birth and death included, has been requisitioned as social and national material. Birth too fits into that picture—the shortage of vitamins for infants.

> On 15 May 1796, General Bonaparte made his entry into Milan at the head of that youthful army which but a short time before had crossed the Bridge of Lodi, and taught the world that after so many centuries Caesar and Alexander had a successor.

The miracles of gallantry and genius that Italy had been witness of in the space of a few months aroused a slumbering people. Only a week before the arrival of the French, the Milanese still regarded them as a horde of brigands, accustomed invariably to flee before the troops of His Imperial and Royal Majesty. That, at least, was what was reported to them three times weekly by a little news-sheet no larger than a man's hand and printed on grimy paper.

In the Middle Ages the republicans of Lombardy had given proof of a valour equal to that of the French, and had deserved to see their city razed to the ground by the German Emperors. Ever since they had become *loyal subjects* their main business had been the printing of sonnets upon little handkerchiefs of rose-coloured taffeta on the occasion of the marriage of some young lady belonging to a rich or a noble family. Two or three years after that great event in her life, this young lady would select a *cavaliere servente:* the name of the *cicisbeo* chosen by her husband's family sometimes occupied an honourable place in the marriage contract. It was a far cry from such effeminate manners to the deep emotions aroused by the unexpected arrival of the French army. Very soon a new and passionate standard of manners sprang into being. A whole nation became aware, on 15 May 1796, that everything it had respected up till then was supremely ridiculous and on occasion hateful. The departure of the last Austrian regiment marked the collapse of the old ideas; to risk one's life became the fashion. People saw that, in order to be happy after centuries of insipid sensations, they needs must love their country with genuine affection and seek to perform heroic actions. They had been plunged in darkest night by the continuation of the jealous despotism of Charles V and Philip II; they overturned these despots' statues and immediately found themselves flooded with light.

I have copied out the first page of *The Charterhouse of Parma*. The exposition continues in a similar style for another five pages before the actual plot of the novel begins.

I picked up the book after my return from Berlin and was amazed by it. What a way to begin a novel—with historical dates! Unheard of. If today an author were to open his novel with trivia of this sort, the critics would call him a boor or a fool. Today, as a rule, literary criticism dislikes particulars and simply cannot abide historical particulars. Prose, stories, novels, fine, but they should occur in a temporal and spatial nowhere, or at least in a nonexistent Hapsburg monarchy. Then they can be self-respecting. History is discredited, a "mixture of errors and violence" that does not lend itself to art. Let us leave history to politicians and journalists.

In the end, even that is understandable. In our times people feel that history is a sort of misfortune. It is seen either as demonic degeneration or a collection of insipid dirty tricks. I once wrote about a generation "impaled by history" and was thinking of myself as well. Let us speak more boldly here: it was we who impaled ourselves on history, searching for progress in it, or, in other words, the fulfillment of our own desires. It turned out that we had to go on paying for years for having signed that contract.

All right, but why did I read the opening pages of *The Charterhouse of Parma* with such delight? What caused that shudder of admiration from the very first words? "On 15 May 1796, General Bonaparte made his entry into Milan at the head of that youthful army which but a short time before had crossed the Bridge of Lodi . . ." What rhythm! You can hear the sound of drums in that line. But it is not only a matter of rhythm here. Those lines arouse a nostalgia for the literature and the times when history could be an adventure. And what astonishing times those were! To set out on a historical adventure, to breathe in the smell of blood, politics, and gunpowder, to cross half of Europe in the saddle, and then later to dismount, hop down, and spend the rest of your life in some quiet little town. And there to be able to think about it all, to write. Without any shame that you were inserting vulgar particulars—facts, places, dates—into artistic material. In 1840 Stendhal wrote from Civitavecchia to Mademoiselle Eugénie de Montijo, the future empress of France: "I personally thank God that I entered Berlin on October 26, 1806, with my pistols carefully loaded and powder already in the pan. To enter the city, Napoleon wore the full dress uniform of a division general. I think that was the only time I ever saw him in full dress. He rode twenty paces ahead of his soldiers. The silent crowd was scarcely two paces from his horse. He could have been killed by a rifle shot from any window."

How much fascination and pride there is in that reminiscence. That is how one writes of a great adventure or a youthful love. And in Stendhal's life the two were felicitously united: he loved Napoleon. He also said that he loved two or three women, and it probably seemed that way to him since it was precisely those two or three he was unable to conquer. Of Napoleon he wrote: the man whom I loved. That sounds especially eloquent coming from an ironic man.

Adventures with history—Cervantes's adventure, Stendhal's adventure, Byron's fatal adventure. But what about us? Isn't it just the other way around for us? Two years after Stendhal saw him in Berlin, Napoleon was trying to convince Goethe that politics is fate. He anticipated our condition. The Greek tragedy of destiny has left the world stage. History and politics will become fate in modern times; they will be the tragic force. The suspicion that it is we who have been chosen by those insatiable monsters for their adventures, that history is their adventure with us and we are only the playthings of history—that suspicion intrudes itself and seems increasingly probable.

I think, is there no end to this? I cannot rid myself of the feeling that I have been taken in and still am being taken in. I'd like to get off and take a rest. Where? In some quiet dignified town in the provinces. But I ask, How is that done? Where do I find it? In myself? To build a little provincial town in myself, to live there apart from the turmoil of words and events, to withdraw, not listen to the radio, to read, prepare myself . . . And die of boredom. "I'm dying of boredom," Stendhal wrote in a letter from a small Italian town, "and no one has done me any wrong, which only makes matters worse."

In the evening in the television room you hear "economic disaster." In the afternoon a hydrofoil arrives at the pier and from inside comes a radio commentator's baritone voice saying "economic disaster." In the morning M. turns on the transistor radio. I awake to the words "economic disaster." It's the same with the headlines in the papers, the same in the speeches of premiers, the deputies to the Sejm, the party bosses. Near the entrance to the pier someone has written across the entire width of the sidewalk: "Today the fish, tomorrow us." Ulcerous eels have been caught. The beaches are empty; signs warn people not to swim or to lie on the sand. The previous government allowed the waters of the bay to be polluted. An ecological disaster. Ecological disaster, economic disaster, social disaster. And the present government is warning us of a national disaster. Yesterday I saw eighty-year-old Mieczysław Fogg go running out of the television room: "It's a nightmare! I can't listen to it!" The announcers alternate between two tones of voice: the crowing of the citizen and the snarl of the policeman. Not only their voices but the expressions on their faces change, from a look of plaintive concern to lockjaw.

In the afternoon the pier is full of men and women sunbathing. In the evening those suntanned people will hear on television of the complete collapse of the market and learn that there will be a coal shortage in the winter. The next day they run out to shop. The stores are empty. There is not a single piece of cake, not a single apple, to be bought. What is available are little hand mirrors with carved frames. "This can make people neurotic," says M. "Women have an archetypal need to buy things; for them there is something otherworldly about an empty store.

Shopping always connects them to life. Now the stores are as frightening as graves. I bought myself a little mirror."

The catastrophe is not yet entirely real. It is present in your words and thoughts; you can feel it in the air, but there are no scenes of collective despair and the promenading crowds seem carefree enough. There has just been a decrease in Western tourists. You don't see many cars with foreign plates. A paradise for Arabs, who are everywhere, and even Turks from West Berlin pull up in front of the Grand Hotel in secondhand limousines. On the whole, things are jolly enough, and the young ladies who are paid in hard currency have no cause for complaint. There are many things that continue to amaze Western correspondents. In Warsaw they filmed the auto barricade held at the traffic circle to protest the shortage of food. Order was kept by a well-organized worker-guard from Solidarity. The vehicles were heaped with flowers, and the demonstration was accompanied by artistic performances, which drew enthusiastic applause from people who had gathered on the streets and sidewalks. "Hunger threatens Poland," foreign correspondents have been reporting, asking in their commentaries, "Do Poles laugh and applaud in any situation?" Goethe saw gravity and levity as the dual foundation of life (I am still reading Friedenthal's monograph), and their interdependence among Poles is clearly more complex than anywhere else.

The government has found itself in a most strange position. The "people," who had before existed in name only, are now going out into the streets. For thirty years the government has been boasting that socialism has brought the people to the center of the city. But that's one thing, and quite another when the *people* go out into the streets. The government knows that the moment free elections are announced, it would cease to exist overnight, and it does not find that very encouraging. The government says that production is falling; it's your fault; you're pushing the country toward a national disaster. It says that after it has itself pushed the country toward disaster for ten years now. A decline in production is fatal evidence against any government: it indicates a poor economy and a lack of social confidence. The populace feels that the present government is a continuation of the one that brought the country to economic ruin. People work poorly under such a government. There are two possible solutions: either carry out swift and profound reforms or leave office. Neither of these two solutions is likely, since governments are not inclined to commit suicide. And so we say, A stalemate. At the worst moments one finds new definitions to prove one is an educated person.

Despite appearances, Poles have a good deal of common sense. The populace understands the country's political situation and its dependence on its good neighbor. No one expects a decision from the authorities that is beyond their means. The government would cause less ill will if it lied less and used spokesmen who were less compromised. Instead, it addresses society via television commentators who have grown either gray or bald in long years of service. The same commentators who in 1968 declared day after day that Poland's main enemy was Zionism, who in 1972 proclaimed an era of prosperity, and who in 1976 went after the workers who had been arrested, today furiously accuse Solidarity of damaging the nation and the state. They have been joined by the weekly columnists. Seeing and hearing all this, anyone who's awake has to think the government does not wish to be straightforward, that it continues to practice deception and uses the same mouthpieces to do it. If it is incapable of telling the truth, it should at least not malign what is true and should change its method and style; since there are shortages of cigarettes and meat, we can safely have a shortage of propaganda as well.

On the cover of a Western magazine, a bear wearing glasses and a cap with a red star is peering at the map of Europe and pointing its furry paw at Poland, grumbling with surprise, "Really now, what kind of country is this . . ." Eight months ago, the cover of that same weekly had a Soviet tank crushing a white eagle. Now the editors publish an article illustrated with maps: Poland's territory sliced away over the course of two hundred years, a diminishing territory that gradually vanished only to reappear for a while to vanish again, and so on. "A nation that cannot be broken" say other articles in other magazines. "The eternal, unbroken spirit of rebellion." The correspondents are racking their brains to figure out what the bear will do with this odd country.

And what will the bear do? No one knows. How can one know what the bear will do? Perhaps the bear itself doesn't know. These are unforeseen circumstances for the bear as well. This makes the government here feel still more uncertain and it blares all its trumpets, to threaten and intimidate. How many thousands of voices shout from radio and television—100,000, 200,-000, 500,000? How many millions of people hear them—10, 15, 20?

Solidarity has 10 million members in the cities and 3.5 million in the countryside. Even if one had to reduce that number by some amount, there will still remain millions of organized members in the movement, who know that the government is either too incompetent or lacks the goodwill to introduce democratic reforms and, at the same time, who know that the bear has spread the map of Europe out before it and is taking a close look at Poland.

Propaganda pours down on that double awareness. All arguments are mobilized; on television you hear about confrontation, bloodshed, the loss of independence. The public is under fire from the trenches. One side uses television as a weapon, with officers relaying dispatches and on-screen orders. The public understands less and less of what is going on all the time and is becoming afraid. That is the point of the operation—to turn society into a public that is afraid and does not understand what's what.

I met S. on Monte Cassino Street. Approaching me with an expression of both delight and good-natured resourcefulness, he announced that a while back, after standing in line for more than an hour, he managed to buy some thread. Before that, he had waited an hour in front of the paper-goods store, but to no avail; there wasn't a single roll of toilet paper left. Then, on his way back, he had spotted the line in front of the dry-goods store and asked people what they were waiting for. Thread. Now he was on his way home, a conquering hero.

Every grownup must come to terms with the prospect that he will cease to be. Now, however, for the first time, I see a new kind of phenomenon—society fearing the end of its own life as a society. For some time now, nightmares have been troubling society's unconscious. Everyone is afraid, afraid to think about the void that threatens them. For the first time in my life I feel a fear that is more than personal, fear on a national scale. Yesterday the government announced that it was withdrawing a few dozen trains from service and that production has declined as much as fifty percent in certain branches of the industry. After this bulletin, there was a deadly silence in the television room. You could feel the fear in the air—the fear of collective death. When, a moment later, there was news about this year's auspicious harvest, everyone breathed a sigh of hope. Some factory had produced 60,000 scythes for farmers instead of the machinery they lacked. Scythes! Now at least a little light is being shed on the matter. Scythes, sickles, flails. To secure food from the earth with one's own hands as in the days of old, perhaps that is more dependable than being in the forefront of steel production. "You should find yourself some village for the winter," I was advised by the far-sighted Tadeusz Konwicki, "some village where there are still huts with wood-burning stoves."

When bicycles were delivered to a sporting-goods store, the line surged forward and broke the door down. Two saleswomen were beaten; the waiting list was torn out of someone's hands, and a woman crumpled it up and swallowed it. We're not breaking down doors yet. On Sunday, at the Bruners' house, I had to exercise moderation at the sight of the homemade tea biscuits and jam. I think it's the first time since the war that I have not eaten my fill. A friend whom we used to meet at the Golden Hive offered me an American cigarette the other day. I took it, thanked him, and then caught a furtive gleam of exasperation in his eyes. You have to be on your toes now to check certain automatic gestures and habits. I should not have accepted that cigarette.

Walking along the edge of the beach, we approached an older man with a pointer on a leash. A moment before, the pointer had been attacked by a large terrier and was now trembling mutely, a doleful look in its yellow eyes. Its master, a sturdy, solid-looking red-faced man, turned to M., who was tenderly calming the dog, and with a smile that revealed his false teeth said that next time he would settle the score with that terrier in his own way. "I've already taught one mongrel a lesson. It knocked my dog down and bit him too. I picked up a pole that was lying by a boat and clubbed it to death." "Sir!" cried M. "You're crazy!" "What? . . . What?" he stammered. M. was pale with fury. "You did no such thing; but even to think up such nonsense is disgusting."

■ S E P T E M B E R
1 9 8 1

Responsibility. I will be responsible for the worst that can happen, since it will have been caused by a political system that I at one time accepted. I have borne that knowledge within me for twenty-odd years. And it is of no great importance whether I might be able to elucidate psychologically what motivated me then or even whether I would want to. What is important is that one cannot cast off the responsibility for those years and that one's later actions do not set one free from it. Only the simplistic interpretations and the incorrect beliefs can be repudiated, but the error allows for no deletion. It casts its shadow back onto the past and one lives with that shadow. I foresee society becoming more acutely aware that the evil of those years is the source and the beginning of the evils that now exist. And then that shadow will grow longer.

Phantoms of the street. When you read about the growing economic problems, it is difficult to picture the reality behind the words. But they are connected with scenes and images more easily spotted in my district than elsewhere because there are no autos here and the streets are narrow. All that is infirm and unwell comes crawling out. I see women barely able to walk on their swollen legs, resigned old men with fearful eyes. Many helpless people look as if they have been dragged out of bed. Sometimes these images of misfortune are accompanied by a street band—five men with purplish noses. Yesterday they were playing "Tango Milonga" on Piwna Street as a gray-haired, half-paralyzed old man made his way down the middle of the street on metal crutches, slippers on his feet and a wreath of ten rolls of toilet paper around his neck. He moved slowly away from a garrulous line in front of the paper-goods store. The lines have gutted the district, bared the innards of the houses.

It's still warm now, but it will be snowing in two months. In the afternoon, whistling and howling, country hippies with long, matted hair and dirty headbands go running down Świętojańska Street. I feel sorriest of all for the old people, myself included. At night especially I think that all this is happening on some wayward star, while nearby, on the other planets, life goes on normally.

The future. It used to be natural and appropriate to have some outline of the immediate future before one, to be able to make a rough definition of it and to live by that sketchy idea. I repeat, this is an ordinary thing, something due everyone. Now that no longer pertains. Every thought about the future is immediately twisted into a question mark. Not a question mark signifying the inherent uncertainty of fate but a sign of our suspension before a menacing possibility that is known and horrible. As a result, that small margin of future time with which we are accustomed to living now seems like a maharajah's luxury. I cannot think that I will finish my book in January or that I will go to Konstancin for Christmas because that smacks of impudence; it would be letting myself go too far. And so I watch myself, setting only the shortest of deadlines; for example, "On Thursday I will go to the market." There is something superstitious about this reduction in perspective, this curtailment of goals. We walk around scared by our double-barreled mortality—by a date dictated by nature and by another that seems predicted for October or December (before I finish my book).

It would seem that relations between people ought to become closer in times like these. Not necessarily. I often retire from the world for days on end and don't reach for the phone when it rings. I am not cutting myself off from people because there is so much that separates us but, on the contrary, because there is too much that connects us. What's new with you? I know, same as with me. Excessive similarity reduces mutual curiosity. Then later I come to my senses and start dialing my friends' numbers again and again, and find none of them home.

Trips. At the Writers' Club people were talking about the scenes taking place in front of the German Consulate on Saska Kępa. People wait all night long to submit their applications for visas to West Germany. Young people predominate in the crowd besieging the building; the number of those on the waiting list runs to four figures. Tickets on foreign airlines have been sold out for many months in advance. In a period of six weeks, four Polish flights have been hijacked to West Berlin, where the hijackers asked for asylum. Around 200,000 people are said to have emigrated this year. Trips seem increasingly like escapes, and one involuntarily thinks of the people who left Poland in 1939 and 1945. And 1968 too. The Polish diaspora is growing larger. Periodically it becomes necessary to slip away from here, as from a trap, to flee the fear and hopelessness. The other day, on my way back from the garage, I walked past two young people, two tall silhouettes against the dark. I heard a snatch of their conversation, a monologue really: "No, old man, now I know for sure that I'm getting out of here. I just need a little time. You see, I'll be turning twenty-six in a month and I've got investments of sorts here. I'll tell you, I even liked it here. I had some all right buddies and a girl, two girls. They both loved me. And I loved them too in a way. You could go mountain climbing or go out boating on the lakes. It was pretty great. And it's not that I don't have a job either. So I just can't be a brute about it and tear it all off in one pull—you see what I mean—I have to sort of untie things."

A dream I remember: I have strangled Goebbels, a cripple, in the Hotel Europejski. He had come to Warsaw incognito at a time difficult to determine—possibly before the war, possibly after. M. and I tossed him wrapped in a raincoat into the Vistula and then returned through a forest. On the way back I said, "We have to take care of everything together!"

We were surprised that we were so calm even though they would no doubt come for us tomorrow. M. said, "Because you never fully believe it can happen."

■ OCTOBER
1981

So as not to paint a one-sided picture, I should mention that the movie theaters and cafés are full, that it's no easy matter to get an appointment with the fashionable hairdressers, and that the people strolling through the Saxon Gardens are feeding the wild ducks by the pond.

The last days of September were beautiful. On warm Saturday evenings Mercedes would pull up to the Rycerska Restaurant with flowers on their hoods; as the newlyweds (white veils, bow ties) got out of the car, they would be greeted at the restaurant's entrance by accordionists playing Mendelssohn's *Wedding March*. The entire city is performing feats of magic to stay alive. Everything must be the way it was before, as if nothing had happened, as if nothing bad could have happened. At times this seems a matter of pure form, of maintaining life's outward pattern. Perhaps audiences would fill the movie theaters even if no films were being shown, people in the park would still make gestures as if throwing crumbs, and newlyweds would pull up in front of nonexistent restaurants. All this gives an impression of something between an agreement to hang on and a struggle for continuity. And there is nostalgia here too, a yearning for a normal, everyday human life. Thirty-six years ago people were returning to this city on foot, to take up residence in houses that no longer existed.

In an issue of *Krytyka* (Criticism) I read an interesting account of a conversation between the editors and a French intellectual, Jacques Julliard. In discussing the intellectual left's attitude toward Marxism, Julliard said, "Totalitarian systems enjoy sympathy and recognition from intellectuals as long as they [that is, those systems] have nerve enough to cover up their tremendous idiocies with a show of self-confidence. All the intellectuals' unwavering certainty disappears at the first sign that those systems have begun to doubt themselves, for example, Khrushchev's speech. The path Sartre took is characteristic and symbolic here."

The intellectuals' unwavering certainty . . . But, on the whole, do intellectuals have any certainty in political affairs? It would be better to say that theirs is a shaky certainty and is, at bottom, a cover-up for their profound uncertainty. Politicians have unwavering certainty. For intellectuals, nonpolitical arguments are the most important thing, and that explains the shock they experienced after Khrushchev's speech. They learned of the acts committed by the world's first Socialist state from the most reliable of sources—one of the culprits. There was no sign of uncertainty in Khrushchev's speech: he provided information about facts that left-wing intellectuals in the West had refused for many years to believe, considering them right-wing fabrications. At the Twentieth Party Congress, these facts were confirmed by the Moscow politburo. The intellectuals were faced with a choice: either to continue to view the USSR as the first land of socialism or to admit that the idea of Socialist justice had been brought to ruin there. There may have been a third possibility: to renounce socialism as a reality and reconcile oneself to the fact that its value is that of a utopian myth. Such choices and acts of self-definition were made by intellectuals in the years that followed (and not only in the West).

The politicians did not lose either their nerve or their self-assurance, which is quite understandable, for they realize that politics has precious little to do with making myths come true and that the widespread belief that a bureaucratic police state can fulfill mankind's moral ideals is one of history's jokes, taken seriously by poets. So very seriously that, while it was still possible to do so, they denied the existence of concentration camps in the USSR and the violation of law in the other countries of the bloc. "I have too much to handle with innocent people who cry out about their innocence to be able to concern myself with the guilty who have admitted their guilt." So wrote the French poet Paul Eluard, whose spiritual purity was beyond doubt, after the death sentences were passed in Prague.

It would be superficial to explain this as opportunism or fear. Was it opportunism or fear that during the war prevented the English and Americans from believing in the existence of Hitler's death camps despite the evidence that had been presented? Probably the turning point does not come when a totalitarian state begins to doubt itself (if it is capable of doubt) but through an earlier collective process of psychological communication. At a certain moment, there occur simultaneous crystallizations of a new consciousness. Khrushchev's speech was a shock for many people, not because it destroyed their unwavering certainty but because it released the uncertainty they had repressed. The fears and scruples that until then had been kept beneath the threshold of consciousness were thrust to the surface by the fact of the crimes and the number of victims. It was a shock of a moral nature.

Politicians react differently. In March 1956 I had the opportunity to observe their reactions at close range. I was in Krynica, in one of the Ministry of Health's sanatoriums, when a few members of the Central Committee arrived from Warsaw with the text of Khrushchev's speech, which had been distributed to the plenum. The text had not been translated from Russian yet. In the dining room some of the party leaders whose Russian was poor asked their colleagues for a precise translation of those segments that at first glance had seemed beyond belief to them. I could see them go rigid. Later on I caught snatches of their conversations. Observing those people, I was certain, however, that it was not the fact of the crimes that caused them dread but only the fact of their disclosure. I was certain that had Khrushchev been overthrown the next day and his speech disowned as a licentious attempt to slander the Land of the Soviets, those same party men would have regained their peace of mind, even though the crimes would have remained crimes. They had been briefly seized by doubt, but not about themselves or because of any moral shock. They doubted whether the system's mechanism was still functioning. As long as it continued to function, any crime could be justified dialectically.

There are some sketchy plans for a winter trip in connection with an invitation to New York. It's a long journey, and I resist the idea. I quarrel with M., who says that it is precisely such surprises that make life worth living. I reply, "Life is only worth living because you were born and for no other reason." She didn't answer. That evening over tea she asked me if that is what I really think.

Monday. In line in the dark for three hours at a gas station on Aleja Sobieski. Five cars ahead of me, in a Fiat, Ch., an old friend from the university. He gets in beside me and we talk, smoking our rationed cigarettes. Each time the line moves forward, Ch. hops out and runs to push his Fiat forward. Then he comes back and sits with me again. In his opinion there will be no Soviet military intervention; a different decision has been made. People with special instructions have been placed at key points in the state administration; they have been assigned to undo things wherever there is any sign of reform and at whatever point progress is being made. These types can't be budged, says Ch.; a system of sabotage has been built into the machinery of state. He assured me that one such character occupies an executive position in the institution where he works (in the communications department). Then we talk about Wałęsa. Ch. takes a sober view: without Wałęsa, Solidarity would fall apart immediately. Wałęsa himself (Ch. calls him Lech) is a man with dictatorial ambitions, primitive, but with the instincts of a realist. He does not want to listen to the intellectuals; he's trying to make it through on common sense now, lying low before making the next leap. I reply that in my opinion Wałęsa still incarnates the spirit of the street and is the hero of the lines. I would characterize him as part king, part holy fool, and with that moustache, which looks painted on, he reminds me of something from a folk puppet show. Then we talk about the war, the occupation, saying that they were endurable only because of a faith in their just conclusion, a faith that does not exist today. The hardest thing for people to bear is the fear of a future that appears as a formless gloom. The gas-station attendants in their light-blue uniforms move silently around the pumps, their gestures automated like those of robots, their eyes seemingly blind, expressionless. The next morning I thought, It is not profound unhappiness or some great pain that I dread, for then you often fall into a kind of half-sleep—I am only frightened by the necessities they entail, going to the post office, filling out forms, and it is those little nightmares superimposed onto true calamity that make your hair stand on end. In adversity a person becomes numb and turns into a pillar of salt. And that pillar of salt is supposed to fill out forms at the post office!

Tuesday. There are rumors afoot that Poland's western borders are in danger of being reviewed. What this means, neither more nor less, is if you don't calm down, we'll let the Germans bite off your right hand . . .

I am no longer actually writing, only taking notes. In this siege-like situation it is beyond me to tackle any large theme. It's cold in the apartment. M. has more and more difficulty obtaining food. Six-hour lines. Some start forming at five o'clock in the morning. If the dismal predictions for this winter prove correct, we will be a ghetto in the heart of Europe. Parallels with the Warsaw Ghetto are multiplying: there too there were restaurants and cabarets, and the appearance of normal life was preserved amid the poverty and the despair in that trap. I observe signs of fear when I eat lunch at the Writers' Club, including some that are distasteful. Yesterday J. began accusing Solidarity of black-mailing the people and the government. He was pale as a ghost; his hands were trembling. I said, "After all, it is the people who are putting up the resistance, take a broader view; you're missing the big picture." He had probably been somewhere, talked with someone, and let himself become frightened. Women have the gift of charmingly turning their weariness into an acerbic War-saw quip. When Marian came unexpectedly to lunch and an-nounced that in spite of everything a splendid thing was happening, Tadeusz Konwicki's wife exclaimed, "I just hope I survive the splendor!" If I make associations with the Warsaw Ghetto, it is because I am also thinking of the deeper kinship be-tween the histories of the Jews and the Poles. Small, stubborn Judea with its God who tested it so cruelly, a crazy nation that would not kneel down before the superpowers. Its misfortune was accelerated by groups of youths who pelted the Roman cohorts with stones at the gates of the city.

Lunches at the club are meatless now, and starting tomorrow, they'll stop serving poultry as well. The government representative on the commission concerned with food supply is named Indyk ("turkey"). Construction has been halted on two modern skyscrapers in Warsaw; many factories are idle throughout the country. Stickers have appeared in Łódź that read, "They were building a Second Poland and they built us into a Third World country." We are soaring to the level of the African countries. When musing on the bankruptcy of Gierek's enterprise, I remembered how in the late eighteenth century King Stanisław August and the mighty mythomaniac Tyzenhauz had decided to industrialize the country and forced the peasants in Lithuania into the newly established factories. The factories were soon closed, and after a while, only bare walls remained amid the Lithuanian forests.

Thursday, G., an actor, whom I bumped into on Długa Street, told me of his run-in with a gang of hoodlums, which had walked behind him insulting him with filthy curses; one of them had kicked him. The street was nearly deserted. Seeing what was brewing, G. came to a stop, and surprising himself he said, as he assured me: "Gentlemen, leave me in peace; my little boy died this morning." The gang walked away.

G. has no children.

I am writing in a car in front of the hospital of the Academy of Medicine, on Nowogrodzka Street. Young women doctors come out, and a little later, a group of nurses. They are all well dressed and in high spirits, and a few are strikingly good-looking. There is a sort of unconscious courage about the care they have taken with their outward appearance and style. They remind me of women from the war years, their eyes smiling, making light of danger. Looking at them, I think of birds and how boring life would be without them. I have been waiting nearly an hour now.

M. is having a cardiac checkup; they have to hook her up to an imported device that will register any new spasms. She is fascinated by this new marvel of technology. On the way there, she was nervously excited and bridled when I said I doubted that the device would have an equally marvelous effect on her nerves. We had been quarreling since the morning; I would make a bad psychologist—I improvidently said that the strain of shopping was diverting her attention from her cardiac arrhythmia and that was why she was less obsessed with her body. A great cry of protest!

Saturday. In his column in *Twórczość* (Creative Work), Dedal writes of the early postwar years:

> We were divided into those who could not imagine living in the so-called new society and thought that either it all would end in a new, total cataclysm or that they themselves would perish, and into those who in turn were unable to imagine that Polish life could go on in the form that it had acquired over the centuries, who thought that everything about it had to be changed, the structure of its economy and the soil, the fabric of society, the landscape, the cityscape, the style of culture, the direction of development, the connections with other cultures, the language, customs, moral code ... How did that division occur? Neither along class and generational lines nor along philosophic lines, and in general not because of any reasons or arguments but according to instinct and character. That does not mean that people with less character immediately supported the "new society" and quickly found places for themselves in it and those with more character continued to resist. Or that the more stupid ones went chasing after propaganda slogans while wiser heads resisted. No, not all. On the contrary. In all fields the people who stood out because of their intelligence, vitality, and receptivity

opted for the new: they were attracted by it and were reaching for an opportunity to act and show what they could do. They made for a minority, but one active to about the same degree as is usually the case when various milieus and social groups divide into the active and those who wait and see. And thus the entire society had undergone a profound division into a minority that had an articulated world view, political representation, areas in which to operate, and the chance to advance and succeed, and an impotent majority that had nothing.

The above is especially worthy of esteem, since Dedal has no personal reasons for stating this not too well-known side of things.

Now the divisions are different—one great, principal division separates society from the authorities. And within society itself?

Good things and bad things happen in this society, as they do everywhere. The old division between the country and the city is now more explicit and painful. It is a peculiar love the peasants have for their fatherland, a love that allows them to look with indifference upon city people racked by food shortages. It is said that out in the country people have everything. Everything is for sale—but only to their own and among themselves. In the press and on television, terrified asses are braying about the need to send children and old people out to the country before winter approaches. To the country! Who would take care of them there, who would feed them, and what would the price be? Let's not deify the "people"; there are dark forces and feelings in them too. Someone threw stones at the windows of a rebuilt Warsaw synagogue, breaking them. Konwicki, who is shooting scenes for his film there, returned pale: "There are people living right next door and no one tried to stop it. How can that be? A country that is proud of its Polish Pope and wants to be on a first name basis with God is, after all, obliged . . ." Someone else says that apparently anti-Semitic moods are also making their way into Solidarity. Given the similarities in the fates of the Poles and the Jews, which are so apparent to me, this seems particularly unbelievable. You leave such conversations with a feeling that the rug has been pulled out from under your feet.

Words and deeds are infectious. A person often hesitates between his own sense of what is wrong and its justification by others. Naturally, frequently the way other people act constitutes a standard. That does not mean that such a person is amoral; it only means that a certain number of people who act in one definite way become a moral norm for him. When we cannot understand our past behavior, the explanation often proves to be astonishingly simple: we did what others were doing. I have observed this both in the way many men behave with women and in professional or political affairs.

Monday. Yesterday afternoon we were at JMR's. Later on we drove Ewa back to the theater. On the evening news, a report that the party has a new first secretary. In a plenary resolution, a promise of open conflict with Solidarity, and again this smacks of a state of emergency. For first secretary they have elected the Premier and the Minister of Defense, General Jaruzelski, who has been sporting dark glasses since the August strikes.

Tuesday. On Świętojerska Street a conversation with the man I share a garage with. Graying, wearing a suede jacket, he owns a Volvo and a summer house on the Pilica River. He said softly to me, "I don't understand anything anymore. They keep changing premiers and secretaries, but I'm still eating potato pancakes all the time."

Reading Paul Claudel's *Diaries*, I think about the paucity of French literature today. The French haven't had a truly outstanding writer for many years now. The same is true in film. They lack the great collective experiences that reach people's inner depths. Their last experience of that sort was World War I, and after that carnage they had had enough blood to last them a quarter of a century. World War II did not plow through as deeply as World War I had. And later their social body was not subjected to the sort of shock Poland knew from war and communism, and America experienced with its black problem and Vietnam. Something is shifting in Europe. Perhaps countries like Poland, Yugoslavia, Spain, and Hungary, which—each in its own way but all intensely—went through fascism and communism, will become Europe's new center of experience. Perhaps today in Poland, amid the spasms and desperate struggles, future forms of community life are being born, forms that at some point the West will need.

Wednesday. Visa formalities at the American Consulate. Around four o'clock in the afternoon, on the way to see Truffaut's *Adèle H.,* we were caught by crowds hurrying to the bus stops. At rush hour, the cars entering and leaving Miodowa Street made sharp screeching turns, people dashed through clouds of exhaust, shouting and slipping nervily between the closely packed cars. You could hear laughter. There were also crowds of people flowing toward the buses from the churches on the other side of the street. One could think this some enormous group excursion hastily leaving the city. Everything was outlined distinctly against the dull air; the street swarmed with little silhouettes performing movements that seemed identical, somehow coordinated. Yet despite that, the feeling was far from depressing. I was struck by a sense of rapid, intelligent vitality and connectedness, the passing faces flushed with laughter or exertion. Life's incredible will. On the way back after the film, things looked different. The streets were nearly dark; the damp road reflected the weak gleam of streetlights, a haze through which people's glances slip with a mysterious ambiguity. A motionless line of figures stood waiting for taxis on the square by the column; a few solitary pedestrians were moving about. There is something disquieting about the way things quiet and slow down; there are some unseen relationships, something cozy and singular concealed in that darkness. Two pot-bellied drunks, their threadbare coats unbuttoned, stagger down the sidewalk. I catch a scrap of their dialogue.

"And did you ever have any backbone?"

"Leave me alone, Zdziś, I can't remember . . ."

Those two have no secrets from each other.

An old woman whom I helped descend a flight of winding stairs at the post office said to me with a smile, "I'm an old woman. I once had a sister and a fiancé, but that was long ago."

New strikes have been called after the incidents in Katowice and Wrocław, where the police broke up the crowds. An instance of the proverbial vicious cycle: the government's poor policies bring the country to ruin—the strikes are a protest against that—and the strikes make matters worse. How to break that cycle? In many parts of the country, conflicts have broken out between management and the workers that are becoming more and more tense, volatile situations that neither the government nor the leaders of Solidarity seem able to control. In recent days I have been hearing the situation described in ways that are unprecedented in my circle—"the social fabric is decaying," "a no-exit situation," "collective national suicide." Someone has also said, "Poland is the first country where communism broke down because Poles have the least unfree society." Rivers of blather pour from the newspapers and television. A certain minister has recommended that people seal their windows with straw and moss to prevent heat loss; after the evening news on television, professors with the faces of psychopaths deliver informal talks on civics. Some journalists are specializing in stories about the rise of barbarism in society. One such incident has been on my mind for several days now. On a street in a Poznań suburb, a man out walking minding his own business was kicked black and blue and then beaten to death in front of his wife and two young children. Killed by a group of young men while a fair-sized crowd of onlookers watched. No one attempted to come to his aid. He could have been saved by one man in whom the reflex to help another had gone into operation before the instinct of self-preservation took over. This man might not have succeeded in preventing the killing, but then again he might have. And even if he were to have paid for that effort with his life, something would still have been saved, some remnant of the idea of solidarity among people. There was no such person in that random collection of people. Or perhaps there were several, and they were just not brave enough to agree to act—that's always the hardest part. The idea that someone can be murdered before a group of onlookers is abominable, difficult to bear. Fifty years ago his chances of being saved by someone would have been greater. The police were less occupied with political affairs and were better at keeping order. Besides, in an incident like this there would practically always be someone present with a sense of social responsibility—a teacher, a doctor, a lawyer, someone who would act like a citizen and do what was right. Not to mention that at that time, the ethical imperative to defend the weak was still widely felt by people. Now the conviction that the weak must lose out is more deeply rooted. There are signs that people are becoming habituated to horror. We are daily spectators of cruelty—executions, murders, terrorist actions—and drinking tea in front of the television, we behold the massacres of the innocents, bodies in flaming cars, the victims of typhoons and earthquakes. Formerly people read about such things, and print created a sense of distance and abstraction. Television and film have abrogated that abstraction, at the same time blunting our sensitivity. As a result, the sight of a person being slaughtered on the street ceases to be shocking; the scene is viewed as if it were happening on screen. And what do we really know about the silence of the crowd watching someone else's suffering. At bottom, its behavior was akin to the way whole societies have acted for decades at a time. Faced with overwhelming violence and force, mankind has conceived of no safer response than silence and observation. Then the only solutions—the only outs—are psychological ones: force gives rise to manifold combinations of assumed attitudes, masks, games, lies. The road to degeneration and perversion. In reconciling oneself to violence, one may feign ethics and rationalism. And cynicism as well. A peculiar sort of "hypocrisy as punishment" arises—punishment for those who still continue to believe in justice. Then one claims that life under the rule of force is neither absolutely evil nor deprived of meaning, whereas all attempts to regain freedom are evil and meaningless. I know such people, ready to smother the voice of protest in themselves and in others. Fear is an opulent fan made of protective coloring. Someone once said to me that the prehistoric monsters, the various antediluvian ichthyosaurs and brontosaurs, did not appreciate or failed to notice the little rodents bustling about on the ground at their feet. They disregarded them. The monsters perished; the rodents survived. Undergoing further mutations, they created the species *Homo sapiens*. Thus we owe our existence to the tolerance displayed by the great reptiles. And who are we in turn disregarding—the mosquitoes perhaps? The flies? Millions of years from now, will the descendants of insects be making large-scale illustrations reconstructing our grotesque forms, those of the two-legged mammals, vertebrates? Will they discover in them any ominous and sublime signs that each of those monsters knew he had to die?

Wednesday. The radiators are already on. The entire center of the city is permeated with the sweetish fragrance of moldering leaves that floats upward from the sidewalks. In the sky a faint sun alternates with a light, warm rain. This was the weather in which a one-hour general warning strike took place. At twelve o'clock the buses and streetcars came to a halt. Polish flags and Solidarity banners were hung on many buildings. Here and there, banners with the word "Strajk." Many bars and kiosks were closed; taxis idled. Police cars patrolled the city. The street corners at the intersection of Marszałkowska and Aleje Jerozolimskie were thick with people staring at the flat, deserted traffic circle as if it were an arena where, in a moment, some action would commence. There were crowds on the sidewalks everywhere. On Castle Square, a line of empty taxis, their hoods turned toward Zygmunt's column. Around one o'clock, in front of the Hotel Europejski's closed café, a line of people stood waiting for the strike to end, while three young people with red and white armbands kept watch on the other side of the glass door. Smiles were exchanged through the glass. At one o'clock on the dot, everything went calmly back into motion.

Friday. Every government is God's deputy on earth. It is no easy matter to hate God for being the cause of human affliction; it is much easier to hate the government in His stead. That is the way things are in many countries that are not badly governed, and it is healthy, since man does not wish to accuse himself but someone else for his misfortunes. And that is why a good government should be bad. Not to the degree where it ruins everything and causes revolts, but so that the citizen can feel superior to it and saddle it with the blame for his fate. The Jews have often played the role of God's deputy on earth. Everywhere there exist people who to this day have not forgiven them. And it is for what those people themselves have suffered at the hand of God that they have not forgiven the Jews. Perhaps it is the Jews themselves who are at fault. They have a mysterious relationship with God, the God who supposedly made a chosen people of them. They are less hypocritical and less inclined to illusions, but at the same time, they have been staggered by injustice once and for all time. Because they represent humanity so drastically, they are so offensive to the eye. I am obviously speaking of the best among them. But in the case of the Jews, it is precisely the best who are hated. There's no point in degrading the lowly: it's the best you have to trample. I always have to stop and think whenever I feel proud that I bear a portion of that people's experience within me. I am not certain that I have that right. Jews who are expert in what it means to be a Jew claim that I am not one.

Saturday. A tape recording of Marian Jurczyk's speech in a furniture factory in Trzebiatów has been broadcast on radio and television. Jurczyk is the chairman of Solidarity in the Szczecin area and was the leader of the August strike in the Szczecin shipyard. We hear Jurczyk's voice saying on tape that the people ruling Poland are traitors to the nation and agents of Moscow. That voice also said that a gallows should be erected to set an example and that three quarters of the party leaders are Jews whose names have been changed.

I had not heard much about Marian Jurczyk before this. I do remember, however, that at the Solidarity congress in Gdańsk, where the chairman of the National Consultation Committee was elected, Jurczyk finished second behind Wałęsa, receiving more than 200 votes. If that tape of his speech is not a fake—as it might be—then at least now I know what goes on inside Jurczyk's head. A person gets up in the morning, eats breakfast, and then suddenly hears news that makes him realize who could have become the leader of an organization, 10 million strong, that is deciding the country's fate.

They don't trust intellectuals. They don't realize that democracy cannot survive without intellectual leadership. It would do them good to study the history of Poland's struggle for independence and freedom. If things go on like this, they will become an enormous body without a head and follow some new Szela* in pursuit of redress for the wrongs done them.

Rain, all the time rain . . . The roofs and sidewalks wet. In front of the stores, lines of people wrapped in waterproof cellophane. Cats are drinking milk again: there's a shortage of certain chemical agents, and as a result, the taste of milk has improved. Industry has had to abandon the production of those food poisons, and cats have breathed a sigh of relief that people have regained their senses.

I should finish the second volume of the *Diary* during January, and that probably means abroad. And what then? I have

---

* The leader of a massive 1846 peasant revolt against the landed gentry.

had a detective story in mind for a long time, which I would call "The Oval Face" and which I would begin more or less like this: "Because my personal needs are modest, because I don't change wives and do not carry money on me, many people consider me a saint. Yes, I reply, I am a saint; it's the cheapest way to live." The narrator would be a man in his early thirties who had been buried alive. The whole thing wouldn't end tragically, however. The day after his funeral, he would return to his wife, whom he had abandoned despite his feelings for her, since in the grave he had by chance unraveled the mystery of their unhappiness.

I don't know if in a couple of months I'll have enough energy to sit down and begin writing again. It's also difficult to foresee what shape events will take in Poland, and it is on them, after all, that the way I live and the conditions for my work depend. I don't even know if I'll have time to write. Last week M. was out shopping for four hours. There was a biting wind that day. She brought back a little cheese, some bread, eggs, and lettuce in a plastic bag. I had been working in my room since the morning. I had a few pages to rewrite and, banging away at my typewriter, had lost track of the time. She came into the room, sat down on the couch without taking off her coat, and burst into tears. I had not seen her so near the verge of collapse since the day I took her to the hospital. Crying, she told me that she had no strength left and that she did not want to come to such a pitiful end. I sat beside her and put my arms around her. I gave her my word that I would help her do the shopping and, if need be, would put off my writing to some other, better time. She calmed down. Straightening her kerchief, which had come loose, she told me that that was not the point. "That's all we need—for you to stop writing. No. It was because of that wind." After lunch, I did the rest of the errands and brought some newspapers home. She began reading *Życie Literackie* (Literary Life). The issue contained an interview with one of the government's press spokesmen, who stated that he had been refused admittance to the party four times, that he did not like people who were only philanderers or only workaholics, and that King Stanisław August had good reason for joining Targowica.* She came into my room laughing and showed me that passage.

■ *N O V E M B E R*
1 9 8 1

The last few weeks before we leave. Rain and strikes, reports of snow in the Tatra Highlands, the apartment dark in the morning. I wake up oppressed by the idea of leaving the country and lie in bed waiting for the clock in the Old City to strike seven-thirty. In that hour after waking, the trip we have planned to New York seems senseless: two people getting on in years will fly nine hours on a winter's day and cross the Atlantic to land in an immense, unintelligible, dangerous city, leaving behind the traces they had spent years making in the only little corner of the world they know well. At this time of year we would usually reserve a room for Christmas in Obory. Now no one knows how long the coal there will last after the holidays and whether the house will be open at all in January. Moreover, I'm not sure whether I would have any luck finding gas there for the return trip to Warsaw. Cars are lining up in front of the stations during the night; people sometimes wait two days to get their tanks filled. And the problems will probably be still worse in January.

Now and then I rise before the stroke of seven, and after my bath, the sense of pointlessness disperses. I set about the small, automatic tasks with which I usually begin my day. I've pushed my writing back an hour, which allows me to help M. with the

---

* The name given to a group of Polish aristocrats who in the late eighteenth century supported Russia's plans to partition Poland.

shopping. I'm not always successful. The day before yesterday I
went for fresh croissants three times. The first two times they
hadn't arrived yet, and the third time they were all gone and so I
brought home some stale bread. An older man standing by the
counter with a wire basket in his hand glanced over at me. "Tell
me, how did they do it? It's the same soil, the same Poland. It's
hard to understand." The women in the lines use a much more
forceful language. Lately I have observed a certain type of
woman—between forty and sixty, stocky, thick-legged, wearing a
wool cap or nappy beret, the grandmother-wife-and-mother
type, with a voice like a man's and a fierce aggressive look in her
eye. They stand on the sidewalks near the food stores from
morning on. Whenever a delivery truck pulls up in front of a
store, a mob of these women runs after it, clomping across the
street with their arms outstretched—to keep their balance and to
keep others from being first in line. When it turns out the truck
has come to pick up empty cartons, they begin to curse. Others
laugh and jeer at them. That causes commotions and quarrels,
the tone of which quickly turns nasty. They especially hate men
carrying children, who are allowed to the head of a line. They
yell that the children are rented, their voices deep and hoarse: "I
don't believe it! I don't believe it! He borrowed them from the
neighbors!" One of those women, with bushy eyebrows and a
four-cornered beret of amaranth-colored wool, stared at me with
a look of venomous superiority when I tossed a cigarette onto the
sidewalk. She picked it up, making a point of sticking her behind
up in the air, and put the cigarette out in a trash can. I didn't say
anything, pretending not to have noticed, but I felt her implac-
able gaze on me. It occurred to me that if there were public
hangings, she would have been there at daybreak, knitting and
squabbling with the women beside her. A *tricoteuse* in a woolen
Phrygian cap.

Standing in line with these women are thin, gray-haired men,
usually silent and somewhat ill at ease. Retired professionals.
Some of them can still remember World War I, which coincided
with their childhood or early youth. I also recognize a few minis-

ters of People's Poland who have been dismissed from their posts, and even one former member of the politburo. A stooped man in a soft hat with a visor: I often run into him in cheese lines. He always comes with a bulging black briefcase. I once noticed him take his place behind a tall man with a cane whom I knew by sight, a Home Army officer, one of those who had been sent to Moscow to be tried.* One is tempted to say that the lines in front of the stores sometimes create living allegorical images that incarnate several generations and eras, as well as various social classes. A week ago in a line for chicken on Bonifraterska Street, I caught sight of a woman I know, one of those whose direct male ancestors had been hanged two hundred years ago in the Old City Market. Advancing right behind her were the wives of some older bricklayers, outstanding workers who had been awarded decorations for helping to rebuild the Old City after the war. Over the years, various kinds of people have been allocated apartments in our neighborhood, either as a reward for their merits or as compensation for the wrongs done them. Food lines have created a perfect equality: former ministers, officers released from prison, the granddaughters and wives of workers, today have the same chance of acquiring a chicken.

It often happens that I spot someone standing a certain distance from a line as if hesitating whether to join it or give up, and who avoids my eyes. Oh, those who are still ashamed ... Humanists, artistic souls. As I approach with my shopping bag, we avert our eyes discreetly so as not to create an occasion for greetings and we quicken our pace, pretending that we have nothing in common with the butter line, or else we cross to the other side of the street feigning a bibliophile's interest in a bookstore window. May God forgive us.

A lovely young woman, the wife of a film director, came to the Writers' Club yesterday for lunch, her face gray and weary after an hour and a half on public transportation from Mokotów. Friends have invited her to West Germany, and she's going for

---

* At the end of World War II, the leaders of the Warsaw Uprising were deported to Moscow by the NKVD.

ten days. She said, "For ten days I want to live like a white person."

On Wednesday morning I was awakened by the song "First Brigade." I had slept until eight o'clock (my blood pressure had changed during the night and I had taken a reladorm tablet). Now the last of my sleep had been invaded by that brisk marching song: "We have thrown our lives and fates on the pyre, the pyre, the pyre!" I turned from side to side, thinking that I was dreaming about some old school celebration. A moment later, however, the voice of the announcer on Polish Radio reached my ears: "Sixty-three years have passed since Józef Piłsudski arrived in Warsaw after his rescue from the Magdeburg Fortress. Patriotic crowds greeted him at the Vienna Station . . ." M. came into the room. "Did you hear that?" For the first time in her life she did not say a word when I lit up a cigarette before breakfast.

Three years ago I described the ceremonies held for the sixtieth anniversary of independence on the eve of November 11 at a meeting of the P.E.N. Club in Warsaw, when Professor Kieniewicz disappointed the audience hungry for a national miracle. Today, three years later, it would seem that the miracle has occurred. The government has decided to observe the November anniversary, shrouded in silence every year until now; there has been a wreath-laying ceremony, and the radio has been speaking warmly on the subject. The papers have carried a story about naming the new Toruń highway after the Home Army. The television commentators, barely able to control their emotion, have announced a competition for a monument to the Warsaw Uprising, which will no doubt be placed in front of the Palace of the Republic at the point where the fighters descended into the sewers. Only spontaneous demonstrations, such as yesterday's march by thousands of people from the Cathedral, are passed over in silence. I have heard that the shipyard in Gdynia has voted to name itself the Józef Piłsudski Yard. In Kraków an enormous procession bearing banners marched toward Wawel Castle, and a handful of old men wearing their Legion caps stood at attention by Piłsudski's coffin in the crypt of the Silver Bells. Had the people gathered at the P.E.N. Club three years ago been able to see these images from the not too distant future, they would have fallen into each other's arms. There would have been no doubt that a miracle had occurred.

It has occurred and it continues. It has all the improbability of a miracle, as well as the leaden weight of truth. The miracle has become a reality, astonishing by the very fact of its existence but, at the same time, morbidly entangled and incomplete. Like a dream. I think of those exhausting, feverish dreams in which one experiences exaltation and dread in rapid succession and in which one walks along a ledge at a dizzying height that almost reaches the sky, yet feeling at the same time naked and afraid that one could come tumbling down at any moment. In such dreams time is confused. As it is for us now. Amid hardship and poverty like those of the occupation, in a burnt-out city you suddenly dream that the radio is playing the "First Brigade." On the wall, a printed proclamation with an old-fashioned crowned eagle—it is 1920; no, it's a racist poster with Falange slogans that pretend to be democratic in my dream . . . Chorales from the uprising resound in the churches. Young bearded men from the paintings of Grottger—it is 1863; no, a dream, a modern radar-equipped police car is parked around the corner . . . Everything is in a whirl, hope and fear, legend and reality, bizarre phantoms. Certain incidents are marked by a chilling surrealism, the true grotesqueness of dreams—take the eleven prisoners in Rzeszowski who went on a protest strike on top of the 40-meter high chimney of a heating plant. They have been sitting up there for three days now, demanding talks with the government. They're going to negotiate from the top of the chimney. No, that could only be a dream. And above the chimneys, banners and forests, the Mother of God hovers in the clouds above the fatherland as she did once before over the battlefield at Grunwald . . . Grunwald? What am I saying? Today "Grunwald" is an association of nationalistic Communists that is supported by Moscow and East Berlin. Is that a dream too? Whose dream? Ours.

A dream miracle . . .

All this is happening in the city to which I came as a fifteen-year-old student a half century ago, a city I wandered for a year enchanted by its legendary spots, its streetlights, the faces of women filled with the intoxicating mystery of sins I had not yet known. Romantic times. Later I began my studies—the hard lessons of loneliness from which I emerged a melancholiac with a completely useless diploma and went right into war. Fortunately, before that happened, I experienced a second enchantment—a face glimpsed by chance through the gleaming window of an Italian ice-cream parlor as I was crossing Nowy Świat, a tennis racket under my arm, on my way home. It must have been early autumn. Yes, love. One of the words mankind has been unable to change. And this time it proved true to its oldest archetypes— pure, lyrical, everlasting. Lasting the whole of my life if my life can be said to have begun with my arrival in this city. Fifty years in round numbers. It was also in Warsaw that I began to write, which seems to me the second phase of my salvation and which has also lasted to this day. Everything in this one city. But what astonishes me is not only that "everything," not only that I experienced the fullness of life in this city that formed me into the person I am now, but that that process shows no sign of ending. On the contrary, it seems to be picking up new threads; the city from which I no longer expected anything, now so real and stripped of mystery, the city I know through and through, having long since ceased to distinguish between its beauty and its ugliness, now that city has suddenly once again enchanted me with something that is inconceivable, beyond belief. I look around, I stop, I ask myself, Is this a dream or not? A singular feeling. As if I were once again that student who came here to discover the wonders of life. My God, how many times are we to begin anew . . .

The miracle has lasted fifteen months and—this we know—cannot be ranked with irrational metamorphoses or sudden cures. It does not multiply loaves; it does not strike sinners down with fire. It is a workaday, down-to-earth miracle, a monstrously long-winded, exhausting miracle. But a miracle all the same.

For fifteen months now, the innards of the nation have been bared, its social, psychic, mental lava, which for thirty-five years had gone uncharted—at best one could make guesses about it. Now those contents are being revealed, and we can see for ourselves what was within. And what will that lava prove to be? Or to put it another way, what would it prove to be were it able to assume its own proper form?

In *A Question of Reality* I said that in today's Poland there endures a half-hidden but persistently vital set of world views and ideological positions that could be considered a continuation of the political forces of prewar Poland. It is not difficult today to distinguish the various mentalities, for example, that of the National Democrat, the Social Democrat, the Communist, or conservative, and even to define roughly who would have been sympathetic to the Christian centrists before the war or who would have been with the peasant left or, conversely, with the military dictatorship, who for the ONR, who for democracy, and who would have collaborated with whatever regime was in power. "Except that today," I wrote, "the administration keeps a lid on that spectrum of positions, the lid of the system that levels everything. Now everyone has been flattened out, everything is one dimensional, individual opinions cannot come out into the open, and a single program is proclaimed for everyone and on everyone's behalf."

But today all that sounds like past history. The lid has been pried off, the internal pressure released. Since I wrote *A Question of Reality*, KOR and ROPCiO* have come into being, followed by KPN,† DiP,‡ as well as Grunwald. Currents from a great variety of groups and trends, frequently with premises that clash,

---

* Ruch Obrony Praw Człowieka i Obywatela (Movement for the Defense of Human and Civil Rights).
† Konfederacja Polski Niepodległej (Confederation of Independent Poland).
‡ Doświadczenie i Przyszłość (Experience and the Future [Club]).

have gone into Solidarity, as happened forty years ago with the Home Army. Thus, something important and difficult is under way, something whose nature is profoundly complex, fruitful yet painful, as birth pangs always are. Amid spasms, cries, and pressure, a new organism is being formed, the social body of the future. At moments one can catch a faint glimpse of its circulatory system and of individual limbs. Everything is still embryonic, unclear, but signs of division can already be seen in what has been joined together.

We say, The opposition and the government, Solidarity and the party. We also say, A line that seeks agreement and an extremist line. To superficial observers, the division here is between the nation as a whole and the authorities as a single entity. The more intelligent, however, look more deeply and see internal conflicts and trouble spots on both sides. And points of convergence too. In the course of my rather long life, I have seen plenty of political crises and today am certain that the essential differences are not those that divide people according to programs, slogans, or tactics. I have actually always seen two forces at work in life and two types of people subject to them. The first I would call the energy of the free individual consciousness; the second, propulsion caused by collective conditions. That doesn't sound too original, but I can't find a better definition. I may have been right in *A Question of Reality* when I said that politics in contemporary Poland is a continuation of the prewar groupings and positions. That's probably true. But today, or more precisely over the years leading up to today, I have learned to see other divisions between people, not only political and philosophical ones, and it would be absurd for me to divide them according to the names they have assumed or by the terms they use—left-wing or right-wing terms, Marxist or Catholic. No doubt they feel that this is what divides them and believe it is so, and words, slogans, and programs seem the important things to them. What, however, seems a hundred times more important to me than someone's views is his relation to the views expressed by someone else. One person may be an idealist; another, a materialist. Fine, let them consider themselves that, and let them argue. But if the materialist says that the idealist must be hanged or if the idealist cries out that materialists must be hanged, then, for me, they're both the same.

At one point I wrote that nothing fills me with greater fear than a Poland that is stupid and ignorant. I have always been afraid of a Poland like that, one full of hatred and intolerance. Now the old specters of chauvinism and fanatic xenophobia are once again on the rise. They had been in hiding under the crust of the earth, in there with the lava. It is more difficult than ever to protect oneself against them, for in the crucible of the struggle, they have been mixed in with the best elements. Overall, it is more difficult than ever to subject Polish reality to rational analysis.

Whenever I attempt to reflect on it, to make some judgment, to ascertain some truth, my thoughts collapse at once into meaninglessness. There is strength, however, in the certainty that time will give things shape. Years from now, everything will be elucidated by culture. Culture has a higher wisdom than history: not only can it interpret facts, but it also posits a scale of values. Intolerance, stupidity, and ignorance have inundated Polish society more than once before, but they have never created the nation's culture. Therein lies its greatness.

Yesterday I spoke to the students who have been on strike for two weeks in one of the buildings of Warsaw University. The strike has spread to schools throughout the country, the students protesting the fact that the Engineering Institute in Radom is being forced to accept as its chancellor someone chosen by the party. Around a hundred people gathered in the university's Polish studies auditorium. Many questions concerning *A Question of Reality, A Warsaw Diary,* and some of my other books.

When the evening was over, one of its organizers, a tall, good-looking young man, led me out through the dark to the Obózna Street side-gate, which was guarded by students wearing red and white armbands. He walked with me as far as the Old City, asking various questions, speaking intelligently and with a certain judicious tact. When I expressed my concern that he was accompanying me out of politeness, he explained that he wanted to see the street where I lived. "You wrote about those places in your *Warsaw Diary*." He had been present two days earlier, when I had met with the students on strike at the Drama School. There the discussion had gone beyond purely literary matters. It lasted three hours. In some of the questions they asked, I detected a touch of anxiety: questions about the reality of winning, the chances in the short run, the long run. One of the people involved in the discussion had used the epithet "intellectual weakness." He said that perhaps the doubts and fears people felt stemmed from that weakness. For the love of God, who put that idea in their heads, the idea that the word "intellectual" has a pejorative meaning and can be used slightingly? As in "intellectual wishiwashiness," "intellectual liabilities." Just like Russia—this smacks of Slavophile peasantomania! The Polish intellectuals—those two words signify moral and mental energy, the source of Poland's vital powers during the last two hundred years of its history. What would Poland be today had it not been for the work of the Enlightenment, the Romantic intellectual imagination, and the social labors performed by the intellectuals during the period of Positivism—Poland without the intellectuals in the Legions and in the Socialist independence movement, the peasant, educational and cooperative movements. Poland without the intellectuals in KOR and in the "Flying University." Come to your senses! No, remember.

For three hours, sixty or so students on benches arranged in amphitheater fashion and me down below at a table. For three hours I tried to assure them that there was a real chance. Hard years were coming, all the possibilities, the good and the bad, were open, as well as those that no one could imagine or foresee, things unpredictable from our narrow vantage. Furthermore, I said that the greatest error would be to hypnotize oneself by analogies with the age of the partitions and the age of the uprisings.

In the course of the last two hundred years, other peoples have extricated themselves from the oppression of empires—the Americans, the Greeks, the Italians, the Belgians—and it has never been written anywhere that Poland is condemned to always bear the burden of futility and defeat. I also maintained that what has been achieved since August, what has already been achieved, is and will remain inscribed in European history as a memorable struggle fought for a society's soul and its rights, and whatever happens, no one can take that spiritual possession away from us. Then a bright, articulate young man, blond and wearing glasses, spoke up from the last row: "I understand. That means there are values for which one must pay the highest price, regardless of the consequences, including the sacrifice of one's own life." I fell silent. The room grew still. "No," I said, "you've misunderstood me. I am not advocating self-destruction." That was all the answer I could muster. It was not an easy moment. My mind had suddenly gone blank. The students seemed to take pity on me, and someone asked what I considered to be the role of the contemporary writer. The void began to fill. I said that I would much prefer to cross out the word "role" and replace it with another, "job." For me the "job" of literature is the work a writer does on himself, the working out of the truth of oneself as a human being, a person, a choice of self among the many that one can become. I think that that was my final remark. Later they invited me to the cafeteria for tea. Little sandwiches were served; two charming young ladies sat down with me and we discussed the theater.

But that night, I kept thinking about the blond young man and how I could have answered him better. I don't know. To nod my head and say, "Yes, including the sacrifice of one's own life, regardless of the consequences," would have been disgraceful. I remember a fragment of Miłosz's conversation with Wat in *My Century* about the *auto-da-fé* of the Polish uprisings, when the heaviest burden of responsibility fell, in the end, on the children. Children with rifles in their hands. I had not elaborated on my answer; it had been too brief. Certainly they had expected more from me. It would have been a hundred times better to have admitted to my own uncertainty and to have answered that I did not know or that I did not know any more than they did. Which does not mean that I have lost hope. I can see it before me, vast and vague; I foresee long years of labor, a labor of character and mind, struggle, effort, fatigue. We can lose today, but we cannot lose forever. No doubt, plans to destroy us already exist, but it is impossible to foresee the mysterious plan of other, still-undisclosed elements and the dispensations concealed in the nature of the world, in the future. The plans for our destruction may run aground on that other plan. We must bet on good and against evil, but we must play the game wisely and patiently. Sometimes a nation wins such battles over two or three generations (in India, which showed the world the power of passive resistance, it was the generation of Gandhi and Nehru that won the decisive victory). A struggle of this sort depends on enormous, sustained efforts of mind and will. It is a struggle for oneself. Not only a struggle for freedom. We ourselves are transformed in it. This is the hard work of creating a new configuration of Polish experience.

Friday. A sudden reversal—at breakfast M. says, "New York is too far away. It's crazy to go." She asks me to reserve a room in Konstancin for January. I agree and telephone ZAIKS. We still have seven days to buy our airline tickets. At eleven o'clock in the evening I try to call New York. It takes half an hour to reach the international exchange. The operator will not accept my order for a call—orders for calls to New York are accepted only after midnight. At midnight I dial the international exchange number and after fifteen minutes hear a recording: "Please-wait-an-operator-will-be-with-you-shortly." For two hours, until two o'clock in the morning, that nightmarish voice keeps repeating its message. I fall asleep with the receiver at my ear; I wake up, I try to read, then I fall asleep and dream I'm in the mountains, then wake up again. "Please-wait-an-operator-will-be-with-you-shortly." I throw down the receiver in despair. A moment later I decide to give it one last try. I dial the number again and suddenly, after three rings, she's there. A female voice, bored but real at last, informs me that it will take one week to put me through to New York. Fine. I give her my number. I'll wait a week.

So, we're not going to New York. In January we will go to Konstancin and perhaps to Obory in February. M. is very pensive, the house is quiet. I read Faulkner in the evening and work on the *Diary* in the morning. I had wanted to end it with the departure for New York. A strange book, impossible to plot. It develops on its own, keeps taking me by surprise, and in fact I'm only a participant in the plot, with no idea of what will happen next. Now I'm curious what the ending will be.

An interview with Professor Geremek in *Kurier Polski* (The Polish Courier). I was struck by the words "a self-governing republic." A beautiful ring to it. As if it were correcting the much-abused expression "In anarchy lies Poland's strength." Yet it only makes me more painfully aware of the current state of affairs, so startling, so incredible. In years of peace, with no war, in an industrialized agricultural country, havoc has been wrought similar to the destruction caused by war. Individuals are being indicted for this. And although there is no doubt that they are responsible, it is the life-destroying system that bears the principal blame. I remember a conversation I once had with a young KOR activist: "It's usually thought that a society creates its leaders. In totalitarian systems, the reverse is true: it is the authorities who create the society. In order to achieve this, they have to destroy everything that had previously been alive and authentic in that society. But, at some point, that newly created society will destroy the authorities who produced it."

Tuesday. One forces oneself to have rational hopes and optimistic thoughts, but dark premonitions twitch beneath the surface. There are more flash points all the time. The student strikes continue throughout the country. The sit-in strike at the Fire Department's Officers' School was broken up immediately, by force, with squads of assault police. The air (by helicopter) and ground operations progressed smoothly, watched by an agitated crowd. It looked to me like a dress rehearsal before a fiery opening night. I have a feeling that the general who donned dark glasses after August will soon be taking them off.

I continue to have many conversations, meetings. One invariable topic draws everything to itself like a magnet. In the morning I carry my *Diary* forward. M. said, "If I feel so relieved after making the decision, that means we shouldn't have gone." "Of course," I say, "you're right." And I think, But how to end the *Diary*? Describe a fictitious takeoff, fictitious stewardesses, follow it up by some inner monologue as the plane soars above the clouds—just the way it would actually have happened—and then just put one sentence at the end saying it could have happened like this but it didn't and we stayed on in Warsaw? Quite a modern ending.

I notice that she looks sad and seems to be waiting for me to make objections, voice my doubts. She gave me a sort of sidelong glance and then I knew: she's afraid of flying over the ocean and wants to shift the decision onto me.

Days of feigned peace at home while throughout the country the flames are being fanned. As of Thursday, we have not said a word about going; we're both avoiding the subject. Besides, there are other things to talk about. The government is to introduce into the Sejm the draft of a bill calling for martial law. Solidarity has issued a standby call for a general strike. No desire can be seen on the part of the authorities to come to terms with society. The students continue their sit-in; threats and lies continue to pour from the television screen. An enigmatic figure, that Premier-Secretary in his general's uniform. What is hidden behind those dark glasses—Poland or Russia? The dreamers whisper that he's a Wallenrod. The skeptics allude to other figures closer in time. The realists say nothing.

The gates of the university and the street corners on Castle

Square are plastered with posters. Those torn off are replaced by new ones. Groups of passersby stand reading.

I have decided not to think about how the *Diary* will end. Circumstances will dictate the ending: it will write itself; I'll only note it down. On Thursday evening I waited to be put through to New York and the call came at ten on the dot. When the international operator called, M. was standing a few steps away from me. She glanced at the phone but did not reach for it. As I picked up the receiver, I felt her eyes on me. I could hear the operator dialing, then static and a rattling sound. Finally, New York answered. Looking over at M., I said slowly, pausing between words, "We're afraid that our coming will inconvenience you." "Don't worry, don't worry," said the voice on the other side of the ocean, laughing. Still looking at M., I continued, "We're supposed to arrive on December the fourth but . . ." Now M. was looking at me. I knew that she could interrupt me, grab the phone. I waited a moment, and then I said, "All right then, December the fourth, at three-fifty-five, American time. Goodbye." Static and rattling. The call was over.

The next day we went to Waryński Street to pay for the tickets we had reserved at the LOT airline office. M. was still very hesitant and at the last minute tried to put the flight off to January so as to be in Warsaw for the holidays. But we were informed that that was impossible, as all flights were sold out until April. We fly in a week; our return tickets are good for three months, and our passports are valid until 1984.

Walking home on Freta Street, I passed a helpless old couple moving toward a poultry store with a long, compact line in front of it. They stopped every few feet; the man would set his bag down on the sidewalk, switch his cane to his left hand, and with his right arm briefly support the woman, who was bent double, her thin, shriveled legs wavering. They did not have the strength to go on. But when I walked over to them wanting to help, they grew frightened and began assuring me that they were in no need of anything, as if justifying their moment of weariness to me. I apologized and walked away. They remained there on the sidewalk, holding each other up in the desperate embrace of the drowning. When I looked back, the man was trying to lift the bag from the ground.

Since we know that this is the way things are, and if we call this old age, without asking why it is that way, if we reconcile ourselves to the inexplicable and undeserved sufferings of children and old people, if we live without expecting any explanation for our uncertainty and with no hope of any reply, then our despair in God's justice is well founded. Whenever I hear religious people speak about God's justice and when I read what intellectuals have written about it, I can't help feeling that their image of God is naïve; they see Him as a person in heaven judging people's actions in accordance with human concepts of justice. It is enough for me to remember the millions who have died and have been murdered to know that God exists and is not just. But since God exists without being just, it is we who must be just. I cannot explain why I am so certain of this, yet I know that somewhere—somewhere else—it will be confirmed. And of that too I am certain.

■ *NEW YORK,*
DECEMBER 13,
1982

News that martial law has been declared in Poland. All communications cut.

About the Author

KAZIMIERZ BRANDYS was born in Łódź, Poland, and studied law at Warsaw University.
His first novel was published in 1946, followed
by nine others, a number of which have appeared in translation. He received the presti-
gious Italian Premio Elba award in 1964, and
his novel *Samson* was made into a film of the
same title by director Andrzej Wajda. In 1966
Brandys resigned from the Polish Communist
Party, of which he had been a prominent member since 1946, and in 1978 co-founded *Zapis,*
the renowned independent literary quarterly.
For the past five years he has been blacklisted
by the Polish authorities—unable to publish in
Poland—and currently divides his time between
New York and Paris.